The Staffordshire Potter;

THE STAFFORDSHIRE POTTER

"Where the minarets are chimneys;
Where the towers are potters' ovens;
Where the plastic clay is fashioned
Into forms of use and beauty;
Where the crusted earth is burrowed
For the wealth of mine beneath it;
Where the very hills are iron;
Where grim workers in the metals·
Make the potter's face look whiter
As they meet him in the highways;
Where the busy sounds of labour
Rise, the best of human incense,
To the throne of the Creator."

WILLIAM OWEN, in "Songs of Labour," 1884.

The Staffordshire Potter

BY

HAROLD OWEN

WITH A CHAPTER ON THE DANGEROUS
PROCESSES IN THE POTTING INDUSTRY BY

THE DUCHESS OF SUTHERLAND

LONDON

GRANT RICHARDS

9 HENRIETTA STREET, COVENT GARDEN, W.C.

1901

TO

MY FATHER

WILLIAM OWEN

WHOSE LONG LABOURS FOR THE WORKING POTTER

HAVE FURNISHED THE MATERIAL

FOR SO MUCH OF ITS STORY

I DEDICATE THIS BOOK

CONTENTS

v

218756

CHAPTER IV

CHAPTER V

CHAPTER VI

CHAPTER VII

CHAPTER VIII

CHAPTER IX

CHAPTER X

CHAPTER XI

CONTENTS

THE STAFFORDSHIRE POTTER

PROLOGUE

THERE is a chain of towns in North Staffordshire, stretching some five or six miles from Longton at the South of the chain to Tunstall at the North, which together produce nine-tenths of the earthenware manufactured in the United Kingdom; and more than half their population of a quarter of a million is more or less directly engaged in, or concerned with, the industry which has procured for the chain of towns the name of " The Potteries." That comprehensive designation was originally bestowed upon them from outside, and though in course of time it became accepted by the inhabitants of the district—to whom the names of Longton, Fenton, Stoke, Hanley, Burslem, and Tunstall, had an individual and sufficient significance—there still lingers in the minds of the people of " The Potteries " a parochial resentment of the hasty generalisation which could not stop, or stoop, to discriminate between municipal boundaries, but merged the identity of each unit into one colloquial, though undeniably convenient, name for all.

Sheffield would have successfully resisted any attempt to describe it as " The Cutleries "; Northampton had acquired an honoured place in history

A

before the circumstance of its manufacture of boots could have filched its good name, and substituted one less euphonious; and the cluster of towns in the south-east corner of Lancashire, whose chief industry has given to Manchester the proud title of Cottonopolis, and enabled her to carve her way to the sea, still preserve their separate identity as Burnley, Bury, or Blackburn, and have escaped the degradation of being lumped together as "The Spinneries." And as to that quarter of the county of Nottingham where Welbeck, Thoresby, and Clumber cluster together in unwonted opulence, it merely exhibits, by accepting the bantering alias of "The Dukeries," that gracious condescension which is the prerogative of conscious superiority, and not a single strawberry leaf in the neighbourhood droops at the familiarity.

One other district in England has suffered the injustice which has been done to Hanley and Burslem and their sister towns. At the other end of the county of Stafford lies a manufacturing and mineral-producing district as uninviting to the eye as that in the North, and travellers who have returned from those remote regions have spoken of their visit to the "Black Country." Yet even here Wolverhampton emerges with proud distinctness from the surrounding darkness;—but Longton and Tunstall, what and where are they?

There are legends to the effect that in the days of stage coaches, those that ran from London to Liverpool and Chester regularly stopped at Burslem and Stoke, and changed their horses; and it is conceivable that the travellers who passed by the smoking potters' ovens—then surrounded by pleasant fields, and now by other potters' ovens—inquired and learned that they were in Burslem, where Josiah Wedgwood lived and worked, or in the town of Stoke, upon the River Trent. But the main iron highways of to-day avoid "The Potteries," and it lies from the path of the travellers who go from London to the North, in an "isolation" that may be "splendid" for the travellers, but is regretted by its inhabitants as the legacy of the cupidity and stupidity of some of their land-owning predecessors. And so, to the Man in the Street, "The Potteries" is a place "somewhere in the Midlands," and if you ask him for a more precise location, he will tell you that it is "part-of the Black Country"; and thus this laxity of geographical expression perpetrates a fresh injustice to the small chain of towns in the North—or to the longsuffering cluster in the South?— of the county of Stafford. But should you come across a man in the street who really knows "The Potteries," and something about it, you will hear that it is a strange place where men fight dogs — and, in 'truth, Americans have descended upon "The Potteries," asking which was the veritable house in the salubrious quarter of Tinkersclough where a certain ill - authenticated encounter occurred, and perhaps have found local guides—anxious to turn an ill-wind to comparatively honest account, at trifling expense of imagination and sacrifice of scruple—to show them ; but assuredly have found many houses in Tinkersclough.

But it is to be feared that there are others who remain in the outer darkness, and have not even heard of that legendary hero, "Brummy"—(a name which suggests that, viewed from the distance of Fleet Street, Birmingham too may be geographically mixed up with the Black Country and The Potteries) —nor of his canine antagonist; and by such "The Potteries" may never have been consciously assigned to any more precise location' than is allotted to Utopia.   But lately, special correspondents have gone down from London to Tinkersclough and its environs, and have written special articles in their newspapers concerning the men and women and children who work in the potteries, and certain evils of lead-poisoning which they have long borne, and others have just discovered, which articles have led in turn to questions and even debates in Parliament, and these newspaper articles and Parliamentary debates may have stimulated geographical research. But at any rate they have quite overshadowed the legend of the Man and the Dog, and given "The Potteries" a new notoriety, and certainly have dispelled any lingering ideas which may have associated it with Utopia.

It is with the industrial struggles of the working potters in this district that the following pages are concerned.   The author has no better claim to tell their story than that the materials which supply it have been peculiarly accessible to him; but whilst he cannot pretend to have made any deeper study of the industrial and economic questions to which it is related than that made by anyone who endeavours to follow the drift of the chief movements of his own time, he hopes that the book may be of some interest to the general reader on the ground of at least an equal endeavour; and he can only ask for the indulgence of any industrial experts into whose hands the book may fall, in the hope that they will be able to winnow some grain from the gleanings he has gathered from a corner of that field in which they have reaped their harvest.

But there are two obvious divisions in the class of general readers who may be induced to read the book: those who may look in it for some corroboration of their own views of the malign influence exercised by Trades Unions upon "trade"—by which "capital" is meant—and those who, sympathising with the efforts of Trades Unions, may hope to find in it some justification of their faith, or who, living in a day when political economy (which theorised on the inevitability of effects produced by mutable conditions) has given place to a broader social science (which challenges the inevitability, and investigates the causes of those conditions, and leaves to statesmanship the task of changing them) take an interest in the labour question merely as a branch of the social problem.

The days of cavilling at the *existence* of Trades Unions are over, and the working-classes of the kingdom are as free in the management of their industrial affairs as they are in the enjoyment of political power. One condition could not exist without the other; and the desire for, and gradual acquirement of the one, inevitably brought corresponding progress in the parallel path. Both movements—if they can really be distinguished—were warmly championed and hotly opposed; but though a generation has been born which found Trades Unions legalised, farm labourers and working-men voting in the security of the ballot, and schools built in part from the money of the rich or the childless ratepayer, into which troop the children of the poor; and though this generation reads as history the struggles and battles which enabled it to come into the world, with the hurly-burly done, and these things accomplished facts, there undoubtedly exists in the minds of the ancient enemies of the democratic movement—who fought in or witnessed the struggle—or of their intellectual descendants, who review the field of buried controversy, a distrust of the powers and privileges conferred on the "lower classes," as workers or as voters, which has not wholly been dispelled by the falsification of the predictions which were made in regard to the use to which they would be put.

To such, the perusal of the detailed story of the aims and efforts of several generations of working-men, engaged in one trade, and concentrated in one district, to work out their industrial progress, may help to dissipate the prejudice which only sees in a Trades Union a sinister instrument, unwisely placed in the hands of working-men by a weak legislature, for "upsetting trade and driving capital out of the country"; and may present an aspect of the activities of such organisations which will lead to some modification of their opinions, even if it does not change their point of view.

In the narrative told in the following pages, there is abundant testimony to the intelligence, moderation, and far-sightedness of the working potters, varied only by such aberrations from the strict path of prudence — as in their emigration movement — as involved no injustice, in intention or effect, to their employers, but recoiled on themselves. Their dealings with their employers have not been those of a disciplined but unscrupulous army of thoughtless labourers, holding helpless Capital by the throat, but those of a body of peaceful, orderly, and self-respecting men, negotiating and fighting for what they believed to be right, with a body of gentlemen who often believed them to be wrong, and still oftener refused their demands, but who were, at any rate, always well able to take care of themselves. The employers of the Staffordshire Potteries have, indeed, generally shown an enlightened appreciation of the right of their workmen to combine— even in the days when there was legal sanction for the fashion which held Trades Unions as "things accursed." So far as their main body is concerned, they have not assumed any lofty pretence of their respect for "the sacred rights of labour" by endeavouring to persuade their Union workmen that they were sacrificing their independence by their foolish combinations. They have implicitly recognised the justice of their workmen's Unions by uniting themselves, and have given practical effect to the recognition by generally seeking to deal with the accredited organisations of the men through their own. They have not sought, in times of crisis, to get at the men behind their leaders, but, on the contrary—and especially in later times—have themselves invoked the interference, and upon occasions have unreservedly accepted the mediation, of the leaders of the men in disputes with the latter. To those, therefore, who are more royalist than the king, the assurance may be given that the employers of the Staffordshire Potteries have not given known utterance to the hope that they could be relieved of the tyranny of their workmen's Unions.

By thus frankly "accepting service" of the complaints preferred by the Unions on behalf of those for whom they acted, the employers of the Staffordshire Potteries have simplified the situation and narrowed the issues that are dealt with in the following pages. The history of the Potters' Unions, therefore, affords an excellent example of how, given a frank and even cordial acceptance by the employers of the existence and official responsibility of their workmen's Unions, those Unions affect the relations between employers and employed, and of the points of conflict that may arise between the two, and allows the general observer to form a judgment upon the reasonableness and justice of the demands made and resistance offered by the one side or the other.

The narrative shows that the disputes between the two sides have not always presented the simple issue of whether more wages could be forced, or less imposed, to be determined by the relative strength of the combatants. The questions of "annual hiring," "good - from - oven," and "allow-ances" involved matters of principle connected with the basis of the conditions of employment and remuneration, and will be admitted to have been at least subjects for legitimate controversy. And even the simple issue of wages has been complicated by a "principle." The working potters fought for higher wages, and thought they deserved them, but they were innocent of any sinister desire—so often strangely attributed to their class—to take the bread and butter out of their own mouths; and had no more deliberate intention of driving the Staffordshire potting industry to Germany than the bricklayers of London ever had of sending the building trade to France. The employers, of course, almost invariably resisted their demands for higher wages, and predicted at each period of unrest that the trade must inevitably succumb to any increase in the cost of production. The workmen, on the other hand, insisted that they knew better than their masters, and that there were other means of preserving the trade than by a reduction in wages, when one was asked for by the employers "to save the trade," and other possibilities of compensating for any increase in the cost of production when the masters contested a claim for an advance in wages on the ground that to concede it would destroy the trade. And, through the latter half of the history of the Potters' Trades Unions, there run these opposing contentions of employers and employed: on the part of the former, that wages must fall with selling prices, or could not rise because selling prices had not risen; and on the part of the employed that such a regulating principle could only be enforced if as much attention were given by employers to collectively keeping up selling prices as was collectively bestowed upon the effort to keep down wages, and that, in such case, both sides would be the gainers. The workmen offered co-operation to that end, and it was refused. The views of the employers prevailed with successive arbitrators over the arguments of the men, and selling prices continued to fall, and wages too, and both sides wondered when the decline of each would stop.

Quite recently, and after the writing of this narrative was thought to be concluded, a remarkable movement in The Potteries opportunely supplied a probable solution to that question. Many employers came to the conclusion that they must look within their own ranks for the greatest enemy of prosperity to their trade. The workmen had named him over and over again in years gone by, and had offered their assistance in coercing him into better conduct, or exterminating him altogether. He was, and is, the "cutter" of the trade. Sometimes he is a man of much capital, sometimes of none. In the former case, he uses his capital as a weapon; in the latter it is the circumstance of his lack of capital that is the motive force, and he is the helpless, though willing instrument. In both cases labour is equally necessary, and often equally ill-paid. The main body of employers are in a condition between the two extremes, and suffer by the deliberation of the one and the helplessness of the other. They have now asked their workmen to join them in fighting a common enemy — the manufacturer who beggars his class by unrestrained and ill-regulated competition—and the Trades Unionists have responded to an invitation which they asked to be extended to them years ago. It is a safe prediction that, if the projected movement becomes ratified and complete, the enemy will either be vanquished or absorbed. Either consummation would be good, but the latter better. At any rate, a position has to-day been reached in which both sides combine to extract the best possible results to each from the trade in which they are engaged. Whether it will yield the full fruits of its promise remains to be seen, but all the indications are favourable. The effort, in itself, is at least a satisfactory outcome of long years of strenuous controversy; and being, as it is, the fulfilment of the hopes and efforts of the leaders of the workmen, is an adventitious aid to the desire of the author to show that the motives and actions of Trades Unions are, whilst necessary to the protection of the class which they are primarily designed to serve, not irreconcilable with the interests of the class which they are popularly supposed to oppose; and it enables him to close his narrative with the fair promise of a future—only usually assured in narratives of a more imaginative and interesting character — summarily described as " Happy ever after."

LONDON, *January* 1899.

CHAPTER I

THE EARLY DAYS OF UNION

IT was not until after the second decade of this century that any attempt was made by the workmen engaged in the potting trade of Staffordshire to exert any organised influence over their employers.*

The possession of natural advantages, arising from the clay-beds and coal-fields found in the locality, fixed the future trade of The Potteries; but though the manufacture of earthenware can be definitely traced to Burslem so long ago. as 1600, the date of its introduction into the district remains uncertain. The rough products of its earlier years belonged, however, in character if not in chronology, to the remote ages of the rudest conception and practice of the plastic art; and the industry, as carried on in Staffordshire, had derived no

---

* There is a paragraph in the London *Star* of Wednesday, November 26, 1792, which says: "COUNTRY NEWS. — Staffordshire. — The workmen employed in the different potteries here have combined to obtain an increase of wages; hitherto the masters have denied their demands, and the men remained inactive, except in punishing some of their comrades, who attempted to work at their usual price. A troop of dragoons has been ordered from Leicester to Wolverhampton, to act should necessity require."—There seems, however, to be no local evidence connecting this with The Potteries, and Wolverhampton in any case would have been almost two days' ride from where any necessity would have required the presence of the dragoons. It probably points, however, to some such sporadic movement as is referred to on p. 15, which has escaped a local chronicler.

assistance from the development of that art in intermediate ages, nor from its contemporaneous advancement on the Continent. Until the earlier half of last century it was still in the rudimentary stage, and there was but little distinction between the character of its products then and those of a century earlier, when Burslem—the seat and home of Staffordshire potting—was marked on the maps as "Butter-pot Town," and an Act of Parliament of the reign of Charles II. regulated the size and weight of the butter-pot which formed the staple item of its manufactures. But with the glazing of the red clay butter-pots, and the subsequent introduction of the finer white clays of Devonshire and Cornwall, began the process of that evolution and development which was soon carried to an immeasurably greater height by Wedgwood and Brindley and their contemporaries, who transformed a handicraft into an art.

This transformation in the character of the work produced no less a change in the worker, and a generation of skilled workmen—of artisans—arose. New processes and methods produced fresh branches of labour, and to each branch a distinctive skill was necessary. For example, the importation from the Continent of the process of making ware from Plaster of Paris moulds produced a distinct class of workmen called "pressers," who were again divided into two classes,—the flat-ware and the hollow-ware pressers. And so, with more than fifty years of progress and education, the beginning of the nineteenth century saw a generation of working potters almost as far advanced from their ancestors of the " butter-pot" period as the letter-press printer of to-day is from Caxton and Gutenberg. And, as the industry became more complex — each succeeding innovation demanding a change in technical method, or the acquirement of a totally distinct practice — the old system by which prices were regulated required constant modifications, and it was to this cause and opportunity, and to the individual disputes which constantly recurred between an individual master and his workmen in the settlement of what price should be paid for a fresh article of production or for a fresh process in its manufacture, that we must trace the beginnings of a workmen's Union.*

* Mr Ward, in his history of the old Borough of Stoke-on-Trent (which comprised practically the whole of The Potteries), ascribes the beginning of Potters' Unions to political agitation : " During the years 1817, 1818, and 1819, when the epidemic of political reform ,was extremely rife throughout the nation, several radical gatherings took place in different parts of this Borough, particularly one at Burslem on 27th January 1817, and one at Hanley on the 1st November 1819," which were addressed "by itinerant orators," and at which "strong resolutions were passed in favour of Parliamentary reform, voting by ballot, and the exclusion of placemen and pensioners from Parliament. Attempts were also made to form political clubs, to carry the views of the reformers into practice ; but most of the manufacturers and respectable inhabitants stood aloof from these associations, either from disapprobation of their measures or fear that the peace of the neighbourhood might be endangered by their proceedings. . . . The demagogues, however, affected to excite no ill-feeling among the working-class towards their employers ; but the tendency of their levelling doctrines, whatever they might profess, could hardly fail to produce such a result, and we do not expect to be contradicted in asserting that from the excitement of that period dates whatever political fervour the Operative classes in this district have since manifested, as well as the combinations or Trades Unions by which they

The progress of this Union was indeed a matter of evolution. It began with those branches of the trade which were most affected by the innovations and improvements in methods of manufacture; and, for a time, the workers in other branches who had been little, if at all, affected by these innovations, or whose condition and affairs had been modified or confirmed in the early days of the general development, remained wholly outside this movement. The whole tendency of the trade, indeed, had been—and long continued so—that the successive changes in process had introduced themselves so insidiously and imperceptibly that it was only by the introduction of some process of a revolutionary character that not only those concerned in that branch, but the workers in other branches, appreciated to the full the change that had passed over their heads. But the genesis of the movement must be traced to the disaffections felt by this or that particular branch of labour feeling that its rights were violated, and that they were adversely affected by the technical development, and very improvement of the trade. A movement, perhaps, it can scarcely be called, for it was but the momentary rebellion or defence of an isolated group of workers in a particular branch, a protest called up by the circumstances of the moment, to be silenced by defeat or satisfied by victory, and then

have since greatly injured themselves and inconvenienced their employers."—These meetings, however, were only part of the general political agitation which culminated in 1832, and their relation to Potters' Unions was only that of the general to the particular.

to cease when the immediate necessity which called it forth had so been disposed. It will therefore be seen how in its conception the spirit of their "movement" differed from that which, in a later day, found in the Trades Unions of Europe and the United States the active embodiment of a principle, rather than the temporary assertion of a right temporarily challenged.

In the year 1824 a generation of potters whose general skill had become hereditary, and who, moreover, being trained in a particular channel, had made that channel or particular branch a trade in itself, combined together to form the first Potters' Union. This Union had for its object the regulation of the prices paid to its members, and it was not long before an opportunity occurred to test its strength. In the following year, 1825, the hands of a number of manufactories struck for an advance of wages. The strike was confined to certain branches of the trade, and it is a fair assumption, from the fact that the Union was by no means complete, and then only in comparative infancy, that the workers in these branches throughout the trade were only affected to a limited extent. The strike quickly collapsed. The effort, indeed, was singularly ill-timed, for the whole industry shared with the general trade of the country a severe depression, and, apart from the conviction of the justice of their refusal to grant the asked-for advance, the masters could very cheerfully accept the alternative of keeping their manufactories closed, rather than keep them open under conditions which might have been absolutely unremunerative. There were soon a few seceders among the working potters, who returned to work upon the old terms, and quickly acknowledged defeat. The main body, however, upheld their demands with courage and resource. They had chosen to fight when their Union was young, with little or no accumulation of funds upon which to maintain their out-of-work members; but, in order to make their financial resources go as far as possible, they hit upon the ingenious expedient of turning the idle hours of those on strike to account, by establishing a manufactory, controlled by the Union, in which the strikers were employed. It was not only hoped that this enterprise would become a source of direct profit, but it was expected, by thus giving employment to those on strike and to a portion of that surplus labour which, owing to bad times, had unfortunately become only too common in the district, to prevent an undue competition for employment on the part of the potters generally, and to check any tendency to weakness or surrender in those members of the Union who had struck. As might, however, have been foreseen, such a spasmodic effort at co-operative production by men inexperienced in the conduct of business—an effort, too, which was only the desperate expedient of a moment, and was not the outcome of any settled or prepared plan—was doomed to failure, and with the collapse of this bold and resourceful defence the whole movement collapsed.

Those sturdy men who had kept their colours flying to the last were only too glad to be able to

B

return to employment on terms much worse than those in protest against which they had abandoned it. Many of the leaders, indeed, were not allowed to return to their employment at all. As one writer, whose bias of mind was certainly not in favour of the men, afterwards said, those who had " actively promoted the strike were looked upon with great distrust by the masters, and were deemed dangerous characters, inasmuch as they would on all occasions be ready to excite a spirit of disaffection among their fellow-workmen, and take every opportunity of raising the price of labour. These leaders had subsequently considerable difficulty in obtaining employment, and some therefore left the district, while others looked for other occupations."*

At a time when an accumulation of five centuries of enactments directed against labour and its combinations had but a few months previously, by the Act of 1824, been repealed by Parliament, and Trades Unions were freed from the ban of the law, though not yet accorded its protection, and when the power to assess the wages of workmen had but a few years been taken away from the magistrates of Quarter Sessions, it is not to be wondered at that the leaders in the defeated movement should have felt the enmity of their employers. But they paid another penalty of defeat — one almost invariably attaching to those who, in industrial warfare, play a similar part — for they who had dared most by the prominence of their

* "Workmen and Wages at Home and Abroad." Ward, London, 1868.

advocacy of the claims of the workmen, and who suffered peculiarly by the general defeat, were maligned and neglected, and in their poverty unassisted by those on whose behalf they had risked their livelihood, and who had willingly followed their leadership when there was a promise of success.

The Union, now deprived of its leaders, collapsed with the strike, and for the succeeding five years no attempt to re-organise any combination was made. Meanwhile, the general trade was recovering from its depression, and work was plentiful. The workmen then began to recover from the demoralisation of their defeat in 1825, and from amongst their ranks sprang new leaders. The Trades Union movement had been stimulated and encouraged in other parts of the country by the Acts of 1824-5, and delegates from Trades Unions from the Metropolis and Lancashire came down to address the working potters on the advantages and duties of union. Amongst others who so influenced them was the well-known Robert Owen,* the socialist and philanthropist of New Lanark; and he, by preaching a larger and more far-reaching gospel of the power of democracy than the local leaders had expounded, or thought necessary to their purpose, infused an enthusiasm into the action of the potters which they had never before felt. They no longer regarded themselves as an isolated body of workmen fighting their battle in a trade

* For an interesting account of Robert Owen's second visit to The Potteries (1840) in his 70th year, when riots took place at Burslem, on the incentive of placards denouncing his "blasphemous principles," *see* Lloyd Jones' "Life and Labours of Robert Owen."

which was confined to one locality, and having no contact with or sympathy from the outside world; but, deriving new courage from the advent in their midst of the advanced apostles of labour from other parts of the country, they felt all the enthusiasm of men who fight for an abstract cause, and have set before themselves an ideal.

And so, in 1833, a new Union, born of an enthusiasm and a determination lacking in its predecessor, came to life, and daily grew in strength. It was formed of branch lodges, each meeting weekly for the transaction of its own business, and conducting its proceedings in a uniform manner, according to the rules and regulations provided for all. At the head of the Union was the Committee of Management, or Grand Lodge, composed of representatives from each branch lodge, and also meeting weekly. The Grand Lodge created funds for general purposes by a small weekly levy upon each member of the branches; but the branch lodges had full control of their own funds, apart from the general levy, and undertook nothing of importance without the concurrence of the Grand Lodge, which in turn consulted the opinion of the branches, through the delegates appointed, upon any matter of general interest or importance. The constitution of the Union therefore encouraged and provided for the spread of its principles so as to embrace every branch of the trade, and it may at once be said that no completer Union has since been formed in the potting trade.

The ranks of the employers had increased with the revival of trade, but though work was plentiful

and production had increased, wages still remained
at the level at which they were at the time of the
collapse of 1825—in some cases lower, but in none
higher—and many of the manufacturers were complaining of reduced profits. Low wages and low
profits both proceeded from the same cause—the
competition prevailing amongst the manufacturers—
and the aim of the Union was, to quote the words
of one of its officials, "to place a check upon the
downward course of working prices by providing
that if the masters were determined, by a destructive
competition to depreciate the marketable value of
their goods, they should not be allowed to lower
the workmen's wages to meet the exigency." That
this aim, arising out of the consideration of the
reaction of competition and low wages upon each
other, was part of the deliberate policy of the Union,
promulgated from the outset, is clear from the
address which was issued upon its formation, from
which we take the following passage: — "The
degradation to which our trade is exposed, arising
from the unfair competition of the capitalists, and
the labour-depreciating system growing out of it,
with the distress consequent thereon, are the main
reasons for this institution. To prevent the recurrence and increase of those evils, to obtain and
maintain a just and reasonable remuneration for our
labour, to resist and restrain oppressive power and
authority, to afford mutual protection, assistance,
care, and consolation to each other in every possible
way, are the main *objects* of this institution."

The workmen here showed that they had a better

conception of the elements upon which the prosperity of the trade was based than many of their employers, but it is a noteworthy circumstance— and one probably unique in the early annals of Trades Unionism — that the Union was welcomed with open arms by a few of the leading manufacturers, who, so far from seeing in its objects anything subversive of the rights or interests of their class, recognised it as an agency by which the trade might be benefited.   One of these enlightened employers, Mr Charles Mason, wrote a letter to a local newspaper declaring that "such was the state of trade through unfair competition among the manufacturers, that unless the workmen came forward for its protection, nothing but ruin need be expected," and promising to use his influence with his brother manufacturers to secure their sympathy and co-operation with the objects of the Union.   As a result of his good offices, a few manufacturers met together, and invited the newly formed Union to send a deputation to them empowered to act in forming a list of working prices for the ensuing year, to take effect after Martinmas of 1833. The workmen gladly responded, and the effect of this revision of prices was to give complete satisfaction to the potters employed by those manufacturers who had thus led the van, and to the Union for the standard set, and the latter promised to use all its efforts in urging the example of that standard upon those manufacturers who had taken no part in the negotiations. But the latter formed the main body of the employers, and had rather less sympathy with what they regarded as the Quixotism of those who had volunteered an advance in wages than they had with the action of their workmen in forming themselves into a Union, and with the propaganda which they had formulated. They regarded their workmen as their natural enemy, and though they spoke of the Union as an "interference" with their business, they could only look upon it as the outcome of their workmen's position; but the action of their fellow-employers was unintelligible to them, and they regarded them as traitors to their own class. When, therefore, the workmen began the campaign for levelling up prices against the main body of manufacturers, they found that the example given by the pioneers had only inspired contempt, and not respect, and it was clear that no general revision of prices would be obtained by a peaceful and persuasive process. The few manufacturers, however, manfully persisted in their principles, and upon their own urgent representation, a Standing Committee was appointed to continue the work which had been performed by the Committee which had fixed the working prices for the then current year, whose labours had come to an end. The Standing Committee was composed of an equal number of representatives of both sides, and met weekly "to fix the prices of workmanship of all new shapes and patterns, to decide upon all new regulations, new modes of work not contemplated in the price list, and to settle all disputes that might arise in respect of work." This Committee—whose functions really entitled it to be called an Arbitration

Board — lasted but a few months, though it did much useful work in a short career. It met with the greatest opposition from the main body of the manufacturers, who now began to feel, through the reiterated demands of their own workmen, the moral pressure of the example so worthily set them by those employers who had sought for an amicable understanding with their men, based upon a broad and far-seeing comprehension of the conditions which would be best for the trade as a whole. But the verdicts of the Standing Committee upon the disputes submitted to it, so much favoured the men that even amongst those manufacturers who had formed part of it, division arose, and their dissatisfaction was supported by the clamour of those who had kept aloof from the Committee, and had scoffed at all its works. The dissentients in the Committee justified their dissent on the ground of the failure of the workmen in their efforts to secure advances from the main body equal to those conceded by themselves, and pleaded that the advances thus given had been given conditionally upon a success; and so they joined the ranks of those employers who had refused to rise to the standard set (and were thus responsible for the failure charged against the men), and they threatened a reversion to the old prices. And then the Union knew that any further temporising would jeopardise the advantage already gained, and, in November 1834, the men employed by those manufacturers who had steadily refused all concessions, came out on strike, and nothing more was heard of a reversion

to the old prices from the disaffected members of
the Standing Committee.

Ten weeks after the commencement of the strike,
those employers who were concerned in it called
a general meeting of their body to decide what
course should be pursued.   They were the more
disposed to come to terms because they saw those
employers who were not involved in the dispute
reaping increased benefits from the general briskness
in the trade, and amongst such employers were those
who had formed the Standing Committee, and who
were, of course, paying higher prices than those
who now sought their advice.   It is, therefore, not
surprising that the general meeting decided that
some advance in prices should be given.   Those
employers who had originally conceded it had
only anticipated what they regarded as the inevitable demands of the men, and had shown a wise
disposition in turning the new Union to good
account by treating it as an organisation which, as
its proclaimed objects showed, was not oblivious
of the general interests of the industry; but they
had been disheartened by the opposition of their
fellow-employers, and had lost faith in the practic-
ability of their own principles, and now saw in the
position brought about by the strike a possibility
of compromise between their own concessions and
the opposition of the main body to any concessions
at all.   The terms proposed by the meeting of
manufacturers were therefore a mean between the
two; but the workmen, encouraged by the evident
yielding of the employers involved in the strike,

persisted in their full demands, and held to the
standard set. Negotiations followed, but the workmen remained firm, and nearly four months from
the commencement of the strike, the masters
yielded, and re-opened their manufactories, conceding the full terms originally demanded by the
men, and thus establishing an equable rate of wages
throughout the district.*

The working potters had secured an advance of
twenty-five per cent. in their wages, and the strike
of 1834-5 is memorable on such material account;
but the incidents which led up to it are even more
worthy of notice, as being concerned with the broad
question—then raised for the first time and remaining
unsettled to this day—of the extent to which the
employed can help the employers in restraining
an evil which nearly all employers have deplored,
but to which nearly all have succumbed, and by
which certainly all have suffered—the evil of reckless
competition, only made possible by the depression
of the wages of the workmen, who thus have a vital
interest in the business methods of their employers.

* It is evidently to this strike that Ward refers, in his "History of
Stoke-on-Trent," in the following paragraph :—
  "The trade had been for some time previously in a very prosperous
state, when the masters were called to encounter a formidable *combination of workmen*, to raise wages and prescribe regulations for their
advantage. The operatives, by mandate from their Union and lodge,
systematically *turned out* in a mass from any manufactory where their
prices and rules were not granted, and the unemployed were supported
by weekly allowances from those who were in work. This proceeding
greatly inconvenienced many of the *masters*, and induced some to
forgo that character, and submit to the dictates of their workmen."
—Ward's "History of Stoke-on-Trent," 1846

CHAPTER II

THE GREAT STRIKE OF 1836

NOT unnaturally, the men were elated by such a signal victory, and they had scarcely begun to reap its fruit before they prepared for another campaign. They felt that a Union which could secure a large advance in prices would be no less successful in combating what they regarded as other abuses in the trade, and they soon evinced a disposition to re-model the system and usages upon which their employment and remuneration were based.

The division in the ranks of the employers, however, had become narrowed by the result of the strike. The pioneering minority were satisfied with that result, because it had brought about that equality in wages which was necessary to their own interests, after the concessions they had made and could not recall, and the opposition which the rest of the employers had shown to any sympathetic action with the Union had convinced them of the hopelessness of pursuing their efforts in that direction; and as to the majority, they only saw in the strike and its result further justification of their attitude towards the Union which had brought it about. The signs of an impending attack by the Union upon the "usages" of the trade, finally closed the breach between the employers. They decided to meet Union by Union, and accordingly, in March 1836, they formed themselves into a body known as The Potteries' Chamber of Commerce.* Its professed object was to "protect the general interests of the trade," but its more proper purpose was indicated in an address which was issued to the members of its own body and to manufacturers not included in its membership, in which the members declared the folly of remaining inactive, and of making no combined effort to counteract the policy of the Potters' Union, which, they averred, "had destroyed the legitimate control of the masters over their business, and exposed them to constant and increasing annoyance."

Both sides were then prepared for a conflict, which was waged on a broader issue than that out of which the workmen had just triumphantly emerged, and which involved practically every manufacturer of importance in The Potteries. The issue was not the simple one of the strike just concluded. The men had secured a liberal advance in wages, and now they determined to go further back and attack

---

* "Many of them (manufacturers) united in the year 1813, under the appellation of a Chamber of Commerce, to advance the prices of their goods, and adopted a price list commencing January 1, 1814, by which the ordinary species of ware are yet regulated" (writing about 1838), "though we believe large discounts have been conceded in many instances, and the nett prices have thus been considerably reduced. In September 1825 a Committee was formed 'for the promotion of measures calculated to benefit the general trade of The Potteries'; but the energies of the manufacturers, as a body, were never fully developed until 1836, a crisis which will long be remembered."—Ward's " History of Stoke-on-Trent," 1846.

what they regarded as unfair fundamental conditions of employment, which had prevailed in the potting trade from the earliest days of its period of development. Their hostility was directed against two customs : firstly, that of an annual hiring-time; and secondly, that which only credited the workman with payment for those articles which came in a perfect condition from the "biscuit-oven."

A few words will be necessary to explain the operation of these customs, and the manner in which they affected the workmen. · It would be difficult to say which of the two was regarded by them as the greater hardship. The "hiring agreement" bound the workman to the master for a whole year. He was engaged at Martinmas in one year, and could not leave his master's employment, except at the risk of imprisonment, until the following November, when the period of his service terminated. It was purely a custom, and there was no pretence on the part of the masters that it was reciprocal in character. An employer could, or did, discharge his workmen when he pleased, but no workman could leave his employment except at the general termination of all contracts in November. And not only was the period of service so fixed, but there could be no alteration of prices or conditions of labour except at Martinmas. Then and then only were prices subject to revision. It was against this system that the men rebelled.*

* In an appendix to a paper read before the Industrial Remuneration Conference in London, 1884, Mr Benjamin Jones says : "Some of the brickmakers in Kent have to sign agreements at the beginning of

The system of "good-from-oven" was their second grievance. It concerned two very important branches of the trade—the flat-pressers and the hollow-ware pressers. By this system, the men in those branches were only paid for the work which came in a perfect state out of the biscuit-oven. The master assumed that whatever ware came out in an imperfect state had come imperfectly from the hands of the workman who had fashioned it, and made no allowance for possible damage to the ware during its passage through the process of firing. It was chiefly during this ordeal of firing, and the accidents incidental to it, that the damage to the ware arose, but the risk of injury was not limited to this process. After it had left the hands of the workman who made it, the ware had to pass through several manipulations, and it was not until its arrival in the biscuit-warehouse, after being fired in the biscuit-oven, that the workman was allowed to inspect what was there put before him as the outcome of his labour. It was not always, indeed, that he was allowed even this satisfaction. The system was capable of many variations, at the caprice of the employer or his manager. An inquiry by the workmen was often unanswered; a protest rewarded by dismissal. The system was defended by the employer on two

every year which bind them not to work for any other firm or employer up to the ensuing September, but the firm does not bind itself to find the men work, neither does it give them a signed agreement. . . . I have known of thoroughly good, honest men emigrating rather than continue to sign this one-sided document. It is a pity there is no Trades Union to induce fair play on the part of the masters." The agreement, which is appended, is a very stringent one, and has as little of the mutuality of a bargain as a theft.

grounds. He alleged, in the first instance, that it was a check upon the unskilfulness of the workman, and, as an alternative, pleaded that the workmen should share with the master the risk of loss. The first defence would have been valid if the test had been applied to the work immediately it had left the hands of the workman; but the fact that the ware was only adjudged after it had passed through other hands and processes in which the risk of damage was notorious and admitted, rendered that defence altogether invalid. The workmen answered the second plea by saying that the loss should only be shared when the fault was apportioned. It was indeed obviously inevitable that such a system, upon which the workman was allowed no check, should have admitted the practice of many abuses. It was asserted by the men that at some manufactories no attempt was made by the employer to distinguish between bad and good ware, but that an average of bad ware was assumed, and deducted from the total amount; and it was an admitted practice by the manufacturers to sell as " seconds "— that is, at a reduced price, as a damaged article— that for which they had refused to pay anything to the workman who made it. It is, at any rate, certain that the system allowed ample opportunities for injustice to be practised on the workmen; and even if more restraint were conceded to the manufacturers than they claimed for themselves, the workmen would have had ground for objection against a system which gave such scope for abuse whilst offering an obvious means of reform. It has been thought necessary to dwell at some length upon this subject, for it will be found to form one of the chief causes of dispute in the trade, and it was at this day far from final settlement.

The employers refused to consent to any modification of the system of good-from-oven on the ground that they "could not allow the old usages of the trade to be broken up," and upon that point the two sides definitely joined issue. But there were some attempts at negotiation upon the question of the annual hiring. The workmen drew up a draft agreement, submitted it to counsel, by whom it was approved, and then to the employers. It re-affirmed the custom of settling at Martinmas the prices for the year, and contained a clause providing that the period of employment could be terminated by a month's notice from either side. The employers rejected the proposed form of agreement, on the ground of the insertion of that clause. They maintained that it had only been inserted in order to enable the workmen "to make fresh demands, and to turn out upon those demands legally." The workmen replied that it had no other object than to be "a means of legal release when the bond ceased to be mutually agreeable," and that as the prices and terms were to be fixed for the whole year, no fresh demands could be made.

The employers, rejecting the proposals of the men, put forth their own. The first clause of their proposed agreement was: "That the said (workman) agrees to be satisfied with what amount of work the said (employer) can fairly and reasonably find him during the said term." There was no variation in this clause from the provisions of the old form of agreement, but the workmen had already objected to it because they had experienced its hardship. Under its protection an employer could keep a workman tied to a situation which yielded him no more than one day's employment a week. If the workman left the situation, it would be at the risk of prosecution; but even if his employer did not deem it worth while to so pursue him, he would be no better off, for he would be asked to present a written discharge to the next employer to whom he offered his services. The employers justified the clause in the following words :— "If what the master deems to be a fair and reasonable quantity of work is deemed otherwise by the workmen, the magistrates will define and decide between the two." But the workmen were not distinguished by their faith in the decisions of the magistracy in disputes between "master and servant" — as they were then respectively described in legal phrase— and they answered the employers by asking "why such a simple question could not be defined and decided in the terms of the agreement itself," and pointed out, reasonably and truly enough, that the employers were maintaining a system which, even if it admitted the remedy suggested, "would make an appeal to law a daily necessity," and so become practicably irremediable.

The third clause in the employers' agreement was, however, entirely new. It was as follows:—"And that in case the said (master) shall at any time

C

suspend the manufacturing of earthenware at the said manufactory, this agreement shall be thereupon suspended till the general work at such manufactory shall be resumed." This was rightly regarded by the workmen as an effort on the part of their masters to re-affirm with greater stringency the system of an annual hiring. The employers had rejected the proposal of the workmen because it provided for a termination of the service upon a month's notice, and now they calmly proposed that they should be allowed to dismiss their employees without any notice at all. There was this further difference, however, between the two proposals—that whereas the workman, when he left his employer after giving reasonable notice, would take his fate in his hands, and trust to all the vicissitudes of his class, his employer could close the entire manufactory, and dismiss all his hands, and then re-open business at pleasure, recalling to his service from any other employment which they might have obtained the men whose agreement, and livelihood, had been " suspended " meanwhile.

This monstrous provision was supported by the employers in these naïve terms: " The sole object of the suspension clause is to authorise the masters to suspend work unitedly, and the workman is expressly authorised to take employment elsewhere during the suspension. For the agreement to be suspended rather than to be cancelled is to the advantage of both parties, because in the first case a week's notice would bring all the men to work again; but in the last much time would be required to hire all the men anew." Upon that it can only be said that each separate agreement entitled each separate manufacturer to suspend work as he pleased, and so provided both for free action in case of any individual dispute, or for a campaign in detail against the workmen. But even if the suspension clause were intended to be only set in force "unitedly"—upon which supposition the authorisation to the workman to find employment "elsewhere" merely attested the humour of the employers—it was an arrogation of a right denied to the workmen, who had proposed the reasonable operation of a month's notice. And as to the mutual "advantage" foreshadowed in the explanation given by the employers, the workmen not unnaturally asked where their advantage lay, in being liable to be suspended from work and wages, though not from servitude? The truth seems to be that the employers devised this stringent clause as an easy means of resisting any demands their men might make, or of imposing any fresh conditions themselves; but they could not have been oblivious of the flagrant injustice involved in the means by which they wished to attain their end, and all the contingencies which they wished to avoid, or to provide for, would have been amply met by the sane proposal of their workmen that a month's notice should determine the period of employment. The men were sufficiently determined in the first instance in their opposition to the annual hiring, in its old form, but they were incensed by this fresh effort to maintain it in its integrity by an added stringency.

The manufacturers, through the Chamber of Commerce, intimated to their employees that on the 5th of September 1836 they would be prepared to enter into engagements for the ensuing year, to commence at Martinmas, November 11th, and they, at the same time, announced that the Suspension Clause would form part of the agreements which those engaged would have to sign. This intimation found an immediate answer from the workmen. The employees at fourteen manufactories, numbering 3500, did not wait for Martinmas to come, but ceased work at once. This was a proceeding unexpected by the employers. Burke said that he could not draw up an indictment against a whole nation. The manufacturers could not contemplate, as a practical step, the issue of several thousand summonses against workmen who had broken their annual agreements by declining to wait for the fall of the knife at Martinmas. The whole body of manufacturers met, and took counsel. The fourteen manufacturers were urged to resist the demands of the men, and the Chamber of Commerce undertook to recompense them for the loss they sustained by their works being closed for the period that intervened between then and Martinmas — a period of nearly eleven weeks. It was fully expected that at Martinmas the number of employers whose workmen had ceased to work would be considerably reinforced, and that a united front of opposition could then be shown to their demands. This assumption was well founded. In the interim, the situation remained unchanged. No negotiations passed between the two sides. The fourteen manufactories remained closed, and the workmen were drawing upon the funds of their Union.

Martinmas came, and sixty-four manufactories were at once closed. The total number of employees now out on strike amounted to nearly 20,000. The average amount of the weekly wages paid at the fourteen manufactories closed in September was £2560, and at the sixty-four manufactories which were affected at Martinmas, £11,238, making a total of £13,798. At this time there were about 130 manufactories in The Potteries, so that only a little more than half of the total number were concerned in the strike, but inasmuch as they included the largest firms, and employed seven-ninths of the labour engaged in the trade, it will be seen that the stoppage of work involved practically the whole industry.

There was no vacillation on the part of the masters in 1836. They proposed no conferences, nor suggested any compromise. The men were of like temper, and it was evident from the outset that the battle would be à outrance. The effect of such an almost complete stoppage in the staple trade of the district was to spread distress throughout The Potteries. The auxiliary trades, though not concerned in the dispute, shared in the disaster, and the shopkeepers had little need to keep open their shops. The funds of the Union only allowed of the distribution of five or six shillings per week to men having families dependent on them, and this fact alone gives a vivid idea of the privations which the potters endured for their cause. Unmarried men could only receive three or four shillings a week, and the working women and children had no share whatever of the funds dispensed by the Union. It early became obvious to the leaders of the men that some help must be sought from outside, and appeals were made to many organised trades throughout the kingdom. In one instance, the appeal was conspicuously successful. The Trades Unionists of Sheffield lent the potters a sum of £2084, and collected £108, which they sent as a gift. This generous example was followed by Trades Unionists in other parts of the country. No less a sum than £3794 came as free offerings to the coffers of the potters, and the handsome loan from Sheffield was followed by other loans which amounted to nearly £2000. Altogether, financial assistance to the amount of £7000, of which about half was given and half lent, came to the potters from sympathisers who were totally unconnected with the potting industry.

Even more gratifying, however, than the generous help of these disinterested outsiders was that which came to them from within their own ranks. Amongst the leaders of the men, and in their general body, were some thrifty ones who had put by what, in the expressive phrase of the district, is known as a "stocking-leg" — that article of apparel conveniently lending itself to the purpose of a purse. They had saved a little money to meet times of adversity, or to console a feeble old age, and when the day of common difficulty came they did not hesitate to refuse to accept the help to which they were entitled from the common fund, and live upon the resources which their thrift had provided them.   Others went still further, and gave their little savings to the common fund.*   Nothing could attest more than such facts as these the determination of the men in their struggle, and their honest conviction of the justice of their cause. But they were fighting a forlorn hope.   No whisper of weakness had been heard from the employers, and the men saw the end in sight.   Their courage and self - sacrifice had carried them far, but it was their financial resources that fixed the final limit to which they could go.   And their resources were exhausted.   There was not one of them that had not undergone great privations, many had already passed through weeks of absolute want, all of them saw starvation staring them in the face. In a week, their unity was destroyed, and with it their Union, for to distribute its funds was its only remaining function, and those funds were now gone. There was a stampede to fill the long vacant places, and manufactories re - opened rapidly, at first by

* "That turn-out extended over a period of no less than twenty weeks, and every possible hardship was endured by the determined operatives before they would bend to the more potent power of their combined employers.   Ruin descended on the homes of many a work-ing potter.   The savings of years were scattered in the space of twenty weeks, and no after-exertions could replace the little hoarded sums, then irreparably lost.   Indeed, to such an extent did the devotedness of the potters extend that every available property,—every household god !—the sale of which would bring cash to prolong the strike, was brought to common centres and immediately disposed of for the general good of the cause."—William Evans, Trade Union Leader, in "The Art and History of the Potting Trade." Hanley, 1846.

dozens, then by twos and threes. And then there
came a rally. The leaders of the men had not
abandoned their leadership, but exhorted the rem-
nant of the men to remain firm. At first, theirs
was a voice crying in the wilderness, and they were
answered by scoffs and reproaches. But they could
point with pride to their own record of effort and
sacrifice in the struggle, and the men reflected that
they who had held out for so long, and suffered
so much, might hold out and suffer a little longer,
in the hope of snatching their cause from final
defeat. At a time when half of the body of workmen had returned to their benches, and a total rout
seemed imminent, a courageous band of several
hundreds had marched to the pawnshops to pledge
the whole of their worldly belongings upon which
money could be raised, and had given the scanty
result to the common fund. Little wonder that
with such examples before them the rest should
take fresh courage.

The action of the leaders did not achieve all that
such devotion may have deserved, but it undoubtedly
left to the workmen some result for their struggle.
It was evident to the masters that the strike was
not over. So far from the partial surrender of the
workmen proving a weakness to the whole body,
the faithful and courageous potters who still fought
on had caused it to prove a weakness to the manufacturers. To the latter, the strike had been irk-
some and costly, and though they had locked their
manufactories and gone to their villas, determined
not to unlock their works until the men came,

subdued, to ask for the gates to be thrown open, they reflected with impatience upon their idle capital and lost profits. And so, after the partial submission of the workmen many manufacturers still remained unaffected, and they could turn their eyes from the smoking ovens and busy yards of rival works, dotted here and there in their midst, to their own silent and idle manufactories with a watchman at the wicket. Those employers, indeed, who had opened their gates to the deserting workmen had been guilty of the same disloyalty to their own class, although they had upheld the terms dictated by the whole body. They had hailed the surrender of their men as a victory for themselves, but had left the remainder of their fellow-employers exposed to the unexpected stand of the faithful Unionists who pawned their clothes for food, and starved when they had no more clothes to pawn.

Here, then, was a situation created for compromise. The masters wished for peace; the men could hold out no longer. Neither side, however, would make any overture, and a suggestion of mediation came from outside. The outcome was that a conciliation meeting, was held at Betley, under the presidency of Mr Twemlow, a county magistrate, and there terms of peace were arranged. So far as the men were concerned, their efforts were directed to minimising the effects of their defeat— for they knew their cause had lost. The meeting did not pretend to be an arbitration. It did no more than enable each side to state its case to a neutral ear, and, after the issue had been thus defined, the combatants came to terms themselves. The benevolent impartiality of the Chairman kept them in good temper whilst they "talked it out." The result of this *rapprochement* was the termination of the strike upon terms that were regarded by the men as little more than a complete defeat. For years afterwards, indeed, it was a bitter lament by the potters that union had brought them no advantages, and that they had fallen ignominiously in the great fight—long remembered—of the winter of 1836 and 1837. But really the men who had made the last stand had plucked a brand from the burning. If they had got all they had asked for they would indeed have won a remarkable victory, but it was absurd to regard as an "ignominious defeat" what was really a compromise conceding to the men important advantages, though giving them far from the full measure of their demands.

The masters held to the hiring agreement, and it was retained, but with this important modification: that the employer guaranteed to his workman sixteen days work per month at least, and that, if from any cause the employer were prevented from finding the stipulated amount of employment, the workman had the power to dissolve the contract by giving a month's clear notice. This, surely, was a solid gain. Before the strike there was no agreement worth the name. An employer might prevent his workmen from doing a single day's work for any other employer during the run of the year's agreement, although he might not provide more employment, on the average, than one day's work

a week. A workman dissatisfied with his employment, and desiring to better his position under
another employer, had to bring to the latter his
"discharge" from the employment of the master
to whom he had been hired — otherwise there was
no hope of obtaining a new situation. Just as in
feudal times the serf was forbidden to roam beyond
the limits of his native parish, but was tied to the
land upon which he was born, so the working potter
had to surrender the freedom of his labour to work
in annual periods. The concession obtained, therefore, of the right to ask for work every other day
in the year (for that is what it amounted to), in
default of which the workman was free to offer
himself to any employer who would employ him
for sixteen days in every month, was, as things
were then, a valuable one.

Again, the masters insisted upon retaining the
system of payment by good-from-oven, but they
consented that that system should undergo these
important modifications: that all ware declared to
be bad by the fault of the maker should be broken;
that all ware damaged otherwise than by the maker
should be paid for; and that the men should be
allowed to draw on account, weekly, a sum equal
to two-thirds of the value of the ware from their
hands then on the premises, unfired. The workman
had still to wait until the ware had come from the
oven before it was credited to him, but there was
one temptation the less to abuse the system in the
promise of the masters that such ware as they
declared to be bad and unsaleable should be

destroyed; the workman still had to accept the decree of the master as to what ware was spoiled by him, and what was spoiled by causes over which he had no control; but for the first time the employer was induced to distinguish between the two. The principle was conceded, even though the practice of it might leave matters much as before. And, on the third point, the workman might claim some payment for his visible work, and not be compelled to go home on Saturday night with pockets more or less empty, to await the time when his work, already completed so far as he was concerned, should undergo a process with which he had absolutely nothing to do.

These, then, were the results obtained by the memorable strike of 1836. On January 20th, 1837, the men returned to work. It was twenty-one weeks since those employed at the fourteen manufactories had struck, and ten weeks from the general strike at Martinmas. It is worthy of remark that during this industrial struggle, which was of far greater magnitude than any which had occurred in the potting trade, and which took place at a time when Trades Unions were regarded with aversion by the general public, and when a strike was looked upon as little better than a rebellion, no outrage upon the person or property of any manufacturer was made. Feeling ran high, and the struggle was a desperate one, but the workmen conducted it with a restraint highly creditable to them.

A period of absolute demoralisation followed. The Union had collapsed like a house of cards, and the principles of Union were held in contempt. The men set no value upon the terms gained at the Betley Conference. They felt that they had been roundly beaten, and that their last state was even worse than the first. They predicted that the concessions announced, rather as an act of grace than as a price for peace, by their employers, would be found to bring them no advantage in practice, however satisfactory they might appear in theory. They felt that they had attempted too much, and the pendulum swung back to the other extreme, for they were cowed, and became indifferent. In this way they helped to fulfil their own predictions. The masters soon saw that they had to deal with men broken in spirit, disgusted at their failure, full of recriminations against each other, and dwelling with bitter resignation upon their own helplessness. The employers were not slow to take advantage of this mood of despair. There was no longer any Union, even amongst the workers of a particular branch; but each manufacturer was left to deal with his throwers, pressers, oven-men, and the rest, as he desired.

The " concessions " made at the close of the strike became a dead-letter, and the workmen had soon reverted to the position they occupied before the strike began. The system of " good-from-oven " recovered its lost abuses; the annual hiring gathered to itself again its old stringency and restrictions. Having re-established these two "systems" in their integrity, the masters proceeded to institute a third. The " allowance system " made its appearance. It was merely a reduction of wages, and the process was complimented by being described as a " system." It consisted in subjecting the wages of the workmen to the method adopted in fixing those of an apprentice. An apprentice was, in the first years of his probation, paid at the rate of a quarter of a journeyman's wages; afterwards he received two-thirds— that is, eightpence for that for which a journeyman received a shilling. The masters said trade was bad, and proposed that the journeyman should "allow" twopence in every shilling. Nominally, by a pleasing fiction, his wages remained the same, but actually he submitted to a reduction in his wages of a little over sixteen per cent. This was not the result of any combined action on the part of the employers, and did not receive the sanction of the Chamber of Commerce as an official body. In truth, that Chamber had, to a large extent, lost its occupation. It existed to combat, by organised effort, the organised demands of their men. But the workmen were no longer organised, and each manufacturer now dealt with his own workmen without reference to the general body of the trade. The " allowance system," therefore, came into existence gradually, but finally involved nearly the whole of the manufactories in The Potteries. And so matters went on for seven years.

CHAPTER III

·MARTINMAS of the year 1843 was drawing near when a rumour went round that at the impending annual hiring the employers contemplated a reduction in wages for the next yearly term. Instantly the potters set about the formation of another Union. But it is certain that they would have done so at that period even if no such rumour had obtained credence. Signs of restiveness and rebellion against the "allowance system" had long manifested themselves, and the threatened reduction merely fixed the moment when slumbering discontent should become translated into action.

The employers had enjoyed a happy independence for seven years, and the twopence which was first "allowed" had become in many cases threepence and fourpence, the amount varying according to the insistence of the employer and the compliance of his workmen. Probably, if no employer had had the temerity to go beyond the twopence, the allowance system would have passed into a settled custom of the trade, like the annual hiring-time and "good-from-oven," and would in after years have been defended as a settled system of trade discount. But by its extension it amounted to an evil which awoke the workmen from their lethargy. Meet-

47

ings were held by the separate branches of the
trade and of the combined branches, and the
potters decided that they must look to union again
as presenting the only means of resistance.   Other
meetings were then held to decide upon the constitution of the Union, and in September 1843
their plans were matured, and the Union came
into existence.

The Union greatly differed in its constitution
from that of 1833.   In the latter, the Committee of
Management, as it was called, was supreme, and
there was little delegation of power or responsibility
to the branches.   In 1843 the Union had at its
head a Central Committee, but it did not possess
the power which was vested in the Committee of
Management of 1833.   Each branch was a Union
in itself, and was divided into lodges, each town in
The Potteries having its lodge.   This was a condition necessitated by the geographical extent of The
Potteries, and was designed to meet the convenience
of its members.   All the lodges possessed the same
functions, which were confined to the affairs of the
town or district in which each was situated.   The
united lodges of each branch elected an Executive
Committee, which superintended the proceedings of
its lodges, and dealt with all matters connected
with the trade it represented.   The Central Committee was composed of delegates elected by every
lodge of each branch.   It will thus be seen that
the Central Committee was a very representative
body; and its functions were to superintend all
strikes, to concentrate the powers of all branches

on a given object, and to act as the mouthpiece of all the branches upon any matter common to them all. It was supported by a weekly subscription from each member of the lodges, but had not the power to raise any other levy amongst the members of the Union. Each branch had full control of its own financial arrangements.

The inception of the new Union was not characterised by enthusiasm so much as by determination. It did not regard itself as the agent of a high destiny, and was not hampered or inspired by any other idea than securing as much wages for its members as it could. It lacked the high incentive of its predecessor, but in the quiet resolve of its methods, and the definite, unheroic character of its aims, it had its compensations for the absence of a loftier inspiration. It was a business organisation, and for a time pretended to be no more. It early inaugurated one new departure, but one which was eminently practical. It determined to speak its voice through the trumpet of the Press, and started a newspaper. *The Potters' Examiner* was the property of the Union, conducted by members of the Central Committee specially deputed for the purpose. The *Examiner* was an unpretentious publication devoted to the direct interests of the working potters. Its conductors were able men, and edited their little paper with scrupulous fairness. They were, first and foremost, men of religious conviction—earnest and honest. They regarded every question from the altitude of a severe morality, and enforced their

D

arguments with Biblical texts, and exhortations appealing to the Christian virtues. Wielding a new power, they addressed remonstrance, by means of "open letters," to offending employers, who received reprimands through the columns of the *Examiner* that, for their length and candour, could not have been uninterruptedly delivered through the medium of personal intercourse. And its contributors, among the rank and file of the working potters, revelled in a similar liberty. A grievance which fell on the idle ears of an employer in the workshop or in his office, found more deliberate and ornate utterance in careful compositions which they sent to their little paper. And not only were the employers singled out for the attentions of the *Examiner*, for in its columns were to be found reprimands to the idle and slovenly workman, and denunciations of the discredit which the Sabbath-breaker and the drunkard brought upon their class. Its contents demonstrated the difference of the attitude of the potters towards the questions of their industry in 1830 and 1843. In the former period they were seized with a sudden reforming zeal, and dreamt of founding a new era and a new order. In 1843 they still laboured towards the same goal, but saw it at a greater distance; and recognised that though it might be reached in time the road was long, and that they could only march with their day, and must leave the days to come to complete the journey.

With men of such views and character it would naturally be expected that they would undertake no rash enterprises, nor pursue any visionary aims, and though in all their direct relations with their employers they showed moderation in demands and deliberation in methods and purpose, yet, in two movements which were more remotely connected with those relations, they lapsed into the heroic and impracticable, and served to illustrate again the wisdom of Trades Unions in narrowing their efforts to their elemental functions. It will be convenient to first deal with their efforts in pursuit of those primary aims—which at first alone engaged the attention of the Union—and to then describe the more diffuse employment of its energies.

The Union which started in 1843 did not witness any general strike in the trade. It adopted the policy of guerilla warfare, and learned to walk before it tried to run. The abuses which had created it had come into existence bit by bit, and the policy of the Union was to reform them by the same process. Good-from-oven, the hiring system, the allowance system, and the breaking of the Truck Act furnished enough scope for all their power, and the potters waged a steady war against them all. That they, like their predecessors in 1836, had a broad conception of both their duties and rights, is shown by the fact that they announced their chief object to be to equalise the price of labour throughout the district. They held that from the competitive state of the trade it was "a matter of injustice to compel one manufacturer to give a good price for labour if others around him were allowed to give five, ten, or twenty per cent.

less than he paid to his workpeople." By this statement of principle—which was in its essence identical
with the aim and policy of the Union of 1833—
they hoped to win to their side the more reputable
manufacturers who had been the last to adopt
practices of which the workmen complained, and
who had only done so when they could justly
plead the exigencies of a competition which had
compelled them to follow a bad example. And
this pronouncement of the men applied with still
greater force to the few manufacturers who had
refused altogether to adopt the "allowance system."
But, whilst thus making a concession and an
acknowledgment which was likely to conciliate the
better class of their employers, the workmen were
careful to explain that when they spoke of "equalis-
ing wages" they only meant that the highest rate
should serve as a standard.

In another direction also they gave an evidence
of their comprehensive policy. Since 1836 there
had been a great increase in the number of pottery
manufacturers in other parts of the country—chiefly
in Derbyshire, Yorkshire, and Scotland. The employees in these enterprises were almost entirely
recruited from among the potters of Staffordshire,
and the Union determined to bring the workers
in those out-potteries into their Union. They
sent out delegates to organise them, and generally succeeded. They had an easy task, for the
rate of wages prevailing in the out-districts gave
in but few cases satisfaction to the workmen, and,
as the delegates found themselves among men who

were almost literally their brothers, they had no prejudice to overcome. The Union hoped, by this organisation and spirit of co-fraternity, to anticipate any evil resulting to the whole from a weakness in its remote parts ; and the potters scattered in Scotland and elsewhere, on the other hand, felt that in their hour of need they had the support of their brethren at home.

The Union of 1843 found, at its birth, a strike already in progress. It concerned two firms alone, but the grounds of dispute applied to nearly all the manufactories — good-from-oven, the allowance system, and the annual hiring all contributed to it. But there was a new grievance added to the list, which was the specific cause of the strike. In the trade the different size of plates are distinguished by separate names. The largest size is called a plate, the next a "twiffler," the smallest a "muffin." One of the employers whose workmen had struck re-christened the series. He called the plate a twiffler, the twiffler a muffin, and the muffin, in the words of the workmen, he "sent to God knew where." In other words, the men were told that they must make plates at the same price as twifflers, and twifflers at the same price as muffins. There was no alteration in the sizes — the nomenclature and prices alone were affected. This is an interesting circumstance, inasmuch as it is the earliest recorded example of a practice in the trade which subsequently became very common as an oblique method of a reduction in wages. Another incident in this strike worthy of mention is that one of the workmen concerned was sent to prison for one month, and another workman for three months with hard labour, for breaking their annual agreements. This circumstance caused much indignation among the potters, and stimulated more than ever their opposition to the custom of an annual agreement. The strike lasted nine months, and was ultimately successful, though at a cost of some three thousand pounds to the Union.

In its early day, the Union embarked on another campaign. Some of the manufacturers — but certainly the least reputable and important—had been in the habit of evading, or breaking, the Truck Act —an Act passed some years before,* which made it illegal for any employer to pay his workmen in any manner than by the coin of the realm. In 1843 the potters asserted, in a letter to the Chief Constable of Burslem, that at some manufactories this Act was being systematically broken. The workman, presenting himself for his wages, was handed so much cloth, the price of which, moreover, was calculated at an excessive rate. One passage in the letter is too striking to be passed unnoticed. It was this: "Cases have been known in which bankrupt stocks of Birmingham jewellery have been introduced into manufactories working on short time, and amongst a people wanting the common necessaries of life. Oh! sir, it is a hard case to witness hungry men and women carrying home pins and brooches at two shillings and half-a-crown each, when the same may be had at Birming-

* Act 1 and 2 William IV. c. 37.

ham at one-and-sixpence per dozen; and, when their little ones meet them at the door, crying for bread, to present them with paste." The evasion of the Truck Act was not confined to the Staffordshire potteries — it spread to the potteries of Derbyshire. Some of the manufacturers there were apparently also shopkeepers. They sold grocery, hosiery, clothing, and general provisions. Some of the employees rarely received any coin in return for their labour. A case was given in which a warehouseman had been compelled to pay his rent with flour, for he doubtless possessed a surplusage of that necessity, inasmuch as it formed the currency in which his wages were mostly paid. In another instance it was averred that a lathe-turner had only received tenpence in money in twelve months. One manufacturer, who presumably kept, as an auxiliary business, a butcher's shop, paid his men with pigs' liver, for which he charged half-a-crown. To check such truly monstrous abuses, the workmen had only one course to take, and they took it. They caused proceedings to be instituted against several employers in the Police Court, and they were convicted, and fined. A system so gross, and one in defiance of the law of the land, could not survive publicity, and with this salutary example, it speedily ceased. It is a remarkable fact, however, that acts which only needed an appeal to the law, which had recently and explicitly forbidden them, to ensure their cessation, should have been allowed to develop into an open practice; and it certainly shows the lengths to which some manufacturers were prepared to go, and their low estimate of the power of resistance of their workmen.

Not less successful was the Union in its war upon the "allowance system." The practice had existed, unchecked, for seven years, and amongst some manufacturers it had come to be regarded as an institution sanctified by time. It had spread to such an extent as to involve risking the preservation of any distinction between a mature journeyman and an apprentice. In many cases, work of an advanced nature, which had always been allotted to journeymen, was given to apprentices, whilst the journeymen were put to do the work of apprentices. Then the manufacturer triumphantly argued that he was obeying all that custom and fairness could demand in paying for apprentices' work at the rate of apprentices' wages. An apprentice, at the conclusion of his probationary period, was offered the alternative of leaving his employ, or of continuing to work at his bench at prices for his emancipation from which he had worked and waited for years. Or, again, a journeyman was told that his services would not be required any longer unless he was content to become an "apprentice." Sometimes he refused, and was supported by the Union. Oftener he went along the line of least resistance, and consented, and then the employer answered inquiry or allegation by a reference to the "voluntary" character of the workman's action. But these were exceptional cases. In the main, the allowance system was enforced without any such devious and circumlocutory devices. An incident of the latter

method was given by a workman in 1843. It is
amusing — but not only that. He applied for a
situation, and was asked if he wished to be employed as a journeyman. He answered in the
affirmative, and was then asked what kind of a
journeyman he desired to be, as there were several
kinds. "There were," said the manufacturer, "some
like those of such a firm, who took provisions, and
there were others, like those of another firm, who
took clothes, haberdashery, and provisions; but the
class to which he wished to direct particular attention was that which allowed twopence in the shilling,
which class was sub-divided into two parties: those
who consented to the twopences being stopped out
of their wages on the Saturday evening, and those
who preferred to compound with their dignity and
receive their wages in full on Saturday evening, but
refunded the twopences on Monday morning. To
which of those two parties did the applicant desire
to belong?"

There was no longer any pretence to uniformity
or stability in the wages of the potters. A dozen
manufacturers, producing identical articles, paid a
dozen different rates of wages. The workmen
placed their finger on the right spot when they
stated that this lack of uniformity in wages was
caused by the irregular prices at which the manufacturers sold their goods. They pointed out that
no manufacturer in the potting trade had any
material advantage over another one. They all
carried on their business within an area of a few
miles, and all possessed the same appliances and

facilities. Therefore, presumably, all could sell their
ware at approximately the same price. But it was
notorious that there were the most striking discrep-
ancies in the prices they asked for their goods.
Therefore, argued the workmen, those who sold
their goods cheaper than their fellows must obtain
their labour cheaper than their fellows. All the
raw material used in the trade had a definite
market price; labour alone (the heaviest item in
expenditure) was not uniform and regular in value.
The low price of labour produced the low price of
manufactured goods, and then the effect was pleaded
as justifying the cause. The workmen, therefore,
may be said to have taken a statesmanlike view of
the question in putting in the forefront of their
programme their effort to equalise wages where all
other conditions were equal. And so they came
back again to the "allowance system"—to them the
source of all evil. They took the opinion of an
eminent lawyer on the subject. He gave it as his
opinion that the allowance system was illegal, and
that all moneys deducted from the wages of the
potters under that system constituted debts re-
coverable at law. He held that a man's wages,
being based upon a certain rate, were inviolable, and
no subsequent "understanding" could make the
payment of a less amount anything but an illegal
stoppage, pure and simple. Common-sense certainly
seems to support that view, and it is in some senses
to be regretted that no steps were taken to test the
validity of the opinion in a court of law. The
system, however, was discontinued, and it is prob-

able that a conviction of the correctness of the
lawyer's opinion had more effect upon the minds of
the manufacturers than any fear which the Union,
as a Union, inspired.   Truth to tell, the system
was repugnant to many of the manufacturers who
practised it.   They had adopted it as a means of
defence when it had become almost general, and
when the workmen had submitted to it; and they
were perhaps relieved at the prospect, which the
efforts of the Union gave, of it being discontinued.
And, amongst the main body, there was no suggestion of any combination to resist the demands of the
men that the system should be abolished.   Perhaps
it would be true to say that the allowance system
perished by its own inherent and indefensible unfair-
ness.   The loss to the workmen during the seven
years of its operation could not have been less than
many thousands of pounds ; and, apart from the
obvious advantage to the workmen by its cessation,
its abandonment contributed in some degree to the
solidity of the trade by helping to check the ruinous
competition among the manufacturers which it had
fostered.   It is an interesting chapter, not only in
the history of the working potters, but in that of
the whole industrial movement, for we can find no
trace in any other trade of the adoption of such a
devious method of reducing wages.   What, also, is
interesting is that the men accomplished their victory
without a general strike, but by means of incessant
appeals and remonstrances, and that they were
assisted in no small degree by what may be called
the "moral force" of public opinion—an element

which, in our own day, has more influence in deciding the issue of industrial disputes than the capacity of the financial resistance of those who are parties to them.

The potters, then, had practically regained the position of 1836; and there they remained. Whilst attacking the allowance system, they had not forgotten good-from-oven and the annual hiring. Both these institutions were repeatedly assailed with protests and arguments and little rebellions, but practically no impression was produced upon them. There was really nothing new to be said about them, though much was said. The same allegations were made about the good-from-oven system in 1843 and subsequent years, as at the strike of 1836. The men gave instances of having produced so many dozens of ware, and finding in the biscuit warehouse a greatly diminished quantity set before them as the amount for which they were entitled to be paid. They roundly asserted that the bulk of the absent ware, though adjudged so bad as not to merit payment, was afterwards sent to be printed and glazed, and turned into a finished article, and then sold. They alleged that in other cases they had pointed out to their employer that what ware was really bad was not bad through fault of theirs, that the employer had admitted the truth of their assertions, but had insisted that the system must be upheld to protect him from loss. If, in admitting the truthfulness of their assertion, he had accorded them satisfaction, the workmen would only have been reaping the fruit of one of the "concessions" of the Betley Conference. That conference, however, was so completely forgotten that its result was never urged by the workmen upon the employers.

In the hiring system there had been no developments: it remained as it was in 1836, and, as we have seen, had been enforced by the local magistracy. It had not, however, extended to the out-potteries. The potters of Scotland and Yorkshire knew no Martinmas; in those places it would have been an exotic, and might not have been appreciated and cultivated by the administrators of the law.* In Staffordshire it was ably assailed by the men. They contended that "it contained no feature which gave it the appearance of legal validity." It was merely a stereotyped form which lay in the counting office, and which the workman signed, or to which he oftener affixed his mark. Above all, it contained no reciprocity of interest; it imposed an obligation upon the man which it did not impose upon the employer.

So the workmen argued, as they had done in 1836, but without avail. Doubtless they were wise in not putting either the fate of the good-from-oven system or of annual hiring to the arbitrament of a strike; but certainly they were wise in keeping both grievances to the front, lest it should be thought they accepted them as fair conditions of employment,

---

* Evidence of Newton, Glasgow potter, Select Committee on The Law Affecting Master and Servant, 1866. *Vide* also evidence of William Evans for much interesting information of the strike of 1836 and magisterial decisions in respect of "annual hiring."

and lest they should become still more hallowed by the passage of time.

The attention of the working potters, however, was now distracted from the consideration of all those matters which had hitherto engaged their attention, and which were legitimate subjects for the action of their Union, by other aims and concerns of an ambitious character, which were fraught with disastrous consequences to their cause.

CHAPTER IV

MACHINERY, AND THE FEARS OF THE POTTERS

UP to the year 1845 the potting industry had remained almost completely unaffected by the scientific and mechanical improvements which had greatly modified some trades, and had revolutionised others. The whole range of mechanical science was almost solely represented in the manufacture of potting by the thrower's wheel—identical in mechanical principle, and practically so in form, with that used by the ancient Egyptians — and the turner's lathe. What contrivances had been introduced had been confined to the improvisations of some ingenious members of the trade, which was a sphere into which the engineer had not yet penetrated. These contrivances, moreover, had not succeeded, and the conviction grew in the minds of the potters that their industry, owing to the peculiar nature of the material employed, would remain a stranger to mechanical innovation. In 1844 and 1845 that conviction began to be dispelled. In the summer of the former year, the news that a manufacturer had obtained a machine which would make toilet "paste-boxes" ran through the district, and, after the incredulity with which it was first received had given place to a realisation of the awful truth, sent a thrill of horror through the working potters.

63

The dreaded thing had come. More, it was said to do its work well. The potters spoke of "a new principle" having been established, and asked where it would end. If paste-boxes could be made by machinery, why not plates, cups, jugs, bowls, and every other article? The obvious answer, at that time, was that no machine had been contrived which would make them, but when the potters asked that question they asked it from the standpoint of morality. To them, machinery was an unholy and an accursed thing. They pointed to the starving populations of Lancashire and Yorkshire, and attributed their misery to the introduction of machinery into the cotton and woollen trades upon which they were dependent, and they drew the same moral from the stocking-frame workers of Derbyshire, and the weavers of Nottingham. Their imagination leapt to prophecy, and gloomy forebodings of streets crowded with unemployed and poorhouses full to overflowing, were indulged in. The employer (Mr Ridgway) who had introduced the machine for the manufacture of paste-boxes, a man widely respected, and occupying a prominent position in local publicity, pleaded that he had not taken the departure without "satisfying himself that it would not displace labour but would modify and increase it." An ominous reference, however, to the "whole agency of men, boys, and ways and means by which his arrangements would shortly be complete," was seized upon by the workmen as a text to illustrate the displacement of adult and skilled labour by boys and unskilled workmen which those "arrangements" would bring about. The paste-box machine seems to have been frightened by the scare it created, and modestly withdrew from public notice, and the potters breathed again. Their breathing-time, however, was not long. The little cloud of the paste-box machine gave place to a larger one. It was announced that a machine had been invented which superseded the flat-presser, and that such a machine was about to be introduced into the potteries. It was no longer a question of paste-boxes and such trifling bric-à-brac, but the commonest articles of the trade, which were manufactured at every pottery in their hundreds of dozens each week, were to be made no more by the hands of the workmen, but by a mechanical monster which only required the presence of a woman or a child to turn out its hundreds of dozens a day. The news created what may truthfully be described as a panic. Reports came pouring in from the out-districts saying that the machine was known there, that it was certain to succeed, that each alteration was an improvement, and that it had given practical proof of its power. It could make six hundred dozens of plates in one day. The potters in the out-districts had written to warn their more numerous fellows in Staffordshire of the impending evil, but it was already upon them. The flat-pressers, one of the largest branches of the trade, were particularly threatened, but the whole trade apprehended the general danger.

The machine was first introduced at the manufactory of Mr Mason, but it was known that other manufacturers were only waiting to see with what

E

degree of success it worked to decide upon its
adoption at their own works. And among the ranks
of the employers were some who dreaded the introduction of machinery as a step in the dark for
themselves, and who perhaps would have been
relieved to feel that their old methods of manufacture, which had sufficed so far, would not be superseded by a revolution to which their minds were
not yet accustomed. They gave their word to their
workmen that they would not introduce machinery
unless they were compelled, in self-defence, to do
so ; and whether a fear of commercial consequences,
or a humanitarian motive were behind that promise,
the men felt that they could rely, in their opposition,
upon the active support of some manufacturers,
and the passive help of others. They made a direct
appeal, in fact, to the interests of the smaller
manufacturers, who, they asserted, would inevitably
be left behind in the race of steam by those manufacturers who had a large capital at their command,
and the workmen asked them to join with labour
in common cause against a common enemy. It is
undoubted that this view of the matter impressed
those upon whom it was urged. The cost of the
machinery so far introduced was, indeed, trivial
enough, and could not have been beyond the means
of the most unpretentious manufacturer, but they
reflected that when once the first step had been
taken, Capital would make the pace. The men,
therefore, were in an alliance with interest and
sentiment on the part of the manufacturers—the
former quality being possessed by those of small

financial resources, and the latter divided amongst the conservative members of a trade singularly conservative in its methods, and those—though it is to be feared, a very small minority—whose views were tinctured by any appreciation of the effect that the introduction of machinery would have upon the men.   Looked at in the light of later days, when the tendency is one of impatience at older methods, and when a feverish succession of mechanical improvements make the methods of yesterday out-of-date, the opposition of the work-man, no doubt, seems strangely hopeless; and, regarded from the standpoint of a broader con-ception of social and political economy, their talk of "a new principle" and their appeals to morality, equally no doubt seem childishly narrow; but it must be remembered that at the time of which we write, the stage coach still performed its daily journeys in many parts of the country, and the lines of railway laid down could be measured by a few score miles.   The potters, therefore, fought an element unfamiliar to them, which they could not look at in perspective, but saw towering over them, threatening and strange.

They turned to their Union to avert the danger. The Central Committee called together meetings of every lodge, "for the purpose of taking into consideration the best means of avoiding the evil which was about to be entailed upon them," and appealed to every potter "to use all legal and constitutional means within his power to obstruct the introduction of these principles into his trade, which must inevitably, if allowed to proceed, bring beggary and starvation on himself and his family."

Perhaps an adequate idea of the gravity of the situation, as it appeared to the Union and its members, is afforded by the fact that what may be called an Act of Indulgence was passed for the benefit of their fellow-workmen who were not in the Union. They pointed out to their brethren that this was no trifling struggle in which they were engaged, and not a question of higher wàges or shorter hours, but one of the "conservation of their lives and homes." They magnanimously refrained from calling them any hard names for not having joined the Union, forgot all the quarrels of the past, and asked that all should join hands. The appeal was not in vain, and the Union grew in strength. Meetings of potters were held all over the district, and the Central Committee was everywhere active. The outcome of the agitation was that it was determined to raise a fund of £5000, by eight levies of half-a-crown per man, to combat the evil.

The application of this fund, however, was peculiar. It was to be devoted to the purchase of land in America, and the emigration of the surplus labour of The Potteries which it was predicted would follow from the introduction of machinery! The levy was at once made, and it was determined that at the payment of the first instalment the employees of the manufacturer who had introduced the machine should leave their employ. Meanwhile, amidst all this hubbub, and before the first instalment had come in, the announcement was quietly made that Mr Mason had withdrawn the obnoxious machine. The effect upon the workmen was that of magic. The second and third levy were paid with enthusiasm, and the campaign, having secured such an unexpected victory, was carried on as a warning to others.

Here we may pause for a moment to say that, in one respect particularly, the gloomy predictions of the men as to the results which would follow the introduction of machinery have been justified by time. The movement was, of course, doomed to failure from the first, and fruitless in the end. The early victories that they obtained were merely over the first waves of the advancing tide, which afterwards, in the "seventies" and "eighties," rolled in resistlessly. A generation was then required to adjust the trade to its altered conditions, and after the first shock, it recovered its equilibrium without having tottered to its fall, as the workmen of the "forties" feared and predicted; but although at first little labour was displaced, and increased production alone was the result, yet as machinery became more general, the ,amount of labour employed ceased to maintain its former proportion to the amount of production, and the altered conditions and prices did not leave the worker in as good a position as a wage-earner as when he made fewer articles by the older methods. All that was to be foreseen, and was inevitable. But the particular prediction to which we refer as having come so unhappily true, was that which related to the effect that machinery would have upon the women workers. The men were concerned to think that their labour would be displaced—they were no less concerned at the substitution of their labour by that of their wives and daughters, but their concern was on a higher plane of consideration. It is exemplified in the following passage, taken from an address issued by the Central Committee: "To maidens, mothers, wives, we say, machinery is your deadliest enemy. Of all the sufferers by mechanical improvements, you will be the worst. It is a systematised process of slow murder for you. It will destroy your natural claims to home and domestic duties, and will immure you and your toiling little ones in over-heated and dusty shops, there to weep, and toil, and pine, and die." It is unquestionable that whatever has been the general effect of machinery upon the potting industry, its saddest result has been produced upon the women of the district. Before the introduction of machinery, the proportion of women to the total labour engaged was comparatively small; and subsequent to the introduction of machinery, it rose to nearly one half; and as the women workers increased in number, so the character of their occupation became more and more unfit to their sex. In certain departments machinery has banished men, and demanded women, and the demand has been supplied, but at the cost of both men and women; for, whilst the former have suffered in wage-earning power, the latter, though new avenues of employment have been opened to them, have suffered no less in the moral and physical deterioration which the character of that employment entailed.

It will now be necessary to retrace our steps for a few months. The movement against machinery had become linked with another movement, which had its origin a short time before, and which furnishes one of the most interesting chapters in the history of the Staffordshire potter. In the first years of the existence of the new Union, trade had flourished, and the potters had, at two succeeding Martinmases, signed their hiring agreements on improved terms. No strike was necessary to enforce this—trade was brisk, there was a competition for labour, and the bidding favoured the men. Then trade fell off, and the unemployed became more numerous. The members of some families had emigrated to the United States of America, and they wrote letters to those they had left behind telling of a land of liberty and plenty, and giving exasperating details of the sumptuousness of their daily fare. Each writer desired to be remembered to friends in The Potteries, and appealed to them to leave the old and worn-out country, and to go to the younger world across the sea. Then some of the letters were published in their paper, and became a regular weekly series. The publication of these letters formed the germ of a movement which afterwards grew to extraordinary proportions, and transformed the Potters' Union into an Emigration Society.

Its inception, however, was not due to the Union, but originated in the abstract speculations of one of their number—William Evans. He was a man of extraordinary energy, and of high moral principle, and exercised a predominant influence in the councils of the Union. He at first urged emigration in the abstract, as a desirable and proper action under suitable conditions, but the idea grew until it mastered him, and he became the apostle of emigration. He convinced himself that they must look to emigration as the panacea for all the ills of the working potters, and, unfortunately, soon convinced the Union, of which he was so prominent a member. The problem he saw was that there were more workers than work, and his solution was that each unemployed member of the trade should be deported to America. Then, when they had depleted their ranks, those left behind would find themselves at an enhanced market value, and those who had gone away would have gone to a better land, where the others would follow in course of time. In theory, no doubt, the scheme was perfection itself, but many good theories are notoriously bad in practice, and, in painting his picture of an idealised future, to be realised by emigration, Mr Evans exaggerated the artistic effects of light and shade. He painted in broad lines, and used two colours — white and black. With the former he irradiated the West; and the old country, and particularly the Staffordshire Potteries, were immersed in the gloom of the latter. This Rembrandtesque effect was viewed by the Executive Committee of the Union, and they pronounced it perfect.

Thus sanctioned by the Union, the idea developed

into a plan, and in May 1844 a Society, called the Potters' Joint Stock Emigration Society, was formed, and registered according to Act of Parliament. Upon the foundation of this Society, the details of the scheme were disclosed to the potters generally. It was proposed to purchase, in one of the Western States of the North American Union, twelve thousand acres of land, payment for which should be made by instalments extending over a period of ten years. As soon as the funds of the Society were sufficient to pay the first instalment on the land, the land would be divided into allotments of twenty acres each, and five acres of each allotment would be cultivated, and buildings erected thereon. Then lotteries were to take place amongst the shareholders of the Society, and the successful ones would be sent out to their allotment, and all the expenses of their migration paid. The lotteries, thereafter, would be continued until the colonisation of the twelve thousand acres was completed, and then more land would be bought, and the operations of the Society continued indefinitely. The necessary capital was to be raised by shares of one pound each, and the whole operations of the Society were to be restricted to members of the potting trade, who alone were eligible as shareholders, with the exception that, at the commencement of the colony, any individual, of whatever trade, would be allowed to purchase an allotment at the original value. This provision was designed to encourage the early settlement of the land, and would not be acted upon when the colony had fairly started.

The Union proclaimed their object, in inaugurating the Emigration Society, to be that of "making labour scarce" in The Potteries. For six months they had been paying £70 a week as "unemployed pay" to unemployed members of the Union, and still the unemployed increased. There was no intention of ceasing to give this relief from the funds of the Society, but they had asked themselves where it would end, and they came to the conclusion that the unemployed condition of so many of their members was merely the symptom of a derangement of the industrial situation — surplus labour. They therefore had determined to go to the root of the matter, and they looked to the Emigration Society as offering a better application for the funds of the Union than their payment to its unemployed members.

The scheme, then, was fairly launched, and public meetings of potters were held, at which resolutions were passed to support the Emigration Society. In a few weeks four hundred individual shares were taken out, and various branches of the Union devoted some of their funds to the purchase of collective shares. Any individual engaged in the potting trade, whether a member of the Union or not, was an eligible shareholder, and many non-Union potters became shareholders.

The scheme, however, was too novel and far-reaching to command universal approval. A proposal to increase wages and shorten hours would have appealed to the general mass as a simple and straightforward movement which they could easily understand,

but their breath was taken away by a proposal to
deplete The Potteries on such a wholesale scale.
The population was essentially indigenous. They
were engaged in a trade which was native to their
soil, and into which no outsiders ever penetrated.
All their associations and interests were centred
in the district in which they were born and had
always lived, and the Emigration Society seemed
to them an organisation which would snap all ties
of family and home. And, apart from this recoil
of sentiment, the plan seemed to many of them to
be necessarily impracticable, because it was bold,
new, and so desperately heroic. It was too plausible
to be trusted—too extensive to be possible. And
so, from its first inception, it begot partisanship.
Its adherents had all the advantages of argument
on their side, and could appeal triumphantly to the
contrast presented by the state of affairs as realised
at home, and the alluring prospect which opened
out to them over the sea, but they were answered
by blank and obstinate incredulity. On the part
of the promoters there was no lack of enthusiasm.
In their imagination they had constructed another
Utopia. They saw their little straggling colony
grow into a village, and then into a town, with
wide streets, and imposing public buildings—a little
civilised state set in the midst of beautiful country,
peopled by an industrious community which would
merely be a large family ; and, in their speculations
on the future development of their colony, they only
stopped short at that point in its progress when
they would have reverted to the old conditions which

they were leaving behind in England, and would have evolved, from the same elements of human nature, a state of society like that which they were about to forsake.

And so, in the glow of their enthusiasm, they laughed to scorn the objections of the unconverted, and the fears of the timid. They encountered some opposition from outside their own ranks. Feargus O'Connor, the champion of the Chartists, and subsequently Member of Parliament for Nottingham, came down to the district to expound a rival plan for home colonisation, but he was laughed at by the supporters of the Emigration Society, and unheeded by those who were opposed to it. The former reflected that they were going to buy land in America at five shillings an acre, and thought it a better bargain than Mr O'Connor's estimate of £50 an acre for land in England; the latter thought that if they left their home at all, they might as well leave it for America as Lincolnshire or Essex. So Mr O'Connor went away again, leaving behind him little more than a further excuse of irreconcilability on the part of the few who actively opposed the emigration scheme, from motives of perversity rather than of principle.

At this juncture, when the scheme had made little progress beyond that which came from the first impetus of its promotion, the advent of the paste-box machine and Mr Mason's more sensational innovation was like a gale of wind to a ship becalmed. Nothing could have been more opportune for the emigration enthusiasts. It is, of course,

impossible to say definitely, but the probability
certainly is that the emigration movement would
have languished to an early death but for the
fortuitous circumstance of the introduction of
machinery. That happy chance was at once turned
to good account by the emigrationists. They had
pointed out already the growing evil of surplus
labour, but now they thundered out this unexpected fulfilment of their prophecies. If labour
was too plentiful before, what would the state of
affairs be now that machinery had come to make
it almost unnecessary? Their appeals and arguments acquired a tenfold force from this timely
development of the stituation, and those appeals
found, in the genuine fears of the potters at the
introduction of machinery, a sympathetic response.
And so the £5000 fund was started, which was to
be invested in the funds of the Emigration Society,
to purchase twelve thousand acres of land, and to
provide for the emigration thereto of all those
potters who might leave their employment as a
protest against the introduction of machinery.
Resolutions were passed by the different lodges,
declaring in so many words that machinery could
only be fought by emigration. Thenceforward the
movement against machinery was merged into, or
lost in, the larger scheme of emigration. Strikes
were condemned as useless expedients, wages and
hours of labour became questions of little moment,
and the ordinary functions of the Potters' Union
were forgotten or neglected in the consideration
of an all-absorbing enterprise.

CHAPTER V

EMIGRATION—AND AFTER

THE Five Thousand Pounds Fund was so called because it was expected that five thousand potters would contribute to it. There were estimated to be between seven and eight thousand adult potters in the district, and in allowing for the apathy of two or three thousand of them, the Union could certainly not be accused of basing their hopes on a too sanguine estimate, and, indeed, were only drawing a just conclusion from the indications around them of the general interest in the movement. It is doubtful, however, whether there were ever as many as two thousand subscribers to the fund, and it is certain that only half that number completed the payment of their eight levies, and so became entitled to a share in the Emigration Society. There were, however, many who took shares in the Society as shareholders pure and simple, and without contributing to the fund. As a matter of fact, the potters had many calls upon their slender purses, and the wonder is that they subscribed as much as they did. If a working potter at that time had answered to all the calls made upon him, directly or indirectly, by his Union, he would have paid away fully one-tenth of his income.

Every potter in the Union paid his sixpence a week to his Union lodge, many of them paid their levies of half-a-crown a month to the Five Thousand Pounds Fund, and others took out their shares in the Emigration Society at the rate of sixpence or a shilling per week.   Then, as soon as the last half-crown levy had been paid, another fund was started—a voluntary subscription for "the persecuted and unemployed," which money was to be invested in the Emigration Society for the especial benefit of all who lost their situations by "persecution"—a wide term, and one liberally interpreted—or as a consequence of the introduction of machinery.   This latter fund, however, made little progress, and amounted in the end to so little that it was merged in the general assets of the Emigration Society, and was not exclusively appropriated to the benefit of those for whom it was created.

The levies having been called in, it was found that the Society had enough capital at its command to purchase 4000 acres of land.   They had set out for the price of 12,000 acres, but that sum not being forthcoming, it was decided to make a start with what funds they then possessed.   Meetings were held, and it was· decided that the first practical step to be taken was the appointment of officers of the Society who should be sent out to America to purchase the land, and to prepare the way for those to follow.   The offices created were those of estate steward, his deputy, and a conductor. Before the close of the year 1845 the officers were selected, and in February 1846 they set sail for

New York. Before their departure they were entertained at farewell dinners and gatherings in every town in The Potteries, and when they left The Potteries for Liverpool the streets were full of enthusiastic crowds who bade them good-bye. Each officer was accompanied by his family, for they had no intention of returning to England, and hoped that when next they saw their friends it would be in the colony which they were going to prepare for them over the sea. Their duty was first to select the land—the territory of Wisconsin had been decided upon as their objective—then to purchase it, divide it into allotments of 20 acres each, and build houses or log huts for the accommodation of those who should next come after them.

The departure of the Land Officers was regarded as an event of great importance, for it gave an air of reality to the proceedings of the Society. The scoffers were silenced, and the doubtful ones saw that there was something in the movement. The conductors of the Society determined to profit by this stimulation of interest in their aims, and proposed that the next step should be the appointment of an Estate Committee to be composed of representatives from each branch of the trade, who, with their wives and families, should be sent out to the colony as soon as the land was selected, to there watch over the interests of their branches, and presumably to also watch over the officers who had just been sent out. It was not suggested, however, that the expenses involved should be provided out of the funds of the Society. As a matter of fact, those funds would not have permitted such a strain upon them. It was proposed that each member of the different branches should pay, for twelve weeks, a subscription of threepence a week, and half of the resultant sum in each branch should be allocated to the expense of the emigration of its representative, and the remainder should be invested for branch shares in the Emigration Society. It was an ingenious plan, for it provided for the development of the colony, and committed each branch to the proceedings of the Society at no expense to the latter; whilst at the same time, by it being proposed to devote half the sum raised to the purchase of branch shares, it directly increased the Society's funds. Perhaps there was no more to be said of the object of the proposal. The interests of the branches were to be guarded rather in The Potteries than in Wisconsin; and as the Land Officers had been specially selected with a regard to their character and trustworthiness, the appointment of a cumbrous Estate Committee of eleven members in order to control the Land Officers, would only have found an analogy in the appointment of a Committee of the Colonels of each regiment engaged in a campaign to control the proceedings of the General Staff. Still, the plan was adopted. There was plenty of time in which to carry it out, for some months must elapse before the Land Officers would have accomplished the first part of their mission, and the discussion of the plan served to keep the interest alive.

Soon, however, a more important subject was

F

presented to the potters for their consideration. The Land Officers were on their way to America to purchase 4000 acres, and to establish a store. They had gone there, however, without the means to accomplish those purposes. The total assets of the Society only amounted to the purchase price of the 4000 acres, and left no margin for all the cost of emigration and all the general expenses. The Emigration Committee, therefore, issued an appeal for further shareholders, and insisted upon the necessity of "regular and continuous funds." Many shares had lapsed, and the defaulters were pleaded with. Their shares had, by the laws of the Society, become forfeit, but the offer was made to reinstate the holders of them upon the payment of the arrears. This offer was in many cases accepted, and brought more funds into the Society's coffers. Still, it was obvious that more money was necessary. Part of the capital of the Emigration Society had been sunk in the establishment of a printing office—where the Union weekly paper was now printed and published—which was expected to produce a profit of £100 a year, but it was long before this expectation was even partially answered. The hollow - ware pressers had shown themselves most active of all the branches in the promotion of the Emigration Scheme, and they were appealed to. It was suggested that they should devote threepence out of every sixpence paid into their Union to emigration purposes. Whilst they were considering the suggestion, the long-expected communication from the Land Officers came to hand. They had arrived at

New York, on March 13th, 1845, after a voyage of
nearly six weeks, and their letter was merely the
diary of their voyage. Still, it served again to
stimulate the movement at home, and the Emigration Committee issued another appeal, pointing out
that retreat was impossible, and they must have
funds to go on.

The hollow-ware pressers then decided to devote
half of their Union subscriptions to emigration. It
was a momentous resolve, for the Central Committee, encouraged by the reception which the
hollow - ware pressers had accorded to their suggestion, now ventured to hint that each branch
should do the same. Meanwhile, another letter had
arrived from the Land Officers. They had surveyed
the land in Wisconsin, and had selected the site for
the new colony. But further than that they could
not go, and others were stepping in and taking the
land which they themselves had chosen. They
must have funds. A general meeting of shareholders was then held, to consider the position, and
some opposition showed itself. Upon a resolution
being submitted to the meeting to withdraw £600
from the bankers, and to send a draft for that
amount to the Land Officers, an amendment was
moved suggesting that "the money should be kept
in hand until the shareholders had decided what to
do with it." Seeing that the resolution only proposed that the funds of the Society should be
disposed of for the accomplishment of the purpose
for which they were intended, and for which the
Society had come into existence, the supporters

of the amendment could only mean that they
distrusted the whole business and did not desire
the continuance of the Society.   The resolution,
however, was carried, and, amidst much enthusiasm,
the colony in Wisconsin received its baptismal name
of " Pottersville," and with that name for a battle-cry,
the discontented ones were routed.   Nevertheless,
funds did not come in sufficiently, and the leaders
of the movement saw that drastic measures were
necessary.

They then revived, boldly and definitely, their
suggestion of a few weeks before, that all the
branches of the trade should follow the example
set to them by the hollow-ware pressers.   This
suggestion came directly from the Central Committee of the Union—it was not the proposal of
the Emigration Society, but the former had latterly
been so absorbed in the aims of the latter, that the
two organisations now scarcely suggested any distinction to the working potters.   The Central
Committee held a meeting "for the purpose of
taking immediate steps to improve the prices of
the district, and also to secure for the Emigration
Society a regular and continuous contribution for
the important purpose of peopling 'Pottersville.'"
It may be safely said that the first-named object
of the meeting was subsidiary to the latter.   No
further steps, indeed, were taken "to improve the
prices of the district," and in announcing that object
the Central Committee was doing no more than
making a concession to its own conscience.   The
meeting lasted for some hours, and finally passed

the following resolution :—"That this Meeting believes that the principle of emigration is the only efficient principle for permanently improving the condition of working potters, and that the same be recommended to the different lodges of the Society, to the end that one-half of the subscriptions to the Union be applied to emigration purposes."

The sentiments uttered by those at the meeting were mainly those of the inutility of strikes and turn-outs.   They looked back upon all the money that had been spent in their Union's warfare, and wished that they could recall the past, whilst possessing the wisdom of the present, and devote all the money to the Emigration Society.   The Central Committee, indeed, although not seeming to be quite conscious of it, was ringing its own knell, and writing its own epitaph.   They pointed to the disunited branches of the trade, and contended that their disunion was only due to the fact that they had not taken part in the emigration movement.   The Union was falling to pieces, and emigration was the only common interest which would keep it together.   So they argued, but they were really mistaking the effect for the cause.   The working potters in their Union were as a large family.   The heads of that family had embarked on a big enterprise, which might have been strikingly successful had all the members of the family joined heartily in it.   But some had looked at the enterprise distrustfully, and kept aloof from it, and so the family was divided ; but surely the heads of that family were responsible for the division.   Those

who had joined in the enterprise were naturally
united because they had committed themselves to
it, but those who had not joined in it pointed with
much force to the emigration enterprise as the source
of the disunion.   The Central Committee asked:
"Who then will dare to say that emigration ash
injured the Union?   It has been the foundation of
our stability, and we must foster and protect it."
Their method of "fostering and protecting" the
Union was to make that Union give half its effort
and wealth to emigration.   They anticipated objections in this manner: Out of every sixpence
paid into the Union, two-pence halfpenny has gone
in the current expenses, and the remaining threepence halfpenny has been "wastefully squandered
in foolish strikes, and in unemployed pay.   The
step that is recommended by the Central Committee
is one that will raise the Union from the ghost of
a combination up to a substantial land and property-
owning body."   The logical outcome of this view
would have been the decision to abandon the Union
altogether, to confess its utter failure, and to devote
all combined effort to emigration.   The attitude of
the Central Committee was not even that of Brutus:
"Not that I love Caesar less, but Rome more."   They
were sacrificing their Union to emigration, but, in
the sacrifice, denounced the Union to which they
owed so much, and which they had previously wor-
shipped as their only means of salvation.   It was
generally conceded that about half of the Union
subscription was necessary to pay the ordinary
expenses, and the Central Committee, therefore,

ought to have considered that in suggesting this
revolution, they were reducing their Union to a
condition which would only leave it a Union in
name, and would deprive it of any power of carrying
out its functions. It cannot be said for them that
this view did not present itself, for it was the specific
ground of objection on the part of those who dis-
agreed with their recommendation. The only conclusion possible, therefore, is that they considered
the Union as no longer of any use or importance,
and were prepared to see it perish in their despera-
tion to save the Emigration Society.

The scheme, then, was formally submitted to the
different branches for their decision, and, in most
cases, speedily agreed to. The Central Committee
appear to have had some uneasiness as to the result
of their recommendation, for they were agreeably
surprised at its adoption. "They had feared," they
said, "that its vast importance would not have
been seen," and that "a narrow policy" would have
prevailed. Fortunate, indeed, would it have been
if their fears had been realised. As it was, every
organised branch in the trade ultimately endorsed
the policy of the Central Committee. And then came
a curious development. The hollow-ware pressers
who, as we have seen, had been the pioneers in
the policy of half-payments from the Union subscriptions, which was now generally accepted by
the whole trade, held a general meeting of their
branch, and decided upon "a separation of the
Emigration Society from the proceedings of the
Union." Their motives in executing this *volte face*,

and repudiating their own action, were obscure. They announced that they had "withdrawn from the Branch and Central Committees, owing to the determination of those Committees to appropriate the Union contributions to emigration purposes," and proceeded to pass resolutions affirming that "in a state of disorganisation they were powerless to obtain a fair price for their labour," and that they should take "immediate steps to organise a Union upon better principles" than the one they had left. They carried out this intention by forming themselves into a branch of the National Association of Trades. Like the Central Committee, the hollow-ware pressers had been reviewing the past, and coming to conclusions, and they decided that a Union of Potters, detached from any greater organisation of labour, was futile. They therefore looked to the National Association as the only agency which would, to borrow a picturesque phrase from their pronounce-ment, "hurl from their guilty eminence the oppressors of their race." But still even they could not shake off the thrall of the emigration spirit, and started a Society which they called "The Mutual Assistance Society for the removal of surplus labour." Their objects and their methods of attaining them were identical with those of the Emigration Society—that is to say, they inveighed against surplus labour as the source of all evil, and asserted that emigration was the only remedy, and they asked for subscrip-tions and shares just in the same way as the Emigra-tion Society had done. The only shade of difference between the two was that the Mutual Assistance

Society did not restrict its operations to emigration to America, but asked why the British Colonies should be neglected, and talked of two hemispheres instead of one. But, upon the slender foundation of this difference, they based violent and very often unscrupulous attacks upon the Emigration Society, whose programme they had so sedulously copied.

Their secession from the Union meant more than their repudiation of the Emigration Society. The Union was rapidly falling to pieces, and the action of the hollow-ware pressers, who had hitherto been its most constant supporters, left it much weaker than before. Lodges were broken up in the different towns, and though amongst their members had been some who were faithful to Unionist principles, they were compelled to be out of Union because their lodge, or their branch, no longer existed. Some ardent spirits thus left standing amid the ruins of their various houses, met together, and proposed that they should build themselves a common habitation, and call it a " Miscellaneous Lodge." The idea was carried out, and formed the germ of yet another revolution in the character of the general Union. It must be said of its leaders that they were amazing opportunists.' The policy suggested by the moment became to them the one and only truth. The Central Committee discovered that they had been travelling along the wrong road all the time in conducting their Union upon "branch principles." They proposed to re-model the constitution of the Union, by eliminating any distinction of branch, and making it a general organisation.

They discovered that hitherto, " owing to the division
of the Society into separate branches, the power of
the Union was also divided," and that their only
chance of salvation lay in the adoption of the
Miscellaneous system. It seems evident that some
such alteration in the constitution of their Society
had become necessary, for the secession of one or
two branches, and the dissolution of various lodges
here and there, had reduced the branch system to
incoherency; but it cannot be said, as the Central
Committee then chose to argue, that the Miscellaneous system was a system of perfection. There
were a dozen different and well - defined branches
in the trade, working under different conditions and
at different rates of wages. A grievance in one
branch did not necessarily involve a grievance in
any other, and, in matters of detail, the flat-presser
had nothing in common with the printer or oven-
man. The union of each branch by itself, federated
into the general union by its delegates to the Central
Committee, was a sane and obvious arrangement,
and one that had really not disclosed any drawbacks. The Central Committee, however, had
become adepts in the art of persuading themselves
that they were only travelling to finality and perfection when circumstances compelled them to alter
their plans, and they formulated the constitution of
the new Union. They proposed that the existing
lodges should wind up their affairs, and that the
emigration shares and funds of each branch should
be disposed of as the majority should decide, and
that then "a Lodge of the new Union should be

formed in each district, composed of individuals connected with the potting trade from the slip-house to the packing-house." A Central Committee was still to be supreme, and to be appointed by delegates from each lodge. Its duties were to "superintend the payment of unemployed and turn-out cases," and it was to be considered as "the highest judicature of the Union." And, finally, the basis of the new Union was to be "that the subscriptions of its members should be sixpence per week; and that one half should go to the funds of the Emigration Society," to be converted into individual shares when the requisite amount had been subscribed, "and that the other half should be appropriated to the payment of unemployed and turn-out cases, together with the incidental expenses of the lodge." It may also be mentioned that the rate of payment to unemployed cases was fixed at five shillings a week, and to "turn-out" cases at seven shillings per week. These suggestions for the basis of the new Union were adopted, the old lodges broken up, and in October 1846 new lodges, under the Potters' General Union, were formed.

The change was quietly effected, and there was no display of enthusiasm. Matters had become sadly disorganised by the successive changes which had supervened, and the old ardent and confident spirit of union had flickered out. Division and chaos had followed in the wake of the emigration movement, and those who now emerged from the wreck of the old Union, and still formed the main body, were mostly those who had ventured a stake

in the emigration scheme, and felt that they would
do better to stick to the ship, and see the voyage
out, than lose all by desertion.   The Central
Committee had announced that at the impending
Martinmas various manufacturers had given notice
of a reduction, and that it was their firm intention
not to submit to any alteration in the rate of wages.
This announcement was merely an admission of
the true functions of the Union—which had lately
been completely overlooked — and figured promin-
ently in the advocacy of the Miscellaneous system.
When, however, the new Union was established,
nothing more was heard of the active opposition
to the manufacturers which the Central Committee
had foreshadowed.   The reductions were made, and
the promised strikes did not take place.   The new
Union merely showed that discretion which is the
better part of valour, for they knew they were not
strong enough to force a fight.

The Emigration Society had now been established
for over two years.   The results which it had to
show were three Land Officers in lonely Pottersville, and they were asking for money.   Their
letters had become more and more urgent in tone,
and at last the £600 had reached them, and their
anxiety was relieved.   Then, whilst they journeyed,
as their letters said, for days and weeks over the
prairies of Wisconsin, seeking the authorities to
whom the purchase money had to be paid, losing
themselves in forests, sleeping under the stars, and
encountering Red Indians, their brethren at home
were preparing to send out to them the long-

talked-of Estate Committee. It had been decided that as far as possible the members of that Committee should be selected, as has been said, from different branches ; but the branch system had since gone by the board, and that distinctive qualification was no longer urged. Inasmuch as the Estate Committee had been suggested to look after the various interests of the branches, it might have occurred to them that the necessity for any Estate Committee had now passed away. But the Emigration and Union Committees revived the idea, with the modification that as far as possible the Estate Committee should be selected from amongst the unemployed, and that the Central Committee should *borrow* the necessary money from the Emigration Society. In other words, the Emigration Society delegated to others the expenses of its own business. There was a little murmuring, though no coherent complaint. The potters probably thought of the eighty weeks which they would have to wait before they were entitled to one share in the Emigration Society by virtue of half their subscriptions to the new Union. However, the suggestion of the Emigration Society was accepted, and eight "persecuted" potters, each having a family, were selected to form the Estate Committee. The new year, 1847, opened with the receipt of a letter from the Land Officers, in which they announced that they had purchased 1200 acres of land, and spoke of shipping their wheat, when the crops came round, to The Potteries! This childish enthusiasm did not strike the potters as

pathetic; they only dreamed again of a store set
up in their midst, which should be stocked with
butter and eggs and bread from far-away Wisconsin;
and when reductions in wages were talked of, they
turned for consolation to their promised 20 - acre
farms. And so once more there came a round of
farewell entertainments, and the Estate Committee
responded to the toasts of their health, and prosperity to Pottersville, as the Land Officers had done
before them.

In the midst of this reviving enthusiasm, the
monster "machinery" created another diversion.
The machine patented by Mr Wall, and pioneered
by Mr Mason, was succeeded by another, patented
by Mr Scott. It was designed to accomplish the
same purposes as its unfortunate predecessor, and
had already acquired in the out-districts such a
reputation that it was complimented by the Staffordshire potters by being called " The Scourge." It
had now arrived in their midst under the patronage
of one of the most eminent firms—that of Messrs
Copeland. Its advent enabled the Central Committee to issue an address reminding all whom it
might concern of their predictions of two years ago,
and asserting that the era of fulfilment had now
indeed commenced. The occasion also served to
justify an appeal for further half-crowns, and elabor-
ate calculations were made as to how many families
could be despatched to Pottersville if only certain
hypothetical sums could be raised. But the Central
Committee gave proof of their wisdom by adopting
a second line of defence. They no longer cried out,

"Bring on your machines, and we will take away your workmen and despatch them to Pottersville," but prepared a petition to be presented to Messrs Copeland, praying them to spare the trade the ill-effects of the threatened evil. It was a significant change of attitude, and its significance was found in the condition of their Union. The *fortiter in re* had given place to the *suaviter in modo*, and, strange to say, the latter method prevailed. Before the petition had been presented to Messrs Copeland, and whilst signatures were still being appended to it, the news came that Messrs Copeland had withdrawn the machine. The Central Committee were puzzled. The enemy had retreated whilst they were suing for peace, and they distrusted the operation, and thought it a manœuvre. Finally, they came to the cynical conclusion that the withdrawal of "The Scourge" was not wholly unconnected with the fact that the general elections were drawing near, and that Alderman Copeland, Member of Parliament, was about to issue his address to the "worthy and independent voters of Stoke-upon-Trent." Moreover, "The Scourge" had not been broken up into fragments, or sold as old iron, but had been oiled and carefully locked away in a room of the manufactory.

The Central Committee, therefore, suspended final judgment, and looked askance at an armistice which they did not dare to regard as a victory. The machine, however, was never heard of again, and the episode of "The Scourge" had no further consequences or influence upon the trade. But, though a detached incident, it is interesting as showing the temper of the working potters at this period, and the little reliance which they placed upon their Union. The machine had been withdrawn, not in deference to the wishes of the men, and certainly not in fear of any action which they might take. It was merely found by Messrs Copeland to cause more trouble than its performances were worth, and was therefore laid aside. The workmen, however, dreaded its consequences, and were relieved at its withdrawal, for they were now disunited and demoralised, and were already prepared to accept machinery as inevitable, and to make the best of it.

The last of the farewell entertainments to the Estate Committee had taken place, and they, with their wives and families—numbering forty in all—departed from The Potteries. They went in canal boats to Liverpool, and the banks of the water-way were lined with thousands of people who waved their adieux to the emigrants. Other boats, containing friends and bands of musicians accompanied them for some miles up the canal, and returned when night came on. The proceedings connected with the departure of the Estate Committee had attracted so much the attention of the general public, that the emigration movement received another stimulus, and the flagging faith of the potters in their venture was revived. The Emigration Committee passed resolutions declaring their intention of adding 80 acres a month to their estate, and providing for the promised monthly ballots to be immediately commenced.

The first ballot was in favour of the Oven-men's Society, who then had to decide which of their number should receive the advantage. The second and third ballots again went to branch shares— those of the hollow-ware pressers — though there was now no longer any hollow-ware pressers' branch —and it was not until the fifth ballot that an individual shareholder was successful. The ballots, however, had spread over a considerable period, and there had been much more than the promised monthly interval between them.

Another auxiliary movement was then started. Under the benevolent patronage of the Emigration Society, though independent of it, clubs were formed to purchase 20-acre farms from the Society, and to pay the passage out of the members of the clubs. Calculations were made which demonstrated, on paper, the fact that by the payment of sixpence per week, every member of the club would, in three years, infallibly be the owner of a 20-acre plot in Pottersville, and the necessary expenses of emigration. Unfortunately, these calculations were based on the assumption that the necessary number of members would immediately join the clubs, and that assumption was not realised. Very few members joined, and taking the highest enrolment of members of the most prosperous club, it would have been several years before the subscriptions would have enabled a single family to emigrate. The club movement speedily collapsed, and not a single individual received any benefit from it.

Whilst it was demonstrating its failure, the re-

G

sourcefulness of the Emigration Society produced another scheme. It proposed that a general store should be opened in The Potteries, with a capital of £250, raised by a thousand shares of five shillings each. The usual calculations were made, and it was computed that the store would sell a weekly stock of £250—that is, an amount equal to its capital, slender though it was—and that a yearly profit of £1750 would result, which would go to swell the funds of the Emigration Society. The scheme was discussed, and resolutions determining to carry it out were adopted, and the potters' store was spoken of as familiarly as though it were already an accomplished fact. It is, perhaps, needless to say that nothing whatever came of it. Whilst it was being discussed, Martinmas of 1847 had came round, and a reduction in wages was first rumoured, then threatened, and finally carried out. The reductions were general, and of such an amount as would, in other times, have produced a violent opposition on the part of the potters. Then the "allowance system" again showed its head, at first timorously, but soon certain manufacturers made no compunction in avowing their purpose. The potters submitted, tamely enough. They could do little else. Their leaders, with doubtful honesty, reproached them for the position of affairs. "If," said they, "you had purchased 12,000 acres three years ago, you would have been in the position to resist these attacks." The potters might have replied: "And if you had not subordinated our Union to the Emigration Society, we should now have been in the position you speak of." But there was no longer any trade organisation worthy of the name, and the opening of the year 1848 saw the potters in a position as bad as that which they occupied between the defeat of 1836 and the revival of 1843. The Union had practically ceased to exist, and the Emigration Society was fast coming to an end.

In March, news was received from Pottersville that the Estate Committee and the Land Officers were at "loggerheads"—a result which might have been foreseen from the first. Pottersville, in short, was sharing the fate common to Utopian experiments, and drifting to destruction upon the rock of human imperfections. The Estate Steward— one of the three original officers—wrote of the Estate Committee: " I am sorry to state that the generality of them are not the wise men of the East, but the foolish men of the West, and whatever unity there might have been amongst them prior to their leaving home, I can assure you there has been very little since they came here." And the financial difficulties at home had their counterpart in similar embarrassments in Wisconsin. The divided counsels amongst the emigrants had become bruited about amongst the settlers in the neighbourhood, and credit was refused. Then they wrote home to the parent Society to complain of the smallness of the money drafts sent out to them, and there was found to be considerable difficulty in legalising the possession of the land by the Society, according to the laws of the United States. So matters went on for another year. The ballots had been suspended, for there were no longer funds available to have given them any effect. The dying effort of the Society was made in the decision to open its ranks to members of all trades. It must have been obvious to its conductors that this step would destroy the last shred of pretence or hope to achieve its purpose. It had been established to remove the surplus labour in the potting industry, and now it was proposed that a bricklayer, carpenter, or a small tradesman, should rank equally with the potter. It was true that it had failed, and lamentably so, to achieve its primary aim, but the step proposed robbed its purpose of any distinctive connection with its very name. Still, its leaders kept up their reputation for opportunism. They spoke of the "local infant growing to national manhood" as a result of opening their doors to outsiders. The Emigration Society, however, did not survive the dangers and weaknesses of comparative infancy. Its ranks were not increased by this general invitation to all and sundry to join in the movement, and in the middle of 1849 the whole organisation quietly collapsed.

The enthusiasm of its inception had been long spent, and its later history was merely the dogged obstinacy of its leaders, and the hope of a few tenacious followers that some good might come out of it. In all, only about twenty families had been sent out to Pottersville, but in the accomplishment of this meagre result a splendid trades organisation had been sacrificed and frittered away. The justifica-

tion for the emigration movement had been the fear
of machinery, and, by a curious irony of fate, at the
collapse of the movement there was scarcely a single
machine to be found in the whole of The Potteries.
In short, the emigration movement had fought a
phantom. The general body of manufacturers were
chary of introducing an element into their trade
the results of which upon themselves they did not
know, but feared. And so it came about that for
the last few years of the existence of the Emigration
Society—that agency which, according to the resolutions passed by the potters, was to afford the only
remedy for the "evil of machinery"—the very cause
of its existence was forgotten, and no longer urged
to justify its continuance. The effect which the
movement had had upon the "surplus labour" which
it was its mission to diminish has been seen. To
place twenty or thirty families "out of the combat"
in five or six years was not a factor to be taken
into serious consideration. And so it may be said
that the nett result of the emigration movement
was merely to destroy all that had been accomplished before it came into existence. There is no
doubt that, after the initial mistake of inaugurating
a movement which it was entirely beyond their
power to make effective, the potters committed an
act of suicidal folly in subordinating their Union
to the Emigration Society, and even in consenting
to any official connection between the two organisations. There is equally no doubt that if it had not
been for the policy of using the Union as a milch
cow for the benefit of the Emigration Society, the

latter would soon have died a natural death from sheer lack of sustenance, and that the Union would not have materially suffered through any reaction of disgust or despair. But as it was, the Union had ceased to have a separate existence long before the Emigration Society languished to its death.

The Union, in its early days, accomplished much, and later, missed a golden opportunity of doing more. There are two facts which attracted but little attention at the time, that are, nevertheless, of prime importance in estimating what permanent advantage was lost to the trade by the apathy of the Union. In December of 1845 the masters called together a meeting of their body to consider the state of trade, and to determine the future selling prices, in view of the advances that had taken place in the price of coal and general materials, in the rates of freight and in the wages of the potters.* The increased outlay in all cases— although in the latter case it was mainly the abolition of the "allowance system"—was accepted as an accomplished fact. The meeting was held, the Chamber of Commerce revived, and some basis of agreement in reference to selling prices was arrived at. A reduction in wages was no more contemplated than a reduction in the price of coal—a matter much more beyond their control. The strength of the Union was then unimpaired, and the emigration

* "In the second and third years of the Union (1844 and 1845) the members secured for the whole of their trade two successive rises in the price of their labour, amounting, at least, to 7½ per cent. of their weekly earnings."—William Evans, Leader of 1843 Union, in "The Art and History of the Potting Trade." Hanley, 1846.

movement had not then occupied the attention of the potters to the exclusion of their more immediate and pressing concerns.   It was the first time in the history of the trade that any serious attempt had been made by the main body of the masters to come to a frank understanding in reference to selling prices, and it therefore offered a golden chance to the Union to inaugurate a new period of common action, for mutual benefit, between master and man. Two months later, in March, the following communication was made "to the Manufacturers_ of the Staffordshire Potteries, under the appellation of 'The Chamber of Commerce,'" by the Central Committee of the Union :—

"We, the Central Committee of the United Branches of Operatives, having heard, with much regret, that in your recent praiseworthy efforts to put an advance on the selling prices of the staple manufacture of this district you have been somewhat opposed by one or two of the cheap-labour traffickers of the district, beg to call your attention to the following resolution passed by us, and which we pledge ourselves to carry into practical operation :—'Resolved, That we, the Central Committee, acting by the instructions of and in behalf of the operatives of these districts, pledge ourselves to assist by all legal and moral means the combination of potting manufacturers entitled the Chamber of Commerce, in their present endeavour to put an advance on the selling prices of their ware, believing, as we do, that such endeavour is founded on the desire to give a fair and equitable price for potting industry, and that those who oppose the same are bad in motive and foolishly and mischievously avaricious in practice.'"

This was a wise and comprehensive resolution, and if only it had been carried into effect, as its promoters pledged themselves to do, a happier history of the potting trade in subsequent years might have been written. The manufacturers had come to recognise that the time had gone by when their first resource, in any endeavour to improve the financial condition of their business, lay in the opportunity which a reduction of their workmen's wages afforded. This was a state of mind for which the workmen themselves, through their action in Union, were responsible. But though the ground was tilled, the seed was not sown. No further advance was made by the workmen beyond the mere passing of the resolution. The temper of the masters was ripe for sympathetic action with the men, and if the latter had followed up their resolution by arranging, or endeavouring to arrange, for a joint conference between the two, it is very probable that their proffered alliance would have been received favourably by the employers, even though the latter might not have been sufficiently proof against their prejudices to make the first advance. The workmen, however, were too absorbed in thinking of homes in the far West to appreciate a possibility which, in other times, would have been hailed as an advance upon all that had been so far accomplished, and the opportunity passed by. Then, as we have seen, division crept into their ranks, the miscellaneous system came into being, and the masters then saw a more direct and ready means of accomplishing their purpose, and seized upon it. There was no longer any need to come to any understanding about selling prices, when each manufacturer could practically set his own standard of wages, and so chaos came again. Each employer played his own hand, reductions in wages became general, and for nearly twenty years the history of the trade can be summarised in the statement that the men were disorganised, wages were low, and trade fluctuated. Some branches reorganised themselves in the early fifties, but there was no attempt to bring about a general union. It was the inevitable reaction, and the general mass of potters were simply disgusted with the very name of Union. It would be useless to dwell upon a period of such complete stagnation, in which there was no single movement worthy of recording, and we will therefore pass to the work of another generation.

CHAPTER VI

THE ERA OF ARBITRATION

THE generation with which we now have to deal was one that witnessed a revolution in the attitude of public opinion towards Trades Unionism, and this change soon induced a corresponding attitude in Parliament. Whilst the potters had remained for fourteen or fifteen years comparatively disunited and helpless, Trades Unions had sprung up in connection with every trade of importance in the country, and the growth of the liberal spirit in politics had brought the claims of labour to the front. It may therefore be well to endeavour, briefly, to give some idea of the relation of the legislature to industrial movements at the period at which we have now arrived, when the potters once more became united.

In the last year of the past century was passed the last law which aimed directly at the suppression of workmen's Unions, and all subsequent legislation on the subject has been in the direction of removing the restraints which formerly existed.

The Act of 1800, however, was very severe in its provisions, and assured the punishment of any workmen who combined in any form to secure an advance in wages, and left no loophole for the most peaceful action which they might take. In 1824 the first blow was struck by Parliament at

the fetters which had for so long restricted the
independent action of the English working-man,
and·the Act of that year swept away an accumulation of five centuries of unwholesome and repressive
legislation. But Parliament immediately repented
of its action, and decided to "hasten slowly," for
in the following year the Act of 1824 was repealed.
The repealing Act freed from penal consequences
any workmen taking part in a meeting held for
settling the amount of wages to be received, or
the hours of work to be followed, by those actually
present at the meeting; but provided for the
prosecution, and the imprisonment on conviction,
of those workmen who "molested" or "obstructed"
other workmen not in an organisation, or who imposed fines for disobedience to any order made by a
Union upon those who were members of it. These
provisions left to the judges a wide discretion as
to what really constituted "molestation" or "obstruction," and as the preamble of the Act itself
spoke of the combinations which the Act of 1824
had legalised as being "injurious to trade and
commerce, and dangerous to the tranquillity of the
country, and especially prejudicial to the interests
of all concerned in them," the judges believed that
they were interpreting the Act in sympathy with its
spirit and intention by according a liberal application to the provisions against "molestation" or
"obstruction." Hence a crop of decisions followed
which were contradictory in effect, and left the
actual position of Trades Unionists in a state of
great uncertainty. It was held, for instance, that

although a strike could not itself be pronounced illegal, yet any combination of workmen which brought a strike about was a conspiracy ; and the judge-made law which followed from the Act of 1825 practically deprived that Act of the protective value which it was intended, or believed, to possess. In 1859, therefore, Parliament again interfered, and a short Act was passed which was designed to put a stop to the idiosyncratic decisions of the judges by declaring that those workmen who pursued their objects "peaceably, and in a reasonable manner," should not be held guilty of obstruction within the meaning of the previous Act; and this was the state of the law upon the question at the time at which we have arrived.

Still, though Trades Unions were no longer conspiracies, in virtue of the special enactments made on their behalf, the common law still refused to regard them as completely legal associations, inasmuch as they were held to be in restraint of trade. Their funds might be stolen by unscrupulous members with impunity, for the law did not recognise their right to the possessions of property ; and just as to-day it does not regard a bet as a contract which can be enforced, so Trades Unions were then outlawed. However, they grew in number and extent, and disposed of vast funds. Strikes and lock-outs were almost daily occurrences, and a period of continuous friction between employers and employed had left little sympathy in the public mind with workmen's Unions. The result of the inquiry into the outrages committed by

Trades Unionists in Sheffield and other places then led one portion of the public to wonder, as an historian of the reign expresses it, "whether the laws of the land and the attitude of society were not in some measure responsible" for the excesses of some members of a large class, whose even innocent proceedings were regarded with aversion; and to ask whether the repression of these associations of working-men, engendering secrecy and all the faults which sprang from it, should not give place to a more enlightened toleration of their pacific purposes: and even that larger section of the voting public which still held Trades Unions in abhorrence felt that the day had gone by when the legislature could safely afford to give only a partial and grudging recognition to a movement which had become an essential part of the social life of the working-classes of the country.* And

* "During recent debates in the Reichstag on the conditions of the working-classes, members of the Government were in the habit of replying to the strictures and criticisms of the Left by the proud boast that in no country in the world had social legislation and reform so far advanced as in Germany. England especially was repeatedly singled out for purposes of depreciation. . . . 'Vorwarts' has now appeared with a powerful leader on the subject, evidently written by the veteran Liebknecht. There is no comparison, he says, In England, organised free development; in Germany, the guardianship of the police. In England, the free right of association, and with this weapon in his hands, the British workman has secured good wages and a higher level of life than his German contemporary possesses. The right of association is a sacred principle in England. Not even the Conservatives think of touching it. . . . The English working-man can say what he likes; he can meet with his fellow-citizens when, where, and how he likes; he can write and read anything he chooses; he can organise as he wishes. In a word, he is a free man, in no fear of political repression, dreading no attacks on his personal freedom,

so, to travel a few years beyond the time at which we have arrived, began that ameliorative legislation which ended in 1875 with the full and final recognition of the complete legality of Trades Unions, and the establishment of the principle that no combination of men should be held guilty of an act which would not be criminal on the part of a single individual.* Some excuse is needed for even

his house inviolable. The German has been robbed of the free right of meeting. He can only meet under police surveillance, and every word he utters is in danger of being twisted into an offence against the law. He is perpetually on the threshold of the prison. He suffers thousands of indictments every year for using words which are only the natural expression of his hatred of oppression. He is laden with laws circumscribing his freedom; he is threatened with money fines, with gaol, with the penitentiary."—The Berlin Correspondent of the *Daily Chronicle*, February 2, 1899.

* There have been several recent decisions, however, which conflict with the accepted meaning and purpose of the Act of 1875. The Criminal Law Amendment Act of 1871 made "watching and besetting" any place for the purposes of a strike a criminal offence. The Conspiracy and Protection of Property Act, introduced by Mr (now Lord) Cross, and passed in 1875, qualified the provisions of the Act of 1871 by the saving clause: "Attending at or near the house or place where a person resides in order to obtain or communicate information shall not be deemed a watching or besetting within the meaning of this section." The judgment of the Court of Appeal, however, in the case of Lyons v. Wilkins, in December 1898, involved the doctrine that though no violence or intimidation was threatened or committed, watching or besetting a house "interfered with the ordinary comfort of human existence" and constituted a nuisance, for which an action would lie at common law, "and proof that the nuisance was only for the purpose of peaceably persuading other people would afford no defence to such an action." A still more remarkable decision, however, was that of Mr Bompas, Q.C., Recorder of Plymouth, who affirmed the conviction, on appeal, of three officials of a Trades Union—Curran, Matthews, and Shepheard—in January 1899 for conspiracy in calling out on strike Unionist workmen in the employment of a Mr Trevelyan. There was no

a brief reference to facts of such common knowledge, but to recall them serves as a convenient landmark in the narrative.

It is in the earlier years of this activity and agitation that the tale of the potters' Unions must be resumed. No definite date can be assigned at which the spirit of Unionism again asserted itself amongst them. In two or three branches, as we have seen, Unions were continued even after the downfall of 1849, and these Unions simply grew, and with them other branches began to unite. In 1854 a new periodical, called *The Potter*, had been commenced. It was a poor production in comparison with its vigorous predecessor, *The Potters' Examiner*, and the difference between the two was illustrative of the difference in the spirit of the workmen at the two periods. *The Potter* had not endeavoured to promote any propaganda, and had merely been called into existence by the faithful few who still kept in the bond of Union despite the indifference of the main body of potters. In 1863, however, the latter began to feel the influence of the general activity, and the dying *Potter* was merged in a more ambitious organ, called *The Potteries Examiner*. It was a very

element of violence or intimidation in the case, but the Recorder appeared to hold that whilst a strike to shorten hours or increase wages was within the lawful pale of the Act of 1875, a strike to prevent the employment of non-Unionists was criminal. The test of criminality, however, in the Act of 1875 is the presence of violence and intimidation, and those illegalities only ; and a strike to prevent the use of wall-paper instead of whitewash on the factory walls would still come within the sanction of the Act—provided it was carried out without violence or intimidation.

creditable production, and, though conducted in
the interests of the working potters, it fulfilled the
ordinary functions of a newspaper, dealt with questions of politics, art, and literature, and reflected
in short the general life of the day. It therefore
occupied a much higher place than its predecessor,
which had paid no regard to any subjects unconnected with the potting industry, and its influence
was proportionately higher.

The Unions grew as Branches. They were quite
separate and independent concerns, and there was
no general organisation. The Branch system was
not cultivated by design, but by the accident of
some branches having preserved their Unions
through all the dark days when Unionism had been
in disrepute, whilst other branches were only just
beginning to re-unite; and there was, therefore, no
general or simultaneous movement such as would
have called forth a general organisation. It was
a matter of gradual growth, and in 1865 the various
branches felt themselves strong enough to once
more attempt a battle with their employers on the
old question of annual hiring.

Trade was just recovering from the depression
which had followed upon the American Civil War,
and the potters felt that a prosperous time for their
employers was for them an opportune one. At the
Martinmas of 1865, all the branches which were
united refused to renew their engagements upon
the old hiring agreement. The employers locked
them out, and matters remained at a dead-lock for
several weeks. Then one branch after another gave

in, and the employers already regarded themselves as victorious. They had, however, made their calculations without a due regard to the determination of one branch which still held out. This was the Union of Oven-men. Their branch was one of those which had gathered up the fragments after 1849, and kept a Union more or less alive ever since, and now it was remarkably strong. Of every ten oven-men engaged in the trade, nine were now members of the Union. The employers were powerless. Every other branch might return to work, but production was impossible without the completing process of firing the ware which those branches made, and there were no oven-men to do the firing. So the employers had to confess themselves beaten. A conference was held between the employers and the representatives of the workmen, at which it was agreed that, for that year at any rate, the custom of an annual hiring should be suspended ; that the system of a month's notice should be substituted, enabling a workman to leave his employer, or the latter to discharge his workman, upon such notice being given, but that prices, as fixed at that Martinmas, were not capable of revision or alteration until the completion of the year. This was all that the workmen had contended for, and the oven‑men were justly proud of a victory for the whole body, mainly obtained by their own determination, which had made a breach in the custom of annual hiring. As it turned out, it finally abolished that custom ; for though, in the following year, an attempt was made by the employers to revive it, the workmen

H

were not inclined to tolerate a retrogression, and the attempt was not seriously persisted in. Moreover, a year later, in 1867, the Master and Servants Act was passed, and as this placed employers and workmen on an equality for the first time in the matter of contracts, the annual hiring system would most probably not have survived a condition of affairs which no longer would have allowed it to be supported and enforced by the imprisonment of the men who broke it. From 1863, therefore, the custom of the trade became that of a month's notice to terminate employment, but Martinmas was still held in reverence as being the period when all prices were fixed for the ensuing year.

The period with which we are now dealing will ever be memorable in the history of the potting trade on account of the establishment of a permanent Board of Arbitration. The principle of arbitration in trade disputes was, of course, not new. It had been acted upon in the potting trade so long ago as 1834, when the Committee of Conciliation was established to deal with a series of minor disputes, but the Committee was dissolved because all the decisions went in favour of the workmen; and whether the victories went only to the most deserving side, or whether other less obvious causes accounted for the good fortune of the men, the masters, as we have seen, soon lost their respect for a process by which they always found themselves on the losing side. Since that day (for the Betley Conference, which formulated the terms of settlement of the strike of 1836, can hardly be spoken of as an

Arbitration Court), the principle of arbitration had never been invoked in the settlement of any dispute in the potting trade until 1867. What was, however, entirely novel in the movement, as far as The Potteries was concerned, was the fact that the Board of Arbitration now set up was intended to be a permanent tribunal, dealing with all disputes, great and small, in the trade, by the decisions of which both sides agreed to be bound.

. These permanent Courts of Arbitration, however, were not new to England, and were of still older foundation in France and other countries. The Conseils des Prud'hommes had their origin in France so long ago as 1285, but it was not until the days of the first Napoleon that they were efficiently constituted. The main objects kept in view in the establishment of these Courts were: — First, to provide a tribunal composed of those competent, by experience, to deal with the matters that had to be decided ; second, to insure confidence in the Court on the part of the litigants, by equality of representatives ; and, third, to make the conciliation and mutual satisfaction of the litigants the paramount object. The last object was perhaps best provided for by the fact that no professional practitioners of the law were allowed to take part in the proceedings of the Courts, and the satisfactory working of the system may be judged by the fact that ninety per cent. of the cases brought before the Councils were settled. These Councils were judicial in character—that is to say, the decisions given by them were binding, in law, upon the parties concerned, and the attendance of either master or man was enforced in pretty much the same manner as the attendance of a defendant is compelled in the Police Courts of England to-day. The matters and disputes with which the Courts were empowered to deal practically embraced every possible cause of difference between master and servant, save one—and that the most important. They had no power to make any decree affecting the rates of wages to be paid. It often happened, however, that disputes upon that ground were referred, by mutual consent, to the consideration of the Councils, and either their recommendations were adopted, or the suggestions made led to the parties themselves coming to a satisfactory agreement.

In regard to legislative attempts to adjust differences between masters and workmen, France was much ahead of England, for it was not until 1824 that the question of the establishment of Courts of Arbitration was seriously considered by the English Parliament.* In that year an Act was passed which, briefly stated, enabled an aggrieved master or workman to go before a justice of the peace, and submit the case to his decision. This step, however, could only be taken when both sides agreed to have their dispute settled in this manner; and if one party to the dispute held aloof from this mode of settlement, the machinery and process necessary to compel his attendance, and to make

* All previous references to arbitration had either been in Acts designed to put down "dangerous combinations," or had been confined to certain trades for special reasons.

the decision legally binding, were cumbrous in the extreme. The Act was never taken advantage of by either side, and the workmen at any rate looked with the greatest distrust upon the impartiality of the ordinary magistrate. Moreover, the Act of 1824 provided "That nothing contained in the Act should authorise any justice of the peace to establish a rate of wages at which the workmen should in future be paid, unless with the mutual consent of both master and workmen." That consent was never forthcoming, and the Act of 1824 therefore practically remained inoperative. In 1867 another Act was passed, authorising the appointment of Courts of Conciliation under the Act, which should be duly licensed and registered, and whose decisions should be binding, but could only be enforced by an application to the justice of the peace of the district. The same objectionable element which had rendered the Act of 1824 useless was thus revived in the Act of 1867, and the predictions made at the time, that the Act of 1867 would be as useless as its predecessor, on account of the preservation of the interference of a magistrate, have since been justified. The essential difference between the two Acts was that the first one was compulsory, and the later one permissive. That is to say, the Act of 1824 did provide, though in a cumbrous and roundabout fashion, for the compulsory settlement of disputes; whereas the Act of 1867 merely gave masters and workmen power to form themselves into Councils of Conciliation — if they cared to do so. This, however, was merely conceding to them a power which they might voluntarily exercise, for there was nothing to prevent masters and workmen forming Arbitration Councils, and agreeing to the awards made, without any reference to the Act of 1867 at all. The Act was confessedly modelled upon the Counseils des Prud'hommes of France, but its promoters missed altogether what was regarded as the supreme virtue and purpose of the French system. The Counseils des Prud'hommes were composed of masters and men, who dealt with disputes in their own trade, and not only enforced their awards, but compelled the investigation of all disputes, whether one party to the dispute desired investigation or not. They were, in a word, judicial in character, but composed of experts. The Act of 1867 made the submission of disputes to arbitration dependent upon the mutual agreement of masters and workmen, for Councils of Arbitration under the Act were only possible where and when both sides agreed to form these Councils, and only after the formation of these Councils was arbitration possible; and, furthermore, the awards could only be effective by invoking the interference of a magistrate. The intention of the promoters of the Act was therefore singularly ineffective in their endeavour to approximate to the working of the Counseils of Prud'hommes, and it may here be said at once that England yet waits for legislative enactment that will establish similar machinery to that which France has long enjoyed in regard to the settlement of industrial disputes by competent and expert tribunals, acting under judicial powers.

Whilst the English legislature was tinkering with the subject, and considering the propriety of conceding to Courts of Arbitration the full and final power of settling their disputes, the manufacturers and workmen of Nottingham, to quote an author of 1867 on the subject,* "had the wit to see that it was not necessary to go to France" (as was suggested in Parliament), "to inquire into the working of a principle which recommended itself by its simplicity to the common-sense of mankind." In 1861 they formed a Court of Conciliation and Arbitration to settle all disputes in the hosiery trade established in that town. It is needless to dwell upon the history of the Nottingham effort, except to say that it was the forerunner of all permanent Boards of Arbitration, and that it was productive of unmixed good to both employers and workmen. More important to this narrative, however, is the fact that it was the Nottingham Board of Arbitration, and the intercourse which existed between its founder and president, Mr Mundella, and Mr William Owen, the founder of The Potteries Board of Arbitration, that led to the establishment of the latter organisation.

In 1867 and the following year, the editor of *The Potteries Examiner*, wrote frequent articles upon the subject of arbitration, urging the consideration of the establishment of a Board of Arbitration upon the attention of masters and men. The matter was formally brought before the various

* Alexander Macdonald, on "The Law Relating to Master and Workman."

lodges of the workmen, and the proposal was made to the manufacturers that they should meet the men in conference, and talk over the scheme. The manufacturers submitted the proposal to their official body, the Chamber of Commerce, and that organisation at once expressed its sympathy with the idea, and appointed a Committee from amongst them to meet a deputation of the workmen. The meeting took place, was thoroughly cordial in character, and a code of rules was at once drawn up, to be submitted to the main body of men and to the Chamber of Commerce. Amongst the workmen not a single dissentient voice was heard, and three-fourths of the manufacturers of the district gave the movement their hearty support. Further Conferences took place between the masters and men, and in July 1868 The Potteries Board of Arbitration and Conciliation came into existence. The spirit of its rules was almost entirely those of the Nottingham Board. The objects of the Board was stated to be "to arbitrate upon any questions that may be referred to it from time to time by manufacturers or operatives, and by conciliatory means to interpose its influence to put an end to any disputes." The Board consisted of an equal number of both sides —ten employers and ten workmen — and out of this number four of each side were elected to serve as a Committee of Inquiry. This Committee really formed a Court of First Instance. Any dispute which came before the Board for settlement was first of all investigated by the Committee of Inquiry, which used its influence to bring about an amicable settlement between the parties, but had no power to make an award if their efforts to conciliate proved unsuccessful. In the latter case, the dispute was submitted to the whole Board, a majority of votes decided the issue, and the issue was binding and final. If, however, the voting was equal—that is to say in effect, if the manufacturers voted unanimously for their own side, and the workmen pursued a similar course — the adjudication of a referee was sought, and his decision upon the case was absolutely final. The whole procedure was therefore simplicity itself, and no less fair than simple.

Here was an organisation created which, in theory, made anything like a serious conflict between masters and men impossible. There was no limit imposed as to what disputes were eligible for decision. Whatever may be said of the wisdom of excluding any decision as to wages from the power of a Board or Court appointed by the legislature, and possessing judicial ability to enforce their awards, there can be no question that to exclude from the scope of a Board of Arbitration voluntarily created, and trusting to the honour of the litigants for the effectiveness of its awards, any decision upon the most prolific source of disputes — the question of wages—would have been to deprive the Board of its most effective opportunity for doing good. Both masters and men loyally obeyed the decisions of the tribunal they had themselves created, and though at the time of its creation the conviction was expressed, by the workmen at any rate, that perfection would only be reached when Courts of Conciliation were entrusted with the power of en- forcing their own decisions, the obedience of both sides to the awards made against them was the strongest argument against the necessity of that for which the workmen hoped—and to this day, perhaps, continue to hope.*

The organisation started under the most favour- able auspices. The manufacturers felt that the time had gone by when they could cavil at the Unions of their men, and the operatives hailed the new Board as promising to be an effective barrier against the necessity which had in times past been reluctantly forced upon them as their only weapon —and one that they well knew to be two-edged— that of strikes.

---

* It is doubtful, however, whether there is a generally favourable feeling amongst the working-classes towards compulsory Arbitration Courts. Apart from inherent difficulties in practice—such, for instance, as that of fixing the responsibility of obeying a decree upon a Trades Union, as a body—there are some serious objections urged against the principle, which is held by many to be a reversion to that of the obnoxious Statute of Labourers of Queen Elizabeth's time. Probably no question better serves to show the cleavage between the principles of those who look on Government as the proper repository of all power with which an electorate may invest it, and those who hold that the legislature has done its share of the work in freeing labour from its old fetters, and that labour must now work out its own redemption by its own power of combination. In February 1899, the Right Hon. C. T. Ritchie, President of the Board of Trade, endeavoured to pro- mote the establishment of a National Conciliation Board, but the two leading features of his scheme were : (1) "No outside interference, either by a Government department or otherwise, and (2) No com- pulsion." His proposals were well received by the Parliamentary Committee of the Trades Union Congress, but the Employers' Parlia- mentary Council "regretted they could not see their way," etc.

The new Board had a very busy time at its commencement. The first case with which it had to deal had reference to that perennial cause of dispute — the system of good-from-oven. The dispute only concerned, directly, one manufactory; but it was felt that the decision would have a wider effect than that upon the parties to the issue. The question raised was not that of good-from-oven as a principle, but turned upon what were the usages of the trade in regard to the payment under the system, the principle of good-from-oven being admitted as a common basis. The Board was unable to come to a decision upon the case, and the matter was submitted to the Umpire. He merely had to decide what particular usages were in vogue at the manufactory concerned, and his decision, which was adverse to the workmen, in no way concerned the general principle of good-from-oven.

Before the case had been remitted to the Umpire, however, a discussion had been raised by the operative members of the Board upon the general question. Some of the workmen suggested that the Board should consider the advisability of abolishing good-from-oven altogether, as the system gave rise to endless disputes, and all these disputes would entail a great consumption of time by the Board; but it was felt by some of their own section that the proposal was too sweeping to be likely to meet with the approval of the employers, and it was not pressed. A manufacturer, however, proposed that "the question should be postponed for the present, but that the Board should hereafter draw up rules to regulate the system or decide whether the workmen should be paid good-from-oven, or good-from-hand," and the proposition was agreed to by the manufacturers present.

After the decision of the Umpire in the case referred to, a special meeting of the Arbitration Board was held to consider the question of good-from-oven. There was great diversity of opinion amongst the employers, but it was generally conceded by them that in dealing with the system of good-from-oven, the principle that a workman should be paid for all ware which was damaged through causes beyond his control, should be admitted and acted upon. A manufacturer, Mr Francis Wedgwood —a descendant of the great Josiah Wedgwood— proposed "That each section of the Board shall bring before their constituents the question of good-from-oven and good-from-hand, so that these questions may be discussed, and a set of regulations prepared by both sides, to be produced for discussion at the next quarterly meeting." This resolution was carried, and the operatives at once set about the task of framing a set of rules under which the system should be worked. In suggesting these Rules, they acted upon the principle, acknowledged by the manufacturers, "That the workman be paid for all ware which is spoiled through causes that do not come under his control, or that cannot be traced to his bad workmanship; but that no payment should be made for work which could be proved to be the fault of the workman." The proposals of the manu-

facturers, however, did not contemplate anything
like the same "indulgences" in regard to damaged
ware as those which were comprised in the workmen's
suggestions. Only a few out of the many possible
causes by accidents to the ware were provided for,
and a curious distinction was made between ware
damaged by the oven-men before firing and after
firing. The manufacturers proposed that if ware was
damaged by the oven-men when drawing it out of
the oven, already fired, the workmen who made it
should be paid for it, but that if the oven-men
damaged the ware—even though they had received
it faultless from the maker—in placing it in the
oven, the man who made the ware should not be
paid for it. It was obviously a purely fanciful and
arbitrary distinction, and struck at the root of the
"governing principle" which had been already admitted by the manufacturers as a fair basis upon
which each side should proceed to draw up its
suggestions for the working of the system. The
operative members of the Board submitted the
manufacturers' proposals to the various committees
of the branches, and these proposals were received
with surprise and disapprobation. Then a meeting
of the Board was held at which the workmen were
to hear the opinion of the manufacturers upon the
proposals submitted to them by the operatives.
The manufacturers plainly said that they could not
entertain the proposals of the men, and were only
prepared to offer to the men the original proposals
which had already been made. The President of
the Board, a manufacturer, said that the employers

"could not admit the principle that all ware spoiled that was not due to the workmen's fault should be paid for." This was in effect, an admission of what the workmen had said : that the proposals submitted by the masters were at variance with the generally accepted principle ; and this was not denied by the manufacturers.

The truth seems to be that in consenting to the framing of the Rules upon the principle referred to, the manufacturers had not quite realised what the effect and consequence of that principle would be, and now saw that it meant little else than an acceptance of the system of good-from-hand. The "principle" had been skilfully worded by the workmen, and threw the whole burden of proof against the workman upon the master. For all ware that came from the hand of the workman, that workman would be entitled, *prima facie*, to be paid for : but "no payment should be made for work which could be *proved* to be the fault of the workman." If this were granted, it would be merely a question of quibbling about terms, but good-from-hand would be a reality. The workman hitherto had been compelled to wait until the ovens were "drawn" before his wages were paid, and the wages he received were based upon what had survived the process of firing, and all the accidents to which it was liable before and after that process. Under the governing principle so lightly accepted by the masters, all that would have been reversed, and the workman would be able to claim his wages as soon as his work was done, and if the master objected to pay for certain of the ware which

was damaged, with him would rest the proof that
it was the workman who had damaged it, or who
had turned it out from his workshop in a faulty
condition. All this was clearly seen by the manufacturers, however, when they had approached the
task of framing their regulations under the
"governing principle," and hence that principle
was abandoned by them. They even urged that
the Board was acting beyond its constitution in
taking any notice of the question at all, for the
Rules of the Board only provided for action by the
Board when a dispute was submitted to them, and,
they said, there was then no dispute upon the good-
from-oven question at any manufactory. If this
were a valid objection, it should have been taken
at the time of the first proposal being made, but,
as we have seen, the resolutions that had been
passed which brought the question before the Board
had been passed at the instance of manufacturers
themselves. And, upon the broader question, it
was a mere quibble to speak of there being no
dispute upon the good-from-oven question. It was
one of the main grounds of dispute in the strike of
1836, and it had remained a ground of dispute ever
since, and had caused more friction and discontent
in the trade than any other incident, custom, or
circumstance connected with it, saving only the
direct question of wages itself. In proposing to
deal with the question of good-from-oven, and to
settle once for all a uniform practice in regard to
the way of carrying it out, both employers and
workmen were to be congratulated upon an attempt

to at once remove grounds of discontent then existing, and lessen the possibility of future conflict; but
the employers were depriving themselves of all
credit for their part in that proposal, and were,
moreover, urging an objection which came too late
in the day, in contending that the question could
not be considered until an actual case of conflict
had arisen. The workmen asked: "Do you then
wish us to strike before you will consider the danger
we can now avert?" And the employers naïvely
answered that "they did not recommend a dispute."
The meeting was fruitless of result. The men complained that the agreement had not been carried
out. They had expected that each side would have
submitted its interpretation of the common principle,
and that in the words of their Secretary, the Board
would "reason out, not as partisans, but as honest
arbitrators," a middle course between the two interpretations. The employers, however, had submitted suggestions which were not inspired by the
governing principle, and had returned a simple *non
possumus* to the proposals of the workmen admittedly
based upon it. The manufacturers, however, expressed the opinion "that they had met the workmen
in a very liberal spirit," and refused to consider any
compromise. And so terminated the first stage of
this first "constitutional" effort to remove the long-
standing grievance of the system of good-from-oven.

The meeting referred to had, by chance, taken
place upon the first anniversary of the formation of
the Board, and it separated upon the understanding
that each side would elect its representatives for

the ensuing year. It was not an auspicious termination of the first year's work; and it is not
to be wondered at that there was, on the part of
both masters and men, some consideration of how
the new movement promised to serve their respec-
tive interests.   The men were keenly disappointed
at the result of their first encounter of any moment
—one, too, that had not depended for its result
upon the verdict of an impartial person who had
been called in by both sides to adjust a dispute,
but which had furnished an opportunity for the
display of those qualities of mutual forbearance
and goodwill which its very existence presumed
to be present, and upon which its successful working depended.   The employers, on the other hand,
had experienced something of the possibilities of a
new *régime* which recognised an equality of their
workmen with themselves to which they had never
before been accustomed — a system which placed
both masters and men on an equal height, and
asked justice to decide between them.   It is therefore to the credit of both sides that the second
year of the existence of the Board was entered
upon with a determination to bring its constitution
nearer to perfection.

The workmen had discovered an incompleteness
in its Rules, and they proposed certain alterations.
In the main, the masters accepted them, and where
they made modifications, the workmen were in
entire agreement.   The Rules provided for the
extension of the scope of the Board — designed by
the workmen to popularise arbitration amongst their

I

class, and by the manufacturers to make all members of their own rank more disposed to join in the movement. Both sides felt it a weakness to their own interests, no less than to the cause of arbitration, to have any important portion of their body holding aloof from the movement, and the revised Rules greatly extended the scope of the Board in this respect. One important Rule now introduced provided: "That the leading principles of the Board should be the continuance of work pending any dispute" — the value and propriety of which is sufficiently obvious to only need mention. The workmen, whilst debating the proposed new Rules, suggested that the Board should immediately proceed to draw up a code of rules, or "usages," for the trade—either to consolidate existing usages, and to bring about a state of uniformity in regard to them, or to agree upon such a code as appeared just and desirable to the Board. The workmen dwelt upon the importance of such a step in the potting trade, because the various interpretations which had existed amongst masters and men as to the "unwritten laws" of the trade had caused many differences; and other Boards of Arbitration, as their first step, had proceeded to define the rules and customs of the trade with which they were connected. The employers' received the suggestion cordially, and a Committee of the Board representing each side, was appointed to draft the Trade Rules. The Committee held many sittings, but found the *pons asinorum* of the problem to be that Rule which would concern the question

of good - from - oven — now revived again. The
Rule proposed by the workmen in regard to it
was a resuscitation of the "governing principle,"
and read as follows:—"That workmen be paid for
all ware which is spoiled through causes that do
not come under their control, or that cannot be
traced to bad workmanship, but that no payment
be made for bad work which can be proved to be
bad by the fault of the workmen." After very
lengthy discussion, this Rule was agreed to, and
the Board proceeded to affirm : "That the Committee of the Board of Arbitration should proceed
with its labours in drawing up Trade Rules, and
that it should take the Rule already agreed to as
its guide in any other Rule it might frame on the
good-from-oven question."

The workmen were greatly elated at this victory,
and spoke of the Rule now agreed to as one that
"took the sting" out of the grievance of good-
from-oven ; and, in fact, they did not conceal the
opinion that it carried them, in theory, to the
attainment of good-from-hand. They regarded it
as practically putting an end to a long-standing
quarrel, which had involved, in their words, "an
injury to the trade and a 'curse to the workmen"
from days long before the strike of 1836.

The Board had now been established three years,
and the Trade Rules agreed upon had come into
force at Martinmas 1871. Various arbitrations—
legacies of minor disputes occurring at that Martinmas—took place during the year, and these were
satisfactorily settled. At a quarterly meeting of

the Board, held in the middle of the year 1872, a discussion arose as to the manner in which the fifth Trade Rule—that relating to the "good-from-oven" question — was being carried out by the manufacturers. The manufacturers then said that they did not interpret the Rule as protecting the workmen from any losses caused to the ware before it was in the hands of the biscuit-oven-men, or even before the ware was fired. The workmen contested this interpretation, for which they claimed that the Rule gave no justification, as it contemplated no limitation or condition except that of the ware being damaged through the fault of those who made it. The discussion, however, though conducted with much heat and spirit by both sides, was mainly an academic one, as the point involved had not arisen in connection with any actual dispute. Still, the incident foreshadowed a complete disagreement as to the whole question of good-from-oven, as modified by that Rule.

Six weeks before Martinmas of that year, 1872, the operatives gave notice of their intention to propose that two of the Trade Usages agreed upon a year before should be altered. The first alteration proposed was in respect to the termination of the trade year, to abolish the institution of Martinmas, and to substitute for the 11th of November the first Monday in August. The proposal was not one of great importance, but the consideration which led to it was that, inasmuch as the trade was always unsettled in August on account of that being a period of summer holiday, it would be as well to

take that unsettled time as a fit occasion for the termination of the trade year, instead of further unsettling the trade three months later on. The second alteration was in regard to the fifth Rule, and proposed that that Rule should be abolished, and that for it should be substituted the following :—
" That the principle of payment for work done in the flat-pressers and hollow-ware pressers branches" (the two branches which worked good-from-oven) "shall be the same as in the throwing, turning, and handling departments — viz. good-from-hand." The manufacturers instantly arose against the proposal, and contended that the question of good-from-oven having been settled by the Trade Rules, it was no longer capable of being arbitrated upon ; and they threatened to break up the Board if the workmen persisted in their proposal. The latter replied, pointing out that the Trade Rules, of which the Rule in question was the fifth, provided for "the right of either party to appeal to the Board to change any Trade Usage at Martinmas," and declined to withdraw from their position. The gauntlet was therefore thrown down and accepted, and upon the result of the next meeting of the Board its future existence apparently depended.

It may seem strange that the workmen should, within a year of its adoption, seek to change a Rule of the trade which they had then hailed with so much satisfaction, and as affording an apparently lasting settlement of a feud which had endured so long. They averred, however, that a year's experience of the working of the Rule had convinced them that it was easily to be evaded by the employers, and was constantly so evaded, to such an extent as to deprive it, in practice, of all that it promised in theory. The case of the operatives, against the Rule, was briefly this: That whereas the Rule threw upon the employer the burden of proof against his workmen, that the ware he (the employer) declined to pay for was bad through the fault of the workmen, the Rule had been applied in an exactly contrary way—that the employer had assumed, or asserted, that so much of the ware was bad, and had stopped a corresponding amount out of the workmen's wages, leaving the workmen to prove, to the master's satisfaction, that the master was wrong. That process was a somewhat exacting one from the workmen, for "proof to the master's satisfaction" was a matter of some difficulty. The workmen recalled the Rule under which the system was governed: "That no payment be made for work which can be proved to be the fault of the workmen"—and asked, unanswerably: "If the workman, then, was expected to pick up his ware, and point to every speck and flaw upon it, and endeavour to convince his employer that those specks and flaws were the result of his bad workmanship, and such as, under the Rule, disentitled him to be paid for it?" There surely could not be a better example of the *reductio ad absurdam* in argument. Obviously, the burden of proof was thrown upon the employer. Then, if that were so, it was the employer upon whom rested the onus of taking his case before the Board of Arbitration in case of dispute with his

workmen as to what ware should not be paid for.
But, said the workman, the master took the law
into his own hands, exercised his own judgment,
and left the matter there. But the workman could
appeal to the Board if he felt himself aggrieved?
Certainly, but such appeal would be a tacit acknowledgment of the right of the employers to interpret
the Rule as they were doing, for his appeal would be
to the Board to say that such ware was not spoiled
through his fault, whereas it was for the master to
establish his case against his workman. But then
the workmen could make a general appeal to the
Board to say that the Rule was being generally
misapplied, and asking for an authoritative declaration to that effect? So they might; but if the
Rule had been misinterpreted, had they any reason
to believe that an "authoritative declaration" in
their favour would be any more respected?—for it
could only amount to a declaration that the Rule
meant what it said.

But the workmen had made up their minds to
a final abolition of the system. They had struggled
against it for forty years, and never once had the
employers answered the argument that it was a
system capable of the grossest abuses, and one
that could not be defended on grounds of justice.
And at last, a year before, they had succeeded,
as they hoped, in putting an end to any possibility
of abuse by framing a Rule which, if observed,
would adequately protect the workmen. But they
had seen that Rule violated and reduced to nullity,
and now they were determined that the whole

system should go, root and branch, for it seemed to them that so long as the principle that there should be any supervision of the workman's work after it had left his hands was admitted, that principle served as the foundation for a superstructure of qualifications and limitations which reduced any Rule based upon it to ineffectiveness. And it is certain that their determination was stronger because of the mortification they felt at the disappointment of their hopes a year before. That, then, was the question as it appeared to the workmen, upon which they insisted that the Board should arbitrate.

Against that view of the workmen, what was the answer of the employers? Well, there was absolutely no answer, in so far as the ethics of the case were concerned. They took their stand upon the point of order that it was a *chose jugée* finally determined, and not to be set aside except in the miraculous contingency of a mutual agreement, in which the Umpire should take no part. It seems pretty clear that the manufacturers believed that in assenting to the fifth Trade Rule they had settled once and for ever the question of good-from-oven. It is equally clear that although the workmen were satisfied with the fifth Rule, and most probably would have remained so if it had been satisfactorily carried out, they had not regarded the adoption of that Rule as finally locking the door on the question if it were not satisfactorily carried out. Unless, therefore, the workmen could be supposed to be contending for what they already possessed, one may justly assume that the employers had disregarded the Rule as to good-from-oven.

The day of the meeting came. The operatives had insisted upon the presence of the Umpire,* as provided for in case of a dispute. The employers, however, refusing to treat the question as a dispute, but as a fundamental part of the Board's Constitution, declined to allow him to take any active part in the proceedings, although acquiescing in his presence. He had expressed his willingness to attend, and his readiness "to do anything in his power which threatened not only the existence of the Board, but also the peace of the district," but declaring that he would not give any opinion upon the question in dispute as his duties were in abeyance "between the settlement of one case and the discussions of another." The Umpire was therefore a passive spectator of the whole proceedings, and, under such circumstances, the meeting was destined to be fruitless of any agreement, as both sides were equally resolved upon the justice of their cause, and their determination to uphold it. It was not an occasion when arguments were of avail, and when the vote was taken it only showed that the ten manufacturers were of one opinion and the ten operatives of another. The meeting then broke up, and the fate of the Board of Arbitration hung in the balance.

Martinmas was drawing perilously near, and the position became critical. On each side notices had been given for an alteration in the prices—on the

* The late Mr H. Tichborne Davenport, M.P.

part of some of the manufacturers for a reduction of wages, and on the part of certain operatives in various branches for an advance. The workmen, however, now announced that unless the employers would consent to the question of good-from-oven being arbitrated upon, they would not consent to arbitration in the cases where notices of a reduction in wages had been served upon them. Thereupon, the manufacturers who were members of the Board at once "locked out" their men. They were amongst the most influential, and employed the greatest number of hands. Those branches which were not affected by the question of good-from-oven had expressed their willingness to arbitrate as to wages, but the manufacturers then refused to consider even their case until the demand of the other branches for arbitration upon good-from-oven was withdrawn.

The situation then appeared to be an absolute dead-lock, and there seems little doubt that matters would have developed to a serious extent, and that the Board of Arbitration would have been, for the time at any rate, dissolved, but for a fortunate circumstance. Since the abortive meeting of the Board upon the fifth Rule to which we have just referred, another meeting had taken place to decide one of the appeals of which notice had been given —an appeal, in this instance, from the flat-pressers employed at a particular firm for an advance. The Umpire was present, sitting as arbitrator; but the hearing of the case was not completed, and the Board adjourned. Since the adjournment the

general situation had grown more serious, as just
explained, by the masters locking out their men.
The Board, however, met again, as arranged, to
conclude the hearing upon the case partly heard,
and this gave an opportunity for the whole question of the fifth Rule being unfolded, this time
before the Umpire sitting in his official capacity,
de novo. The employers urged that they would
not have taken the trouble to have conferred upon
the Trade Rules agreed upon if they had thought the
operatives intended to endeavour to alter them the
following year—an argument which was of weight
as going to prove the belief of the employers in
the permanent character of the Trade Rules adopted.
They, however, weakened their case by saying that
whilst they were prepared to arbitrate upon other
trade usages, they would not consent to arbitrate
upon the usage of good-from-oven. The distinction was obviously an inconsistency, for either their
argument as to the permanent character of the
Trade Rules applied to all, or to none. The workmen, on the other hand, added to the strength of
their arguments by referring to a decision of the
Umpire upon a case heard three months previously,
in reference to a dispute concerning wages. He
had then said: "I must express the reluctance
with which I have performed the duty of making
this award. I believe that our Board may be
usefully employed in the amicable settlement of
disputes arising out of the non-fulfilment of agreements, or out of the misunderstanding of the terms
of such agreements, out of the breach of one of

the Board's Trade Rules, or of some recognised custom of the trade, or in the definition and interpretation of these Rules and customs; and in such matters I willingly discharge, to the best of my ability, the duty of giving a final decision. But I am not so sure that it is wise for our Board to attempt to fix the rate of wages, which must depend upon so many and constantly varying circumstances, and cannot be regulated by the decisions of a Board, however influential." The operatives now recalled this pronouncement, and argued that if the view of the employers were to be upheld — that trade usages could not be arbitrated upon; and, on the other hand, if the view of the Umpire were accepted —that the Board should not consider the question of wages—there would absolutely remain no justification or reason for the existence of the Board at all. Finally, after prolonged discussion, the employers agreed to abide by the decision of the Umpire as to whether the fifth Rule was one upon which arbitration was permissible — a course which the operatives had urged without avail at the previous meeting upon the question, and to which they now renewed their consent.

The Umpire then announced that his decision would be in favour of the employers' view, holding that "the employers were right in their contention that the question of good-from-oven cannot, under the present Rules of the Board, be the subject of arbitration."

With this decision the operatives were forced to be content. They loyally submitted to it; the lock-out was withdrawn, the cross appeals of employers and employed were arbitrated upon, and the Board went on as before. Perhaps no further excuse is needed for having entered so fully into this controversy than the fact that it was the last chapter in the long struggle upon good-from-oven. The question has never since been raised as a direct issue, and the practice of the trade remains to this day substantially the same as that which led to the agitation for the repeal of the fifth Trade Rule.

CHAPTER VII

WAGES AND SELLING PRICES

THE period with which we have been dealing, and particularly its later years—1871 and 1872—had been one of unexampled prosperity in the potting trade. The Franco-Prussian war had practically brought the Continental production of pottery to a standstill, and given a corresponding impetus to the manufacture of pottery in England; but the potting industry only shared with every other trade in the country a period of prosperity never since relatively surpassed. The potters sought to take advantage of this flourishing state of affairs, and at the Martinmas of 1871 they appealed to the Board of Arbitration for advances in wages. It is important to notice the method of appeal. Each branch selected an individual case by which the whole question, so far as it concerned the workers in that branch, should be decided. If it was decreed by the Umpire that the members of the appellant branch employed at the firm selected for the appeal, should receive the advance in wages asked for, it was understood that every employer who acknowledged the Board was bound to concede a similar advance to those members of that branch in his employ, and the obligation was honourably carried out. The effect of the award was, however, even more widespread, for those employers who had refused to join the Board found it extremely difficult to exempt themselves from a rate of wages which ruled at so many of the largest and most influential manufactories in the district.

The case of each branch was the subject of an entirely distinct and separate arbitration. The appeals of the workmen were based upon these general grounds: that the main tendency of wages in the potting trade had been of recent years, to decrease, so that for the same amount of labour performed less money was paid, and they sought to have their wages raised to former prices — in some cases going back as far as the rate of wages paid in 1836 to justify their claim. The arbitrations were therefore inquiries into the detailed prices of the various articles made by each branch, and the principle which governed the arbitrations—and one accepted by both sides—was that the prices to be given should be decided by precedent in cases where a knowledge of previous prices was available, and in the case of new patterns or new modes of working the prices to be given should bear an actual relation to the work involved. It therefore came about that an advance was given upon certain articles, and refused on others, and the general effect of the series of arbitrations was to bring about some approximation to uniformity in the working prices of each branch. The workmen did not base their appeals upon any proof of the increased profits of the employers, though, of course, the general prosperity of the trade could not fail to be an underlying thought in the minds of both parties as a circumstance which made the time an opportune one. The workmen merely took each article in dispute in each branch upon its own merits, contrasted the price paid then with prices paid in former times, showed in what way altered conditions of working had affected the capacity of an ordinary workman in regard to those articles, and the Umpire gave his decision entirely upon those considerations.

The average advance in wages decreed, taking all the branches together, was about $8\frac{1}{3}$ per cent., but the point to be noticed is, that not only was there a disparity between the amount of the advances asked for and granted as between the different branches, but that discriminating and detailed inquiry was made into the various prices of each branch, and the awards varied accordingly. It is certain, however, that after the awards had taken effect the prices paid at most of the manufactories in Staffordshire approached more nearly to uniformity than had ever been the case since 1836.

The advance given in 1871-2 remained unchallenged by the general body of manufacturers for four years. There can be no doubt that during that period the potting trade, like every other industry in the country, had lost some of the prosperity which it enjoyed in the golden years of 1871-2, and that potting manufacturers were, in 1875-6, selling their goods at prices below those of four years previously. The decline had been gradual and fairly general, but not uniform in degree. That is to say, all classes of earthenware, and all articles of the same class, had not suffered a diminution in selling prices to the same extent. Still, the prosperity of the trade had been generally declining from an unwontedly high level. In 1875 there was some talk amongst the manufacturers of an appeal to the Board of Arbitration for a general reduction in wages, but the hope that trade would revive prevented any definite movement among the body in that direction. At Martinmas 1876, however, forty - eight manufacturers gave notice of appeal to the Board for a general reduction in wages of 10 per cent. The grounds upon which the reduction was asked were: "(1) The depressed state of trade; (2) The increasing foreign competition; (3) The generally reduced prices at which goods are now selling; (4) That while from time to time, when trade was good, advances in prices were made, on no occasion has any reduction been made when trade has been depressed; (5) That in numerous other trades in North Staffordshire, and throughout the country, workmen have submitted to reductions in wages, and that the cost of living is considerably lower at the present time than when the various advances were given."

It will at once be observed that the grounds of the appeal introduced a new element into the consideration of what circumstances should govern and decide appeals to the Board for any alteration in wages. The employers based their appeal, in short, upon circumstances and conditions with which their workmen had nothing to do, and which excluded from consideration altogether any question

K

of the value of the work performed as judged by the labour necessary to perform it. They introduced the principle that the wages of their workpeople must fall with a fall in selling prices. Now, this principle—called the "sliding scale"—has been adopted in several trades, particularly in the coal trade, but its operation has generally been accompanied by a minimum below which the wages of the men should not fall. Moreover, it has only been applied to trades that are governed by a market price, such as the iron and coal trades, which are concerned with articles having a definite and standard value. The difference between such trades and that of potting is obvious. The potting trade is concerned with a multifarious number of articles, and its selling prices are largely deter mined — unlike the prices in the coal and iron trades — by the competition of the manufacturers themselves, and are not affected by any of those special circumstances which result in fixing a definite market price in the other trades mentioned. Moreover, in the iron and coal trades — which best serve as an example of contrast—the selling prices are matters of common knowledge upon the various exchanges connected with those trades. The prices of coal and iron are as easily ascertained as that of wheat, and are all affected by special and universal conditions from the operation of which the potting trade is excluded, for it fluctuates only in general sympathy with all commerce. Again, the relation of wages to the value of the article produced and procured, in the case of iron or coal, may be

easily ascertained or established on account of the
directness and simplicity of the operation by which
labour, at the furnace or in the mine, gives effect
to capital, and completes the commodity for the
market; and the determinable character of the
connection between wages and selling prices in this
respect, together with the circumstance that the
markets furnish standard prices of standard goods,
renders the principle of a sliding scale in such
trades a comprehensible and convenient method
for the control of wages. But in the potting trade,
the operations and processes by which the ware is
produced are complex and numerous, the number
of articles concerned is enormous, and their qualities
are of immense variation, and the prices of those
articles being finally determined by the individual
circumstances of each manufacturer, are not regulated by any conditions which could fix a standard
of such precision and reliability as to decide what
share of the selling price of each article should fall
to each workman for the particular process performed by him upon it. There are therefore
practical difficulties to any satisfactory application
of a sliding scale to wages in the potting trade;
but even if it were possible for some system to be
devised by which the principle could be adopted,
there would be still objections to the fairness of
any such method so long as the workmen were left
without a guarantee that the manufacturers would
collectively endeavour to keep up selling prices,
and not reduce them by their own competition.
Without such a guarantee, the principle of a sliding

scale practically converts the workmen's wages into an insurance fund, sheltering the manufacturer against loss; and throws upon labour the burden of providing, at its own cost, the profit of capital. Its injustice to the workman is that it singles out the commodity of his labour, from all other commodities—(such as materials and rent)—the price of which may be altered and adjusted by the employer to meet conditions of trade which may be entirely brought about through the action of the employer himself, but in which, in any case, the workman can take no possible part. It makes of his wages a margin and a reserve within the limits of which the employer may speculate, helps to relieve the employers of the primary obligation of basing the selling prices upon the rate of wages and general cost of production, and subjects him to the temptation of reversing the sound and natural principle upon which all trade should be based, by causing him to speculate upon the possibility of, and ultimately to rely upon, being able to suit his wages to the selling prices which in active competition he himself chooses to fix. It therefore acts, by providing a last resort against loss, as a direct incentive to ruthless and reckless competition which, up to a point below which manufacturers would compete and speculate at the risk of loss only to themselves, would be checked by a stable rate of wages.* We have, of course, touched upon

* The following gems of mixed logic, taken from the case of the employers in the report of this arbitration of 1877, deserve to be rescued from the comparative oblivion in which they reposed :—

a question of wider interest and application than its effect upon the relations of the workmen and employers engaged in the potting trade, but it is a question which was now introduced in the first general arbitration that had ever taken place in the trade; which ran as a "motive" through all succeeding arbitrations; round which has centred nearly all the subsequent controversy between master and man in the potting trade, and upon the satisfactory adjustment of which, it is not too much to say, depends the stability of the wages of the working potter, and the prosperity of his employer.

The difference between the principle now invoked by the manufacturers, and that which governed the arbitrations of 1871-2, will be clearly seen. The workmen, in the earlier period, had taken stock of the decline in wages which had been going on for a number of years, and had asked the Board of

The Umpire having spoken of the difficulty of obtaining reliable information as to the actual selling prices of pottery, "Mr Shaw [a manufacturer]: It was a question of supply and demand. The men that could not get orders sold lower, and thus it was. . . . If, as the manufacturers of The Potteries, they were to agree upon a fixed price so far as they were concerned, 'and put on a price *sufficiently remunerative* to themselves, *they would ruin the trade* of the district in a very short time. The Umpire: Taking the prices, is there no means of settling the matter? Is it not possible to establish a sliding scale of wages?—Mr Clarke [a manufacturer]: There is this peculiarity in the potting trade, that wages form so large an element in the [cost of] potting that it would be an exceedingly dangerous matter to alter wages to the selling of goods.—The Umpire: For what reason?—Answer: For the reason that prices of *materials* so change that wages have to be changed to govern them. An adjournment for half-an-hour for lunch was then agreed to." No wonder !

Arbitration to declare that the prices then paid were not equivalent to the work done. They had not, as we have said, relied upon the prosperity of the trade for the success of their claim; they had asked the Board to grant them what in later days has been called a "living wage," and they got it. But in 1876, the employers based their appeal for a reduction upon the assumption that the advances given in 1872 were given as only fairly applicable to the prosperous conditions of trade then prevailing, and as being intended for revision when trade, in the course of its constant fluctuations, showed less flourishing circumstances.

Accepting these premises, the manufacturers certainly proved their case before the Umpire.* The arbitration took place in January 1877, and lasted two days. The manufacturers confined their case mainly to the broad issue that trade had declined, and that selling prices and profits had been lowered. The first statement was capable of proof from official figures, available to the workmen. The second statement was one proof of which was entirely in the hands of the manufacturers, and the accuracy of which the men had no means of disproving. The manufacturers showed that the American trade —with which the forty-eight manufacturers appealing were mainly concerned—had steadily declined since 1871. They made a great point of the American

---

* The late Mr J. E. Davis, for some years Stipendiary Magistrate in The Potteries, and afterwards legal adviser to Scotland Yard. He was the author of the article on "Labour" in the Encyclopædia Britannica.

tariff being accountable for the decrease in exports
to America, and asserted that a reduction in the
cost of production was necessary in order that they
might hold their own in the American market.
But they told a tale of widespread diminution of
trade as a result of increasing foreign competition.
They alleged that in consequence of the advances
in wages in 1872 they had been compelled to raise
their selling prices, and evidence was given on their
behalf "that it was under cover of these advances
in selling prices that foreign competition has been
developed, which has since resulted in replacing our
goods to a very great extent in foreign markets
with the productions of Germany, France, Belgium,
Denmark, and Holland — countries which, up to
that time, we had only known as producing for
home consumption and not for exportation." It
is an indisputable fact that during the arbitration
of 1871-2 the manufacturers never urged that they
would be compelled to raise their selling prices if
the advances asked for were conceded, and there is
no evidence to show that the rise in selling prices
was to be traced to any cause more remote than
that trade was exceptionally good. We may anticipate a remark made by the Umpire, in giving
his award, which dealt with this issue: "The manufacturers alleged that the last advance was forced
on the trade by their being compelled by their
workmen to make a considerable advance in wages
in consequence of the activity of trade and the
demand for labour in 1872. If that were so, and
the state of trade was not sufficiently remunera-

tive, although undoubtedly brisk, in 1872, to warrant a rise in wages without a corresponding rise in prices, it is manifest, judging after the event, from the rapid decline after 1872, and the continued depression to the present time, that the advance ought neither to have been asked for, nor conceded." We have already said that that plea was never urged by the manufacturers in 1872, and this fact is only consistent with the statement that the workmen did not base their claim upon the prosperity of the trade at that period. The Umpire then proceeded: "It was suggested on the part of the workman that the rise of selling prices subsequent to the rise in wages of 1872, was 10 per cent. I can only say that if the manufacturers put on so much as that, or any greater increase than 4 per cent. (which would have been rather in excess of the increased cost to the manufacturer occasioned by the increase in wages, taking the latter at 10 per cent.) the alleged consequent falling off of trade cannot properly be attributed to the upward movement in wages."

The manufacturers, however, proved their statement of the reduction in selling prices beyond a doubt. The workmen attempted to meet the evidence given upon that point, but failed. They had, indeed, no material at their command by which they could test the statements of the manufacturers in regard to selling prices and diminished trade, and they frankly admitted the weight of evidence upon those particulars to be against them. The Umpire held that the manufacturers had

proved the first three grounds of their claim—the
depressed state of trade, the increasing foreign
competition, and the generally reduced prices at
which goods were then selling. The fourth point
of their claim was, however, fiercely contested by
the men, as being untrue. They alleged that after
the general advances given in 1872, their wages had
been subjected to individual modification, and that,
with the advancing wave of depression, breaches
had been gradually made in the comparative uniformity attained in 1872, so that reductions had
been as frequent as advances. This view seems to
have been accepted by the Umpire, who held that
"the fourth ground had not been fully sustained by
the manufacturers."

The Umpire, admitting the weight of evidence
given by the manufacturers in regard to the depression in trade and the reduction in prices,
nevertheless held that it was "inexpedient" to
make any alteration in prices. The strongest part
of the workmen's case had appeared to him to be
that in which they had contrasted "the inevitable
vicissitudes of selling prices and of seller's profits,
with the permanent character of wages." He apparently foresaw the disadvantage which would have
arisen from making wages march *pari passu* with
selling prices and profits, for he recalled the contention of the workmen that "they had not sought
for an advance on the ground of temporary prosperity, and so rejected the claim for a reduction
to meet a time of temporary depression," and
refused to adopt the plea urged by the manu-

facturers that "the advances of 1872 were to be looked at as having been unduly forced upon the employers." The Umpire, therefore, seems to have taken the same view of the matter that has been urged above — that the advances of 1872 were regarded by both sides as merely fixing, as far as possible, standard and uniform prices, and that there was no thought on the part of either masters or men at the time they were given that when, in the ordinary course of its fluctuations, trade declined, those prices should be altered to meet those altered conditions.

But the Umpire, though thus indicating his views upon the broader question of how far altered conditions of trade should modify wages, declined to interfere with the prices then paid on other grounds. He called attention to the fact that the appellant manufacturers had exempted certain branches from the notice of reduction. The explanation of this fact by the manufacturers was that those branches against which they had not appealed for a reduction were those which, in 1872, had not received an advance, but the Umpire said that he regarded the adjustment of prices in 1872 "as operating fairly for all branches, and putting them, as far as was possible, on an equality with one another," and he regarded one condition of the success of the appeal as a *sine qua non*: that the reduction asked for must be proved to have the effect, if granted, of leaving all the branches in the same relative wage-earning capacity as they occupied in 1872; and he held that the distinction made between the different

branches' would destroy the equality which had
been brought about in 1872.   Upon that ground,
he decreed that the contracts for the then current
year should remain as if no notice of reduction had
been given; and his award, therefore, by being
based upon the unforeseen weakness in the case of
the employers, did not involve any decision upon
the general issue raised by the manufacturers: that
the wages of their workmen should fluctuate with
the prices at which their employers sold their goods.

The employers were keenly disappointed at the
result of their appeal, and the workmen corre-
spondingly elated, and both were equally surprised.
The employers looked at the broad fact that they
had based their claim for a reduction upon certain
definite grounds, that the facts given by them in
support of those grounds were practically indisputable, and had been accepted, but that, notwithstanding their proof, the case had gone against
them ; and they were disposed to regard as mere
casuistry the reasons given by the Umpire for not
giving effect to the burden of evidence admitted
by him as being in their favour.   The workmen,
on the other hand, found to their astonishment
that, though they had been unable to make much
headway against the claim advanced by the
manufacturers, they had secured a verdict upon
grounds which they had not urged upon the consideration of the Umpire.   Still, the employers
faithfully observed the award, and looked forward
to the time when they could renew their appeal
with greater chance of success.

One immediate effect of the award of 1877 was an increase in the application of machinery to the trade, and it will be appropriate here to say a few words in continuation of the general subject of machinery from the point at which it was last mentioned — the agitation of 1844 and the few subsequent years. It was not until more than twenty years later. that machinery became, not general, but in any sense a serious factor in the trade. But, by that time, there existed a Board of Arbitration, and the workmen availed themselves of its machinery for a wise purpose. They did not endeavour, as their fathers had done, to resist the introduction of machinery, but accepted it as the inevitable development of a scientific age, and took pains to secure that what would benefit their employers should not injure themselves.

In 1872, two cases, dealing with the effect that the introduction of machinery had had upon wages, came before the first Umpire of the Board (Mr Davenport, M.P.). The hollow-ware pressers of a certain firm appealed for an advance on certain articles on the ground that through other articles being made by a machine—called "the jigger"— only the heavier work, and that which was the least remunerative, was left to be made by the manual labour of the hollow-ware presser. The case was argued before the Umpire, who gave his verdict in favour of the men, at the same time laying down this principle—and asking that the Board should accept it:—"That the removal of the hollow-ware presser's good work to the 'jigger' justifies the workmen in asking for compensation in the shape of an advance in prices on those articles not removed to the 'jigger.'" It would be impossible to imagine any principle more simple or equitable. There was yet another case, in which the action of the Umpire was even more decisive. A hollow-ware presser in the employ of another firm, appealed for an advance upon certain articles upon the same grounds. Obviously, the same principle governed it. The workman pleaded that he had lost by the change caused by the introduction of machinery, and the employer denied that he had seriously suffered. The Umpire ordered the wage-books of the firm to be shown to him, and he took an average of the workman's earnings for twenty weeks before, and twenty weeks after the transference of certain articles to the machine. The result of the investigation showed an average decrease in the workman's wages of seven shillings per week since the introduction of the machine. "These figures," said the Umpire, "cannot be contravened. They show very clearly that the workman has suffered loss"—and the effect of his award was that the workman should be restored to a position of the same wage-earning capacity as that which he had enjoyed before part of the work which he used to do was made by machinery. The verdict of the Umpire was, however, merely the formal expression of the unanimous opinion of the Board itself, for, on the motion of an operative member of the Board, seconded by a manufacturer, a resolution was passed, without dissent, affirming

"That the Board considered the case came under the principle laid down by the Umpire in the previous case, affirming that compensation should be allowed to workmen when good work is taken to the 'jigger.'"

Nothing could exaggerate the importance of these two cases, for they gave to the trade a precedent from which it would have been difficult to have departed in later times, and settled a principle, accepted by both parties as eminently fair, and one which should have secured, for all time, the recognition by the employers that where a workman suffered in earning power through the introduction of machinery—cheapening production to the employer—he should be compensated for the loss. Strange to say, however, not once in the subsequent proceedings of the trade—until the arbitration of 1891, when the Arbitrator (who was, curiously enough, the same Arbitrator as in the case referred to in 1872), practically brushed it aside as occurring "nineteen years ago"—was this principle and the authoritative pronouncement of it recalled by the workmen. In after years the question of the introduction of machinery, and of the loss which the workmen had suffered by it, became a matter of vital importance to the case of the operatives, and, though they had had bequeathed to them this priceless precedent, they had either completely forgotten it, or were guilty of an extraordinary injustice to their own cause by not urging that it should be acted upon. If they had recalled it, one fails to see how it could have been argued away by their employers, and, certainly, succeeding Umpires could not have failed to have paid regard to a principle so far-reaching, which had been accepted by both sides on the very first occasion when the effect of machinery upon wages had received dispassionate consideration. The principle then laid down was, in later years, notoriously departed from, but no blame can be attached to the manufacturers—except it is assumed that they should have shown a degree of magnanimity uncommon in mundane and controversial matters— for not having themselves recalled, and acted upon, a decision of such vital importance to their work-people, who themselves had forgotten it.

The increase in machinery since 1872 had been fairly gradual, but after the award of 1877 it became increasingly general, for the employers, prevented by that award from decreasing the cost of production by a direct reduction of the workmen's wages, sought for other means, and determined to achieve their object by increasing the use of machinery; and the workmen saw it increase, and their wages suffer in consequence, but did not challenge its extension and effect by insisting upon the adoption of the principle laid down for their benefit in 1872.

CHAPTER VIII

THREE years passed, and at Martinmas 1879 the manufacturers agreed that the time had come for them to attempt to accomplish that which they had failed to obtain in 1876-7—a reduction of 10 per cent. They therefore sent in an appeal to the Board, supported by no less than seventy-eight members of their body. At the arbitration of 1877, it will be remembered, only forty-eight manufacturers were parties to the appeal, and the workmen made a strong point of the partial character of the movement among the manufacturers. The general character of the appeal of 1879, however, convinced the workmen that they would have an even more difficult task than they had in the former arbitration in opposing a claim made by nearly every employer of importance in the district.

The first step to be taken was the selection of an Umpire, by both sections of the Board. The name of Lord Hatherton was suggested, and he consented to act as Umpire, but first desired to have some common basis, acknowledged by both sides, upon which he could proceed. A deputation of masters and men therefore waited upon him. They informed him of the nature of the question which he had to decide. He asked for a standard, upon which they

160

were agreed, and they answered—both masters and
men—that they were agreed that he should take
the selling prices and wages of 1872 as a standard
—that he should go back so far, and no further, and
accept evidence dealing with the state of trade
from that period up to that of the arbitration.

It is difficult to imagine why the representatives
of the workmen thus readily acquiesced in a course
of procedure against which they had protested at
the previous arbitration, and one which, in all future
arbitrations, they emphatically repudiated. The only
conclusion possible is that they did not quite appreciate the gravity of the step they were taking,
nor recognise the position of helplessness to which
they were reducing themselves. They had narrowed
down the issue to practically one point—Had selling prices decreased since 1872? Well, obviously
that was a matter upon which they could offer no
authoritative evidence. There were as many different selling prices, for the same goods, as there were
manufactories. Not only did the workmen possess
no knowledge of what the selling prices of any
manufacturer were, but, for prudential reasons, and
owing to a not unnatural jealousy, every manufacturer was careful not to reveal to his rivals in trade
the prices at which he sold his goods. The only
evidence possible, therefore, upon the issue agreed
upon, was the statements of the various manufacturers as to by how much per cent. their selling prices
had decreased since a given period. How were the
workmen to controvert those statements? Clearly,
they could not. They had therefore, by so narrow-

L

ing the issue for the convenience of the Umpire, practically reduced an arbitration to the level of an *ex parte* motion; and, for all effective purposes, having once agreed upon the "common basis" that the appeal should fail or succeed by the test of the change in selling prices since 1872, they might just as well have asked the employers to furnish the Umpire with comparative lists of selling prices, and have quietly retired until he had perused those lists, and given his verdict in the only possible way that they permitted.

The arbitration lasted for five days. In opening the proceedings, Lord Hatherton gave an early indication of his mental attitude towards the question which he had to decide, and showed that, even if the workmen had not agreed to have a common basis so far as a certain year was concerned, they would have had considerable difficulty in persuading him that a reduction in selling prices was not a justification for a reduction in wages. After alluding to the simplification of his work by the agreement "to start with the basis of the prices of 1871-2," he went on to say: "We may say and do as we like, but there is an inevitable law that where there is a great demand for labour, the workmen will be in a position to claim, and will eventually get, an increase in wages; on the other hand, when employers find it necessary to restrict the sphere of their operations, or get alarmed for their capital, and consequently do not employ the same amount of labour as when trade was good, the inevitable result is that, make what strikes you like, before

long wages must be abated. When trade is good,
there is a demand for men, and wages will rise;
when trade is bad, and there is little demand for
men, wages must fall." By thus foreshadowing his
views, the Umpire clearly indicated that he would
not be influenced in his decision by any consideration of a "living wage" for the operatives, for he
was evidently a firm believer in the theory of an
inelastic "wages fund" and the other then current
doctrines of political economists, who called upon
workmen to be the passive spectators of a delicate
system of economical mechanism by which their
wages were considerately adjusted without any effort
on their own part, the perfect working of which they
were asked to admire, but which they must on no
account touch, lest their clumsy fingers should throw
it out of gear.*

The formal statement of appeal contained substantially the same reasons as that of 1876. It
was as follows :—"(1) The depressed state of trade;
(2) the effects of foreign competition; (3) diminished
profits; (4) that while trade was good, advances
were made, and there has been no reduction in
consequence of bad trade;, (5) that in numerous
other trades workmen have submitted to a reduction, and the cost of living is cheaper than when

---

* "With regard to his own workmen, he had no fault to find with
them for any unwillingness or unreasonableness, and he had only put
it down (their opposition to a reduction) to the fact that they had not
studied the matter, and hadn't the knowledge thereon. But if they
would only study the political economy of the matter, they would be
willing to co-operate with them (the masters)."—Mr Pinder, manufacturer, Arbitration of 1877, p. 9.

the present scale of wages was authorised." A comparison with the claim of 1876 will reveal two deviations from that of 1879. In the former appeal, the third clause was, "the generally reduced prices at which goods are now selling," and now the manufacturers did not speak of reduced selling prices, but of diminished profits. In clause 4 of the appeal of 1876, the manufacturers were more emphatic in their statement that no reduction had been made in consequence of bad trade, for they then asserted that "on no occasion had any reduction been made when trade had been depressed." If by this they meant a general and simultaneous reduction, then they were only stating that which was true, but the whole tendency of wages from 1846 down to 1867-8 had been to decrease, and only the arbitrations of 1872 had checked the downward tendency.

The evidence given by the employers to support their appeal briefly consisted of the statements that since 1872 prices had been declining, and foreign competition had increased. The workmen endeavoured to show that since the date of the last arbitration business had improved, but the Umpire, recollecting the "common basis," declined to restrict his view to the later period. Some of the witnesses for the employers, however, said that even since 1876 prices had receded, and none spoke of any improvement in prices since that date. So long as they confined their evidence to the decrease in selling prices, the employers were on safe ground; but they made several excursions

into other directions, and advanced arguments and
contentions which were as absurd as they were novel.
Several manufacturers urged that a reduction in
wages would be for the benefit of the workmen
themselves.   One manufacturer vaguely said:
"With cheaper production there would be increased
profit on the capital invested, and enhanced earnings
.for the workman.   They had no desire to reduce
wages, except as it would be a mutual advantage."
Inasmuch as they proposed to "cheapen production" by reducing wages, one fails to see how the
advantage could very well be of a mutual character.
Others, however, attempted to prove their paradox
by pointing out that if wages were reduced the
manufacturers would be better able to compete with
foreign-made goods, by which they alleged they
were under-sold, and they argued that trade would
thereby be stimulated, and the workmen would
share in this "increased prosperity."   To this the
workmen might have returned the answer that
they could only recoup themselves from the loss
which a reduction would entail by working more
hours for the same money, but extra work would
mean increased production, and that, in its turn,
would inevitably lower prices, and, presumably,
wages again.   The manufacturers were therefore
inviting them to take a first step to bring about
what promised to be a series of reductions in wages,
whilst endeavouring to persuade them that they were
only doing that which was necessary for their own
good.   Other manufacturers urged that they were
already carrying on their business at an actual loss,

consequent on being compelled to accept unremunerative prices, and they urged that the reduction
was necessary in order that they might be able to
accept orders at the rate of selling prices then
prevailing; but they made no attempt to show
that a reduction of 10 per cent. in wages would
make the current selling prices remunerative, and
therefore failed to show that the reduction asked for
would restore stability to their business.   Another
manufacturer—and a member of an eminent firm,
Messrs Josiah Wedgwood & Sons — said that his
"dead" expenses had increased (and by "dead"
expenses he said, in answer to the Umpire, that
he meant "travellers' expenses, new designs, rent,
rates, taxes, bad debts, interest on capital, and allow-
ances"), and he urged that inasmuch as those
"dead expenses" were necessary in order to increase
his business, and secure more orders, "there was
no reason why the workmen should not bear their
share of the cost."   This, surely, was an amazing
doctrine: that the workmen, having made the goods,
should suffer a loss in their wages in order to help
the master to dispose of them.   The principle of
the workmen "bearing their share in the cost" of
the administrative expenses of the business could
be admitted if they also participated in its profits;
but, in the absence of that circumstance, such a
contention suggested the suspicion that the manufacturers, looking around them to diminish their
outlay, regarded their workmen's wages as offering
the readiest means of accomplishing their purpose.
One of the workmen's representatives thus com-

mented on the claim: "The novelty of the claim
is that he wants to meet the increased cost of dead
expenses out of the wages. I contend that that
is not paralleled by any demand usually made by
employers to justify a reduction in wages. In an
eminent firm, of the description of Messrs Wedgwood's, designs and novelties have a substantial
value; they constitute a special element in the
financial worth of such a house, and if Mr Wedgwood
spends thousands instead of hundreds of pounds in
strengthening his trade, he is only doing what the
founders of the house did, and that founder would
not have reduced his workmen's wages because he
paid Flaxman to bring out some of the beautiful
designs which helped to make our potting trade
one of the wonders of the world."

We have referred to these points, not because they
in any way affected the issue, but to show upon what
debatable and dangerous grounds the manufacturers
stepped when they departed from the safe plateau
of the question of selling prices. There they were
invulnerable—once the fairness of the principle was
admitted, as it had been. Still, even upon this
point their evidence was contradictory. One manufacturer handed in an invoice of goods sent out in
1873, amounting to £100, and said the same goods
in 1878 would only fetch £70. There was, therefore,
a decrease in selling prices of 30 per cent., and
he added that, "the money that came back from
the goods sent out did not provide cash for the
wages." Now it was stated by several manufacturers
that the wages formed 40 to 50 per cent. of

the turnover, so that the manufacturer obviously
" proved too much " by his assertion that " the
money which came back "—*i.e.* the turnover—did not
provide that which was only half its amount. The
manufacturer then went on to assert that " a 10
per cent. reduction in wages would enable him to
sell without loss, *though not at a profit.*"   His various
statements were, therefore, mutually destructive ; but
it was a feature of this arbitration that the statistics
quoted were given in the loosest possible fashion.
When the employers made a comparison of selling
prices, they compared those of 1873 and 1878-79.
Now the selling prices in 1873 were at their highest,
but the advance in wages had been given the previous year, 1872 ; and surely, in order to make any
comparison relevant, it should have been one between
the prices at the period of the advance and those
upon which they then sought a reduction.

One admission was made by the leader of the
manufacturers of which the operatives' representatives did not take sufficient advantage. The workmen had asserted that wages had decreased since
1872, owing to the introduction of machinery. The
leader of the manufacturers denied this, saying that
though the workmen in certain branches were now
paid less per dozen or per score of articles, made
by machinery, than they were paid in 1872, when
made by hand, they were still able to earn as much
money for the same length of time worked, inasmuch
as they could turn out, in the same time, more
dozens or scores of the same articles by machinery
than they could when making those articles by hand.

What, then, did this mean? Clearly that the manufacturer was able to produce more ware at less cost
than formerly, and therefore could afford to sell his
goods at less cost. The operatives, however, could
really make little effective use of this point, inasmuch
as they were quite ignorant of the extent to which
machinery, by cheapening production, had benefited
the employer. No figures were given upon this head
by the employers; they contented themselves with
saying that the proportion of wages to selling prices
had increased, though clearly the cost of production
had been modified in their favour by the introduction
of machinery. Still, the workmen had no data upon
which they could give any definite contradiction of
the figures given by the employers—except in one
instance.

The employers had given a list of the exports
from the port of Liverpool to the United States,
from 1866 to 1878, extending the list given at
the previous arbitration down to the latter year.
The figures for 1876 were 61,124 packages; for
1877, 69,951; and for 1878, 64,461. The workmen
pointed out that these figures only related to one
part of the trade of The Potteries—the American
trade—and that they showed, as will be seen, an
increase since the date of the last arbitration. They
also produced other figures, the official figures of the
Parliamentary returns, showing the total pottery
exports from England to all parts of the world, not
in packages, but in money value. These figures
were: 1876, £1,771,179; 1877, £1,852,992; in 1878,
£1,794,218. Again, the imports showed a decline

during those years: 1876, £336,980; 1877, £279,888; 1878, £113,056. The year 1877, therefore, showed a marked improvement upon the previous year, and 1878 still showed increased exports and diminished imports, as compared with 1876. The workmen contended, therefore, that the masters were asking for a reduction in a rising market, and the employers again met them with the statement: "Yes; the exports are greater, because the selling prices are less." So the whole question was narrowed down again to the state of selling prices, and upon that point the manufacturers alone had any knowledge. They selected their own particular invoices, and put them forward as samples of the whole. They may or may not have been; the workmen could not say. The Umpire said: "We have to deal with the broad question of whether trade is in such a state that it will not stand present wages. The masters have said it will not; it is for the workmen to show that it will." The workmen tried to do so by quoting the only figures at their command—the official and reliable figures of the Parliamentary department—which showed an increase of trade, but the masters disposed of these figures by an allusion to selling prices.

Then the workmen urged their second defence; that, since 1872, various branches—particularly the printers and oven-men—had, by altered modes of working, suffered a loss in wages. In the case of the oven-men, the Umpire said that further evidence was unnecessary to convince him of the contention, but the workmen gained nothing by this point, for

the Umpire ruled: "I have nothing to do with
the disproportion of wages at separate works, or in
different departments, nor how much any class of
men earn"—as he must consider the trade as a
whole—"though that might be a subject for separate
arbitration." The position, therefore, amounted to
this: The masters appealed for a reduction in wages
because selling prices had decreased since 1872,
and it was part of their case that wages had not
decreased since that period. The workmen answered
by saying that the employers had already, in the
intervening years, reduced wages, and asked that
these reductions should be taken into account. The
Umpire, deciding between them, ruled that though
the decrease in selling prices since 1872 was material
to the issue, and favourable to the employers, the
decrease in wages since 1872 was a matter of which
he could take no cognisance, "but which might
be a subject for a separate arbitration."

The workmen, therefore, saw themselves forced
to narrow their defence to the limits of inquiry laid
down by the Umpire—the question of selling prices.
They appear to have awakened to some sense of
their weakness in assenting to the introduction of
this question as the principal factor in deciding the
dispute, and their last words in addressing the
Umpire were an appeal to him not to allow the
question of selling prices to govern the rate of wages.
They based their appeal upon the general interests
of the trade—of manufacturers as well as workmen—
contending that "if the men must suffer with the
masters, they must rise with the masters, and wages

must be proportioned to profits," and that would involve constant uncertainty and disturbance in the trade, and asking whether it would not be better for the trade, as a whole, that an even and steady rate of wages should be maintained.   They also predicted that no good would accrue to the manufacturers if the reduction were granted, as a reduction would only be a sign of weakness in the trade, would increase competition, and encourage the customers of the manufacturers to expect and to insist upon a proportionate reduction in the selling prices.   The masters, as the appellants, had the "last word" at the arbitration.   They urged that a reduction of 10 per cent. in wages was necessary to the salvation of the trade, and that, when a time of prosperity came round, they would only be too willing to give back to their workmen that which they now asked should be taken from them.

In less than a week the Umpire gave his award. He decided in favour of the employers' appeal, and decreed a reduction of wages of $8\frac{1}{3}$ per cent., or of a penny in every shilling.

The arbitration of 1879 is interesting, not merely as an integral chapter in this history, but because its direct effects are felt upon the trade to-day. Twenty years have passed since Lord Hatherton decreed a reduction in the wages of the workmen, and the rates of wages now prevailing in the trade are nominally those which followed upon Lord Hatherton's award.   Actually, they are less.   The continued increase in machinery has involved a continuous decrease in wages, and the introduction of new shapes and patterns, demanding a revision in prices, has had a similar effect. We are, however, more concerned with the immediate effect of the award. So far as the manufacturers are concerned, it does not appear to have brought them much immediate gain, for in the following year they again spoke of the decline in selling prices. The amount taken from the workmen, therefore, by Lord Hatherton's reduction, appears to have either been distributed amongst the pockets of the customers — the "middlemen" of the trade — for their exclusive benefit, or to have been dissipated amongst the general public who bought the ware, but who must have remained in ignorance of the infinitesimal benefit which had accrued to them through Lord Hatherton's decision. At any rate, it is certain that the trade, as a whole, reaped no benefit from that award. The workmen certainly had lost a penny of every shilling of their wages, and the employers disclaimed any benefit from that award by pointing to continually falling selling prices. The essential point to discover, therefore, is whether the reduction in wages had had anything to do with the decline in selling prices— whether the latter was the consequence of the former. If that were so, then it is clear that Lord Hatherton's award was an unmixed evil for both employers and men. It is obviously difficult to prove the connection between the two circumstances, and to show that the reduced selling prices were a direct result of the reduction in wages; but there are strong grounds for assuming that the

connection existed. In the golden year of 1872,
trade was so brisk and prices so remunerative, that
all the employers were content to ride on the
crest of the wave. Then, when trade declined to
a more normal level, each employer sought compensation by competition with his fellows, and
selling prices declined, but no proof was ever
given, nor the statement even made, that the
selling prices had declined below the level which
prevailed previous to the unusually high prices
of 1872. In 1876, however, the employers saw
they were approaching a limit beyond which
further reductions in selling prices would be dangerous, and, aware of the difficulty of recovering
lost ground in that respect, they sought to fortify
themselves against loss by obtaining, through a
reduction in wages, a further margin within which
they might compete. The award of 1877, however, checked their hopes in this direction. And
what was the immediate result? That for the next
three years there was no further decline in selling
prices, and an increase in the general bulk of trade
done. At the arbitration before Lord Hatherton,
the comparisons of selling prices were not made
as between 1879 and 1876—(for the appeal of
the manufacturers was at Martinmas of that
year, although the arbitration did not take
place until January of 1877)—but the employers
had to go back to 1872 in order to show that
they had declined. There can, at any rate, be
no doubt that whether or not it was a result of
the refusal of the arbitrator of 1877 to reduce

wages, trade improved between that period and 1879. The employers, however, were more fortunate in the Umpire of 1879. He had to decide upon practically the same facts as his predecessor, and he came to a totally different conclusion. If he had restricted his view of the case to a comparison between 1876 and 1879, the result might possibly have been different, but, by the strange folly of the workmen in allowing Lord Hatherton to go back to 1872, they were practically submitting a decision in their favour by one Umpire to the review of another Umpire — and Lord Hatherton looked at the matter from a different point of view to his predecessor. That difference of view made all the difference in the decision, and the employers had then obtained what they wanted — the assurance that they might rely upon falling back upon their workmen's wages when selling prices were low. Surely this was an incentive to further reductions in selling prices? Negatively, the least that can be said of it, is that it was at any rate not calculated to restrain competition, but to rather diminish the restraint. Looking, therefore, at the experience of the three previous years, when trade had been fairly maintained, even after the Umpire had declined to decree that which the employer said was necessary for the salvation of the trade (*viz.* a reduction in wages), and paying due regard to the probabilities of the effect of Lord Hatherton's award, it does not seem a rash assumption that subsequent reductions in selling prices were encouraged by Lord Hatherton's award, even if they were not a direct effect. In later days, it certainly became an accepted belief of the trade that if Lord Hatherton had refused a reduction, it would have "stiffened" the manufacturers in their dealings with their customers, would have reduced reckless competition amongst themselves, and would have given stability to the whole industry. And that certainly seems a common-sense view to take, even as a prediction.

As for the effect of the award upon the workmen, it is sufficiently obvious not to be dwelt upon. The name of that estimable peer, Lord Hatherton, became synonymous to the potter with injustice. "Lord Hatherton's pennies" are spoken of to-day, and remembered as a stolen birthright. But, at that time, the workmen only thought of the decision as one which would have but a short-lived effect, and which must be reversed at the first opportunity. The following Martinmas was, of course, the earliest opportunity that presented itself, and they took it. They not only wanted their "pennies" back, but they were determined that the next arbitration should be fought out entirely upon the issue of whether selling prices should govern wages or not.

CHAPTER IX

THE BRASSEY ARBITRATION, AND THE
STRIKE OF 1881

AT Martinmas of 1880, each branch sent in an appeal to the employers for a return of the reduction decreed by Lord Hatherton the previous year.

The appeal of each branch was distinct and independent, and though each asked for the same thing, they gave varying reasons for it. The object of making the appeal one from each branch, instead of a united effort, was that the workmen had awakened to the danger of allowing the precedent set by the employers to become a practice—*viz.* that of setting all branches on the same level, and asking for a uniform reduction upon all—because they saw that the method was merely the outcome of the "selling price" principle. The branch form of appeal was therefore not only an effort to keep up the traditional custom of the trade that each branch should be separately dealt with, but was intended to cut the ground from underneath the employers on the question of selling prices. The employers, however, by refusing the branch appeals *en bloc*, practically made the arbitration, which necessarily followed the refusal, a general question, and each

M 177

branch, whilst giving reasons peculiar to itself why, of
all others, it deserved to succeed in its appeal, vainly
insisted upon its right to have a separate award.

To each branch appeal, the employers sent a
separate reply, in every case refusing the request,
and in some cases answering the reasons given by
their workmen *seriatim*.   These appeals and the
replies are interesting because they practically sum-
marise the issue between the two sides, as presented
by them to the Umpire.   There were two grounds
common to all the appeals: (1) that trade continued to improve, and (2) a protest against wages
being controlled by selling prices.   There was also,
in the replies of the manufacturers, one clause
common to all, but vague and enigmatical: "The
improvement of trade applies to certain markets
only, and the goods have been sold at the same,
and, in many instances, at less prices than were
obtained in 1879, and has been of more advantage to the workmen than to the manufacturers."
Wherein had lain the advantage to the workmen
was not explained.   The appeals of several branches
alleged that they had, by altered modes of working
and "count," lost all the advantages of the advance
of 1872 long before the reduction of 1879.   To this
the employers returned a flat denial.   The flat-
pressers made one claim peculiar to them—that the
reduction decreed by Lord Hatherton bore with
special severity upon them, inasmuch as the reduction applied to their gross earnings, and they had not
been able to reduce the wages of their attendants,
whom they paid.   To this the employers replied

that it was their own fault that they had not reduced the wages of their attendants.

The references to selling prices, however, were of most interest, but the employers only permitted themselves to allude to this question in a few instances. Answering the hollow - ware pressers, that "the selling prices of manufacturers have not regulated the rate of wages," the employers said : " Workmen's wages have always been regulated, and will continue to be regulated, by selling prices. The hollow-ware pressers must know that the manufacturer cannot and does not pay a higher price for making than he can recover in his selling prices." Of course he could not, and did not, but the more proper way to put it would have been : " The manufacturer cannot and does not sell his goods at a lower price than he pays for them to be made." But the employers' answer really summarised their point of view of the whole question : that wages should be subsidiary to selling prices, and not that selling prices should be subsidiary to wages, and the general cost of production. The reply of the manufacturers to the hollow - ware pressers upon this point cannot be said to have been an answer, or to have been any contribution to a solution of the ethical problem of whether wages should be governed by selling prices. It was left to the turners, however, to make the most exhaustive reference to this question. In their appeal they said : (1) " That the general reduction awarded by Lord Hatherton was contrary to the practices of the trade ; (2) that we deny it is possible to equitably rule our wages by the rising and the falling of the markets, there being no clear and definite means of ascertaining or gauging such rise or fall; (3) that it is unwise to attempt to regulate the rate of wages by reference to a standard which is cloudy, shifting, and elastic, there being as many differences in qualities of goods and of selling rates as there are manufacturers engaged in the production; (4) that under such a scheme working potters are at the mercy of so few or so many figures as the masters choose to disclose; (5) that in any trade where prices regulate wages these prices are easily ascertained in open market." To this series of arguments—which put the case for the workmen with great force and point—the employers returned no answer whatever.

The Umpire selected was Mr Thomas Brassey, afterwards Sir Thomas, and now Lord Brassey, Governor of Victoria. Nothing but praise can be said of the manner in which he conducted the case; he was patient, vigilant, full of inquiry, and soon showed a remarkable grasp of the bewildering details and technicalities which were submitted to him, connected with a trade to which he was a complete stranger.

The case of the workmen may be summarised under three heads: (1) increase of general trade, as shown by Government return of exports; (2) individual evidence of smallness of earnings; (3) protest against selling prices ruling wages. The figures quoted to show the increase in exports and a decrease in imports of earthenware since 1876, were not, as they could not be, disputed by the employers; but the most interesting part of the proceedings of the arbitration—which lasted for three days—was that which referred to the question of selling prices, because, from the award of Lord Brassey, it is clear that he regarded that question as of vital consequence to the whole case.

The objection to the "selling price" argument was sympathetically listened to by the Umpire. He had always interested himself in industrial matters, he was the author of a valuable book on "Work and Wages" and of other publications on the industrial problem; he had filled the office of Umpire in many industrial disputes; he had a broad mind, and could appreciate, if not accept, the contentions of the workmen that the selling prices of the manufacturers should not govern their wages. The representative of the turners—whose appeal had dealt lengthily with the question—raised the definite issue. He revived an item of forgotten history, which has been dealt with in this narrative in its proper place, that previous to the great strike in 1836, an influential employer had written to a local newspaper "complaining of the unfair competition to which manufacturers were subjecting themselves by under-selling, and by reducing wages to meet the results of their unwise competition," and appealing to the men to combine to raise wages where they were low, so that competition in selling prices might be checked. In 1836, therefore, manufacturers looked to an increase in their workmen's wages as a protective measure for themselves, in order that they might maintain their selling prices, but in 1876 they had reversed the effort, and for the first time asked that wages might be lowered so that they might lower selling prices. In the interval of forty years, the representative of the turners contended, "there was nothing to show that the principle of governing wages by selling prices had any recognition," and he challenged the manufacturers "to produce any of the appeals of the workmen in 1872 in which they based their demand upon the profits of their employers, and the high selling prices which prevailed," a challenge which was not accepted. Therefore, the principle invoked in 1876, which was then repudiated by the Umpire, was a new one in the trade. So much was un-answerable. Then came the question: Even though a new departure, is it a fair one? Upon this point, he argued: "If the idea simply means that the employers are to have the sole control of the figures —their own books—then the proposal is fallacious and one-sided. It has nothing workable and mutual in it. Last year employers gave us certain invoices. We do not say it was so, but by selecting the selling prices of the worst goods an argument in bad times may be easily drawn adverse to the workmen. It is clear that if the rule of governing wages by prices must exist, it would not be a fair one if we did not have good as well as bad prices taken and averaged to get at what should be the rate of wages. But even supposing employers say all the selling prices, good as well as bad, shall be included in the reckoning, the unwisdom of the

rule so far as the employers' own interests are concerned is soon found out. Suppose an employer
went to a great expense for new shapes and designs,
and as a just reward for his enterprise he obtained
a very high price for the finished goods; having
laid down the principle that selling prices shall rule
wages, the workman would demand to follow. And
if the employer said 'No, this high profit is the
result of my enterprise, and I am entitled to all the
margin above profit on common goods,' then the
obvious reply of the workman would be, 'I may
walk with the employer in the valley, but the atmosphere of the mountain top of best trade results
is held as being unsuitable to my constitution.'
Yet, I cannot help sympathising with the employers
on this point. For the man to claim a higher rate
of wages for the few hours he is engaged in placing
a number of plaques in a sagger because the plaques
realise a large profit is nonsensical. But how are
selling prices to guide at all if not throughout?
The employers would be the first to resent the
logical result of their own theory. If I reduce the
matter to an absurdity, it is because the rule all
round is absurdly impracticable. Besides, there is
the main fact still unsettled; what is to be the
starting-point? How much wages must be proportioned to certain rates of selling prices? As the
articles are legion, the initiatory work would find
enough work for the wit of all the Umpires that
ever sat. Philadelphian lawyers would be nowhere.
As a matter of fact, the standard is absolutely un-
reliable. It is asking that something may be

measured that contracts or expands even while the rule is applied to it; and I must affirm, in the language of the appeal, that it is unwise to make the attempt to regulate potters' wages by selling prices." The Umpire, though agreeing with much of the foregoing, asked what circumstance should govern the rate of wages if selling prices did not, and the representative of the turners replied: "The basis of the wages rate has been, as far as any basis has existed, a fair living rate for a British artisan, consideration being paid to skill, physical effort put forth, and to immeasurable loss through health being undermined." The rates of wages paid in various branches differed, but thirty shillings a week had been looked upon by the average potter as a fair rate below which he did not wish to fall, whilst in the higher branches the possible wages amounted to more. Therefore, "either you must take this rather loose and general idea of a skilful workman receiving from £1, 10s. to £2, 5s. a week, which, though not a scientific rate of wages, has existed hitherto, or, if the employers take the selling prices as the basis for regulating wages, they must adopt it with all its logical consequences."

This, then, was the view presented by the workmen to the Umpire as to the question of their wages being governed by selling prices. As it would seem, the arguments by which it was supported were, if not unanswerable, at least of sufficient weight to have merited some acknowledgment from the masters; yet it will scarcely be believed that the employers did not vouchsafe one single word of direct reply to the arguments which the workmen addressed to the Umpire upon this point. They studiously avoided any reference to it, but went on quoting their selected invoices, as instances of reduced selling prices, as though it were a matter of common acceptance that the decree of the Umpire should depend upon the isolated invoices of goods to which they made reference. They had not the excuse for this omission that the Umpire himself paid no heed to the arguments of the workmen. On the contrary, he displayed the greatest interest in all the references made to the question of selling prices throughout the inquiry, and again and again, by his comments upon the views of the workmen, gave an opening, if not a challenge, to the manufacturers to make some attempt to meet argument by argument. What, for instance, could more clearly show his appreciation of the workmen's views than the following remarks, made upon the third day of the arbitration :—" I think I shall sum up all that can be said about selling prices regulating wages, by saying that whilst they contend for the principle that wages depend upon the selling prices, the employers at the same time must admit that the application of the principle is attended with a peculiar, *if not an insuperable difficulty*, in the case of trade in earthenware. The number of articles is so great, the prices differ so considerably for the same goods made by the different makers, and supplied to different markets, that the situation differs materially from what presents itself in the

iron trade, where the prices are determined publicly
by negotiating on Exchange?" This was practically a summary of the arguments of the workmen
themselves, but coming from the mouth of the
Umpire himself, it is inexplicable that no attempt
was made by the manufacturers to answer the
arguments of their opponents, endorsed so fully
by the judge called in to decide between them.
But even the remarks of the Umpire just quoted,
though directly addressed to the manufacturers,
elicited no response. One can only assume, therefore, that they were unable to answer the arguments
of the workmen, and bowed to the opinion of the
Umpire that "the principle was attended with a
peculiar, if not an insuperable difficulty!" And
they did not endeavour to minimise that difficulty.
On the contrary, their whole attitude at the
arbitration confirmed the view of the Umpire.
What was the cause of the difficulty, almost "insuperable," attending the application of the principle
that selling prices should govern wages? To quote
the Umpire again, the difficulty was the "multitudinous number of articles," and the varying prices
of each manufacturer. One would have expected,
then, that the manufacturers would have made
some attempt to minimise the difficulty by showing
that definite and general information as to the
effect of selling prices upon wages was available,
by showing the direct relation between the two,
by showing the proportion which one bore to the
other, and by showing how they were interdepen-
dent, and how one reacted upon the other. But

they did nothing of the kind. To have given such information, it is obvious' that two sets of figures would have been required — *viz.* the total amount of wages paid, and the total value of the ware produced. Then the relation which one bore to the other would have been seen, and the figures would have had some value, and such information would have diminished the "difficulty" of which the Umpire had spoken. But what was the attitude of the manufacturers in regard to these two points? Asked to give information as to the total amount of wages paid, one manufacturer said: " I cannot tell, and if I could, I would not." Asked as to whether, if the principle were admitted, the manufacturers would give such general information as to selling prices, as would enable some definite basis to be established, another manufacturer said: " I am not prepared to say that I would consent to any person comparing my prices with those of other manufacturers." This then was the position: The manufacturers asked for wages to be governed by selling prices; the workmen argued, and the Umpire agreed, that such a course was next to impossible; and the employers, leaving the contention unanswered, proceed to prove its absolute truth by refusing to give any information upon the two factors which alone entered in the case— wages, and selling prices. Anything more farcical it would be impossible to conceive, for it reduced their claim that selling prices should govern wages to absolute nonsense.

What, then, was their answer to the workmen's

appeal for the return of " Lord Hatherton's pennies"? They admitted that trade had increased, but answered that selling prices had gone down. They adduced no figures of any value in support of their statement, and refused to give those figures which alone could have proved their contention. It was left to the workmen, therefore, to endeavour to throw some light upon this vital question. The only figures available to them were those published by the Government, available to the world. The Umpire himself was convinced of the way in which the workmen were handicapped. "Everyone," he said, "must sympathise very much with those who advocate the cause of the workmen in the extreme difficulty to which they are subject in endeavouring to assess profits"—or ascertain selling prices.* However, they did the best they could, and went to the only source, and at the same time the most reliable source, of information open to them. And the Government returns showed that in the case of exports to America, the value per package had been steadily increasing since 1868, and this they considered as *prima facie* evidence that selling prices had increased, and not diminished. It is true that the manufacturers replied that the increase in price was because the ware itself was of a higher quality,

---

* "The rate of profit in business is a subject of great importance to the labourer. In many trades the want of correct information as to the profits realised by their employers constitutes a great difficulty for workmen. They do not know when to press their demand, nor when to acquiesce in reduction in the rate of remuneration for their labour." — Sir Thos. Brassey, M.P., "Report of Industrial Remuneration Conference." London, 1885.

and of a more expensive kind, and though this
assertion was combated by the workmen, it may
well have been true.   But surely the best answer
to be made would have been to have given full
and frank information as to the relation between
wages and selling prices, and not to have com-
. pelled the workmen to go to the only meagre source
of information open to them to combat a point
raised by themselves, whilst they themselves possessed all the information which was necessary to
decide a question which they said must be judged
according to the knowledge which they alone held,
but which they refused to impart to the judge to
whom the question had been submitted.   The
workmen had done the best they could to enlighten
the Umpire upon the question of selling prices so
far as it related to the foreign trade, but the result
was rather an inference than absolute evidence
of fact.   But as for the home trade, they had
not even enough information at their command
to enable them to draw an inference.   They
could merely point to the increased revenue of the
country, to the steadiness of the money market, to
the fact that for the third time in a century Consols
stood at par, and to a good harvest, and argued
that even if the employers of The Potteries
had not gathered the fruits of this general prosperity, "ordinary economical laws made it a
certainty" that it would ripen and blossom for
them soon.

The workmen were hopeful of the result.   They
had proved their case, so far as it was possible for

them to do so. The Umpire had refused to give separate awards for the separate branches. He said he could only consider the trade as a whole, and could not listen to the technical circumstances which variously affected the various branches. And so the workmen confined themselves to the general lines laid down by the Umpire, and dwelt upon the Board of Trade returns, as irresistibly proving general prosperity in the trade. The Umpire himself appreciated their importance. On the third day, he said: "The most important points are really contained in the Blue Books, and the figures that we have with respect to packages. The Blue Books give us figures not only as to the exports, but as to the import trade also. These are broad figures"—such as he had asked for. He admitted their importance, and they were favourable to the appeal. And, as to the question of selling prices, we have quoted his opinion upon that point—that it presented "a peculiar, if not an insuperable difficulty." And really these were the only two factors which he had said would decide the question in his mind—and his subsequent award showed that he was concerned with little else.

The workmen, therefore, had some reason for hoping that they had established their case to the satisfaction of the Umpire. The arbitration came to an end, and they waited for the award. It is difficult to say whether they were more disappointed or astonished by the result, for the Umpire "regretted the necessity which compelled him to decide against the appeal of the workmen."

The men accepted Mr Brassey's award very sullenly. He was known to hold broad views on industrial questions, and to sympathise with the combinations and efforts of working-men, and this knowledge of his tendencies and sympathies had led to a hope which his remarks and inquiries during the progress of the arbitration had considerably strengthened — the hope of victory. It is not untrue to say that they were ten times more surprised at Mr Brassey's refusal to restore to them "Lord Hatherton's penny" than they were disappointed when that nobleman deprived them of it. The inquiry before Mr Brassey had been much more exhaustive than that before Lord Hatherton ; the workmen's case had been prepared with greater care and in greater detail, the figures they had been able to quote were more in their favour than those which they had been able to lay before Mr Brassey's predecessor, and, moreover, they had secured a sympathetic attitude on the part of the last Arbitrator towards their objection against having their wages regulated by selling prices which Lord Hatherton had been far from manifesting, and they could not understand how the verdict could have gone against them.

The employers had won a great victory. They had contended, for the second time, that wages must be governed by selling prices, and again had they succeeded in that contention. Their first success was not so much to boast about — Lord Hatherton had never betrayed any appreciation of the "insuperable" difficulties which that contention involved, but had wrapped himself in the ample folds of the comfortable creed that labour was a straw which must be blown about helplessly in the gusts of competition. But their second victory was much more notable, for they had forced their contention in the teeth of one who had rejected it, and who had vainly called upon them to justify it.

It seems to us that whatever right the workmen may have had to question a decision which they had invited, they had good ground for criticising the reasons by which it was arrived at; and that criticism could easily have been disarmed if Mr Brassey had taken a simple course. We have seen that he repudiated the feasibility of applying the test of selling prices to decide wages, and yet actually invoked that test in coming to a decision; we have seen that his main objection to the application of that test was not so much one of principle as the peculiar difficulties—"almost insuperable"—which such a test offered in the potting trade; and we have seen that he sympathised with the workmen in the difficulties which beset them in encountering and answering that test. We have seen, on the other hand, that the employers made no attempt to answer the objections, or to diminish the difficulties which their repudiated doctrine offered. It appears, therefore, that where Mr Brassey missed the simple course to which we have referred, was in omitting to put this clear issue to the employers: "You say that selling prices must govern wages. Well and good. Then, if you enunciate that principle, you must supply such proven facts as alone can give it effect." If that course had been adopted, either the contention of the employers would have fallen to the ground, unconsidered, or would have been supported by such facts as would have enabled proper consideration to have been given to it. But the workmen had good ground for dissatisfaction at seeing the contention prevail, without being supported in evidence. For there could be no fairness in any method of arbitration which accepted broad and general statements, capable of proof, unsupported by that proof. Mr Brassey had again and again dwelt upon the difficulty of applying the rate of selling prices to wages in the pottery trade, as was done in the iron trade, because of the fact that in the latter trade, where the custom alone prevailed, the selling prices were not only ascertainable by the workmen, but as easily ascertained by them as by their employers. In the pottery trade, to which the same rule was desired to be applied, that information was contained only in the closed book of the employers, which they declined to open to the knowledge of the workmen whose wages had to be governed by its contents. If the employers insisted that they could not disclose the information at their command, then they had no right to insist that their version of it should be binding upon those against whom it was directed. It was quite possible that their version of it was unimpeachable and correct; but, for the workmen, there was the uncomfortable alternative.

It is true, however, that Mr Brassey would have

N

had some difficulty in giving effect to his appreciation of the inapplicability of the "selling price"
doctrine to the issue, because he did not regard
himself as a Court of Appeal from the decision of
Lord Hatherton, but felt that, that decision having
been given, he could only consider how circumstances had changed in the interval; and, if the
circumstances had not changed, he could not
revoke the verdict of his predecessor by declining to apply a principle which his predecessor
had accepted.

The workmen, however, were angry with arbitration. Their leaders had had some difficulty in
persuading them to appeal to it for the settlement
of the claim upon which Mr Brassey had just
decided, but they had accepted it, though with
misgiving, and now it seemed to them that the
result had justified their distrust. It would, of
course, have been wrong of them to have assailed
Justice because she had decreed that they were
wrong, but they directed all their anger against a
system which they felt denied them justice. And
so, one by one, the different branches sent in
notices announcing their withdrawal from the Board
of Arbitration. Their leaders argued with them
until they had almost argued themselves out of
leadership, and then accepted the position. But,
in the course of the following year, 1881, they endeavoured to instil into their followers the conviction that arbitration was a splendid thing—if only
properly carried out—and they proposed that an
effort should be made to reconstruct the Board

upon lines that would give an equality to the men. The men listened sullenly, and agreed, half convinced. Conferences were hastily arranged between masters and men, but the masters showed no disposition to recreate the Board. The men had wilfully destroyed it, and must take the consequences. No doubt it would be re-constructed, but these things took time. So the masters spoke. Meanwhile, Martinmas was drawing near, and the men were determined to get their pennies back. The Board of Arbitration was still suspended in mid-air—the men unwilling to appeal to it again, without the insertion of fresh rules in its constitution which they thought would give them a fair chance ; the masters, flushed with recent victory, well content with things as they were. Then Conferences were abandoned, and the months drifted on to Martinmas. The men sent in notices for a return of their "pennies," the masters returned a solid refusal, and there was no Board of Arbitration to decide between them. The only possible result was a strike. On the eve of Martinmas, a mass meeting of potters was held. Their most influential leader exhorted caution, "and advised thorough and searching arbitration, so that all would be convinced of the justice of decisions." But his voice was drowned in the general clamour. Amidst the wildest enthusiasm, a resolution was passed, "That we cease work on Thursday, November 10th, unless upon the prices and wages paid before the award of Lord Hatherton." It was already the 9th of November, and the strike had begun. Meanwhile, the employers had met, and they, too, were determined. They passed a resolution pledging themselves "not to commence work at any higher price or altered terms," and added two others of even greater stringency: (1) "That any manufacturer having given notice of a reduction in workmen's prices, in order to bring such prices to those of other manufacturers, shall be at liberty to use means for obtaining such reductions." (2) "That we undertake, during the continuance of the present difficulty, not to engage each other's workmen unless such workmen present a written discharge from their late employers."

Four weeks passed, and the rigours of winter were upon them, before any voice was raised to call upon reason. Then the leaders of the men, risking their popularity and influence with their followers, dared again to mention the distrusted name of arbitration. The men howled against it, and the leaders protested that they meant a different arbitration from that to which they had previously given their allegiance. Then a mass meeting of workmen was held, and the leaders won over the men by uttering the magic words "Sworn accountant." They still protested against the doctrine of selling prices, but felt that that principle having been affirmed by two arbitrators, they had lost ground which they could not recover. In the words of their leader: "They had now to recognise that the procedure of the Board was completely changed by the last two decisions, and they must see whether it was possible to adapt themselves to the new conditions which had been forced upon them. He advised that they should make the effort." They made the effort by passing the following resolution :—"That if the employers will consent to a sworn accountant investigating the books of manufacturers, chosen for the purpose ; and further, if some mode of regulating the relations of wages to selling prices can be agreed upon (as that is now to be the principle of the trade) this meeting is willing that the dispute shall be settled by arbitration." This resolution was sent to the employers. A Conference was arranged, and the two sides met.

The employers consented to the appointment of an accountant, who should ascertain whether the nett selling prices from Martinmas 1880 to Martinmas 1881 were reduced, or otherwise, as compared with the prices ruling between 1872 and 1876, or during any one year within that period, and promising to give or refuse the advance, in accordance with the result of the investigation of the accountant, the men returning to work, meanwhile, on the old terms. The workmen objected to the years fixed by the employers, as they would be certain to tell against the men, inasmuch as from 1872 to 1876, and particularly at the beginning of that period, prices were higher than they had ever been in the trade. They suggested that if a definite period should be fixed, it should be the year when wages were advanced, previous to the Martinmas of 1872, or 1878 to 1879, the period upon which Lord Hatherton determined the reduction—and the latter period was urged by the workmen's leaders as offering the fairest basis of comparison. But the greatest divergence between the proposals of the men and the suggestion of the employers lay in this: That the men had suggested the appointment of an accountant, "as part of the machinery of the Board," and responsible to the Umpire, whilst the masters had proposed, or assumed, that the entire issue should be left to the accountant alone. Strange to say, nothing appears to have been said as to who should select the material upon which the accountant should proceed, or what and how many firms should be chosen as examples; but probably the workmen appreciated this omission in the following reason, given by the leaders of the men, why the proposals of the employers could not be accepted: "That besides being deprived of an Umpire to settle the dispute, the workmen would be able to advance no reasons, and deal with no facts, but must simply allow the accountant to deal with the figures derived by him from the employers." The employers hesitated to consent to submit the case to the arbitration of an Umpire, and meanwhile asked the men to define exactly what they meant by asking that a sworn accountant should be allowed to investigate any statements "adduced in evidence." Then the men met again, and said that they meant "that the inquiry before the Umpire and the accountant instructed by him be not restricted to any particular year, but that evidence be allowed to be tendered or called for to enable the present selling prices, the present prices for labour, and the present cost of materials to be compared with any former year on which evidence is accessible, bearing upon the present conditions of the trade. Further, that evidence be allowed upon any questions relating to the modes of working in the different branches concerned in the arbitration, or of any alteration in those modes of working which have any influence upon the amount of work to be performed for the same or for different rates of payment. But that no inquiry shall be made into the business returns of any particular firm, or into the profits or losses of such firms." The last sentence of the statement was designed to conciliate the susceptibilities of those manufacturers who feared that an investigation into those circumstances which they had insisted should govern the dispute, should extend to a revelation of their individual business position, and indicated that all that the workmen desired was such information as, according to the contention of the employers themselves, was necessary to decide the issue.

The employers, however, refused to submit the case to an Umpire ; they restricted their concessions to the investigations of an accountant, and they threw the responsibility upon the workmen, " who had broken up the Board." The leaders of the workmen had already cried on their behalf a loud *peccavi*, had pointed out that the men had distrusted arbitration, because they had felt it had not given them a fair chance, and now they were prepared to submit their case to an extemporised arbitration, conducted under the same rules as those which had governed the Board, with the exception of the advantages which they felt an accountant's investigation would give them. But the employers remained obdurate, and repeated, "It was you who broke up the Board." And so several more weeks passed by. But the workmen were not only fighting the ranks of the employers. The Russians boast of their General Fevrier; the employers had on their side the persuasion of December. It was because they had felt that in the termination of the trade year at Martinmas they had to encounter not only the determination of their masters, but the allied help of November and the impending winter, that the potters had in times gone by tried, without success, to change the termination of the trade year to the more propitious days of summer; and it was because they were now experiencing the disadvantages and the hardships which that period imposed upon them, that they had during this strike of 1881 proclaimed one of their terms of surrender to be the change from Martinmas to Midsummer. But that was merely protesting against superior armament whilst the war was in progress. A cheerless Christmas had passed, and another year was on their thresholds; they did not wish it to enter to see their empty cupboards, and so they returned to work—defeated.

CHAPTER X

PIECING TOGETHER THE SHATTERED IDOL

THE workmen found that it was easier to destroy than to rebuild the Board of Arbitration. They had not returned to work for more than a few weeks when their leaders made proposals to the employers for the reconstruction of the Board. The employers replied that the strike had so seriously interfered with their business, that they could not devote any time to the work of reconstructing the Board. The leaders of the men, however, were determined in their efforts, and in June of that year, 1882, they succeeded in arranging a Conference between the delegates of the men and the representatives of the employers. The workmen submitted to that meeting "a few general principles" which they thought should be clearly set forth in the Rules of the new Board when the time came for its constitution to be arranged. These "general principles" indicated the workmen's view of the inefficiency or incompleteness of the constitution of the old Board, and therefore represented what they regarded as necessary to a final and perfect Board of Arbitration. They had thought it had given them an equality of opportunity when it was

first established in 1868—or, at all events, when its
Rules were revised two or three years later; but the
introduction of the element of selling prices had
since made it manifest to them that the Rules of
the Board must be altered so as to contemplate
and provide for all the exigencies of that new
factor in the government of their wages.

The workmen therefore proposed: "(1) That, if
they were to accept the altered mode of dealing
with potters' wages, as brought about by the two
last arbitrations, it would be necessary to lay down
some basis which would show the proportion of
wages to be paid under given conditions of trade.
(2) That the Board or Umpire, should have full
opportunity to verify any figures or statements made
in evidence, providing that such verification be not
allowed to interfere with or expose the private business affairs of any firm. (3) That those questions
that specially affected each branch, such as the trade
usages and changes in modes of working, should
be allowed to form a part of future arbitration on
the wages question. (4) That each branch of the
trade be dealt with by the Board upon its own
merits in those questions which concerned that
branch alone." The two last proposals meant
briefly this: That whilst general wages might be
affected by the general condition of the markets, it
should be open to each branch to submit facts,
special to itself, to an Umpire, modifying the
general effect produced by the application of the
commercial standard. This proposal was the outcome of the experience gained in the arbitration

before Mr Brassey. Each branch had then come forward with its own special grievances—grievances that had nothing to do with the amount of exports or imports, but which arose mainly from actions on the part of the employers, wholly unconnected with the question of selling prices which they insisted should alone govern wages; and Mr Brassey had answered them that he could take no notice of these "technical questions," as all he had to do was to decide upon the "general question" of the state of trade. The workmen, therefore, found themselves in the position of being unable to show— or, at any rate, of deriving any advantage from showing—how, from causes unconnected with selling prices, their wages had been affected, and Mr Brassey told them that the "technical questions" of their different branches were subjects for other arbitrations than that over which he was presiding. To the potters, however, it mattered very little by what causes their wages were reduced, if the effect was the same, and they could not understand why any distinction should be made in the processes when, to them, the only vital question was the result. And, certainly, to the average mind, it seems curious that the masters should have been able to plead for a reduction in wages because selling prices were low, but that the workmen should have been prohibited from retorting that reductions had already been made through different modes of working, increased count, or more direct methods, in carrying out which reductions employers had failed to invoke the authority of the principle by which they now insisted the same result should be effected. And so the workmen, in trying to re-establish the new Board, endeavoured to secure that that side of their case which was of a positive character, and upon which they could speak with authority, should be deemed worthy of a hearing by an Umpire. They had accepted the principle forced upon them by the employers, and now they desired that the employers should accept their contention—that each branch had its own characteristics and differences, and that an Umpire's award should not sweep like a harrow over all alike, and take no note of the irregularities of the ground.

The employers listened, and said little, but their attitude in regard to the proposal as to branch distinctions did not encourage the hope that they would accede to it. So the workmen's representatives returned to their leaders and told them how matters stood; and one branch of the workmen, in petulant temper, and rather careless as to whether a Board were re-established or not, passed a resolution, declaring that as they were convinced from the report of their delegates that the employers would not agree to a separate consideration on the part of the Umpire of the circumstances of each branch, they "would have nothing more to do, for the present, with the proposed Board of Arbitration." Still the leaders struggled on. The movement was one entirely dependent upon themselves. The employers had no reason to desire the re-establishment of the Board—they had but recently had proof of the powerlessness of their workmen when they resorted to other methods, and a Board of Arbitration would only bring the combatants together, and give them equal ground. Besides, disputes with workmen were not a part of their business, but rather a hindrance to it, and a Board of Arbitration was a court which encouraged litigation. And, on the other hand, the workmen had to go back to 1872 to recollect when the Board of Arbitration had brought them any positive good—and then its proceedings had dealt only with branch questions, as separate questions entirely—and they were only interested in the present movement for the re-establishment of the Board because their leaders told them that arbitration was an enlightened and proper method of settling disputes, in those progressive days. And so the leaders of the men persisted in their task, receiving scant encouragement from their followers, and helped by no *rapprochement* from the employers. They drew up a set of suggested Rules, embodying the "general principles" which they had spoken of at the Conference, and sent them to the employers.

There was, however, in the suggested Rules one very significant omission. The first general principle they had spoken of was that which proposed to "lay down some basis" for the settlement of wages in accordance with selling prices. But the proposal was received so coldly by the employers, or, perhaps, one should say, opposed by them so strenuously, that the operatives, desirous above all things of re-establishing the Board, and working to reduce contentious material to a minimum, omitted altogether, in their proposed new Rules, any reference to this

principle.   The new Rules then merely asked that
an Umpire should have power to test the evidence
submitted to him, and that each branch should have
a "right to claim a separate arbitration upon any
question that especially concerned its interests,
modes of working, trade usages or privileges; and
further, that the right be allowed for any branch to
appeal for an advance upon any special grounds
that it might consider justified an advance, and that
no arbitration be complete unless the particular
grievances of each branch might be thus separately
dealt with upon their own merits," whilst it should,
of course, be perfectly understood that the general
question, as it related to the condition of the
markets, might be arbitrated upon, as one case for
all the trade.   Then they suggested three new
Trade Rules: (1) That after Martinmas 1883 the
annual engagements should commence each Midsummer; (2) that the question of the proportion of
apprentices to journeymen in the oven-men's branch
should be considered a subject for arbitration; and
(3) that an appeal from any branch working under
the system of good-from-oven "for an alteration of
that system" should be considered a dispute subject
to the general Rules of the Board.

Another Martinmas was now drawing near, and
the men had decided, arbitration or no arbitration,
to send in notices for the return of their "pennies."
The manufacturers returned the expected answer:
"That, considering the present selling prices, and
the state of trade generally, they were unanimously
of opinion that an advance in workmen's prices

could not possibly be made." The leaders of the men then gave urgent counsels of prudence to their followers not to repeat the mistake of a year ago, and to the employers renewed their appeal for an effort to be made to establish a Board in time to deal, even retrospectively, with any difficulty that might arise at Martinmas. The employers then gave their reply to the suggested Rules of the workmen. They pronounced them to "contain suggestions which would undermine the foundations on which the trade had hitherto been conducted, and to be such as could not be entertained"; and they expressed the opinion that if the workmen would send in more acceptable Rules, the Board might possibly be in working order for Martinmas 1883.

The employers gave no hint as to what were the suggestions contained in the proposed new Rules which would "undermine the foundations" upon which the trade had hitherto rested, and we can trace no reference to the matter at a later date which throws any light upon the reasons they had for their view. The workmen asked to be informed what the "suggestions" referred to were, and they received a reply which charged them with the fault of delay in reconstruction. They again wrote asking for an explanation of the "suggestions" which would undermine the trade, and, for reply, the employers merely repeated the resolution containing the opinion of which the workmen had asked an explanation.

In the absence of this explanation from the employers themselves it will be necessary to examine the "suggestions" contained in the new Rules, in the endeavour to discover what revolutionary principle they contained such as the employers had affirmed, but not indicated. As we have seen, the workmen had purposely omitted any reference to fixing a basis by which wages should be governed in relation to selling prices. They had abandoned such a Rule out of deference to the employers' feelings upon that sore subject, and in the hope of removing what they thought might prove to be the greatest obstacle to the re-establishment of the Board. As we think, however, they made a great tactical mistake by the omission. They had accepted the new conditions "forced upon them by the last two arbitrations," and were prepared to see their wages governed in the future by the advance or decline of selling prices; and as the two quantities had now to bear a direct relation to each other, the workmen had proposed that the Board should fix the ratio, and the basis from which the relation should be regulated. That, of course, was an obvious necessity if the system was to be carried out as a permanent method of settling wages. The employers had said selling prices must govern wages, and the workmen had fought at two arbitrations against the equity of the proposal. Then they had accepted it, and naturally asked that the employers should sit round a table, with the representatives of the workmen, and suggest in what manner they proposed to arrive at the end they had in view. But, by withdrawing their original proposal that some basis should be established, the workmen relieved the employers of a difficult task, and threw the whole question into confusion. They had, in fact, really asked the employers and the Board to undertake the impossible, and their request simply demonstrated the absurdity and the "impracticability," to quote Mr Brassey, of the selling price doctrine. How could a basis have been arrived at? There would first have been the initial difficulty of deciding at what year and at what rates of wages and selling prices they should commence, and before that critical and essential agreement was arrived at — if it ever could have been—we fear that many Martinmases would have passed. But supposing that preliminary difficulty to have been disposed of, how would the process have been continued? Would the selling price of each article have been taken, and a certain proportion of that sum have been set aside as a fair share for the workman who made it? But the articles were of a "multitudinous" number, and the prices, according to the employers, were ever changing. Then, again, the prices of each of these articles differed at nearly every manufactory. Would the employers consent to reveal their price lists to their workmen, and their rivals? We think the question might safely be answered in the negative. But, if there was not uniformity in selling prices, how could there be uniformity in wages if the first quantity, at a general arbitration, was to govern the latter? Then again, even supposing this labyrinthian difficulty could be shown to possess a direct path to its solution—would that

O

be the end of the matter? Would not the employers be inclined to retort, if selling prices were proven to have increased, that, from certain other causes, profits had nevertheless diminished; or would not the operatives endeavour to convince an Umpire that even if selling prices were lower, the general cost of production had decreased, and manufacturers could therefore still afford to pay the same wages with decreased selling prices? And if either of these contentions could be seriously supported, would any Umpire take the responsibility of excluding them altogether from his consideration, and confine himself to the terms of a Rule which might no longer be equitable in its operation? The plain truth is, of course, that if the operatives had persisted in their demand for "a basis being established," they would have forced the employers to admit the absurdity and impossibility of their own doctrine by declaring their inability to suggest how it could be carried out. Probably the workmen merely indicated their sense of humour in the original proposition, and gave proof of their sense of pity in withdrawing it.

We have said that by withdrawing their suggested Rule, the workmen threw the whole question into confusion. They had practically admitted the principle, but omitted to provide for any way in which it could be carried out. In the Rules which they did suggest — and which were, as we have seen, rejected by the employers — they distinctly contemplated that their wages should be regulated by the condition of the markets, into which general question, of course, that of selling prices would mainly enter, in the following words :—"That while the general question, as it relates to the condition of the markets, may be arbitrated upon as one case for all the trade, each branch, etc. etc." Their course was clear—either they should have accepted the principle as a scientific and permanent guide to an Umpire, and insisted upon knowing in what way, by what means, "and to what extent the condition of the markets" was to affect their wages, or they should have excluded that proposition altogether, for the proposition itself was of no assistance in settling the difficulty which it contained. As it was, they were endorsing and perpetuating a proposition which Mr Brassey had described as "impracticable," after having protested against it, and after abandoning their demand that some coherent method of applying it should be defined. And, in future days, they saw the difficulty in which they placed themselves; but it is clear that at this time their one anxiety was to re-establish the Board and to make the points of conflict between themselves and their employers as few as possible, and to this end they surrendered much of the strength of their position. And so it became a vague and general understanding that wages and selling prices had something to do with each other, but what their exact relation was, or how the selling prices could be ascertained, and how the knowledge, when ascertained, was to be applied to wages, no man ever knew.

Still, this "principle" of fixing a basis between

the two was not included in the set of Rules to which the employers objected, and there seems no ground for the belief that in an access of virtue they objected to its omission. What remained, then, to justify their opinion? There was the Rule recognising the individuality, so to speak, of each branch. Surely nothing in that could have "undermined the foundation on which the trade had hitherto rested," for the Board of Arbitration, when first formed, rested entirely and absolutely upon the principle that each branch had its own case, and deserved an award based upon its own circumstances. The next Rule provided that an Umpire should have power, and full opportunity, to verify any figures or statements made in evidence. That, surely, was an elementary principle, which should not have needed affirmation, and was not one to be described as of a far-reaching or revolutionary character, for it modified its own effect by the addition of the words "providing that such verification be not allowed to interfere with, or expose, the private business of any firm." Then, in the suggested new Trade Rules, the first one was that Martinmas should give place to Midsummer. It involved no inconvenience to any soul whatever, and no manufacturer has ever given any reason why Martinmas should be the object of so much veneration, above any other day in the calendar, as a convenient period for the beginning of the trade year. The workmen desired to abolish it, on the grounds of the hardships which, in certain eventualities, it involved for them—of which they had had bitter experience in the previous winter. There therefore only remained, so far as one can intelligently see, the "suggestions" that the number of apprentices in the oven-men's branch, and the question of good-from-oven should be questions capable of arbitration, which the employers regarded as involving a revolution in the trade. Much might be said, though little is necessary, to show that the employers over-rated the influence and importance of these two suggestions; but, for the purposes of re-establishing the Board of Arbitration, a trivial objection on the part of the employers was as much an obstacle as one based upon grounds of supremest right and wisdom. And so Martinmas passed by, with the Board of Arbitration still unformed. The men, however, continued at work, and looked forward to the opportunity which next year might give them, when the Board would undoubtedly be in existence. But it was not until 1885 that the efforts of the leaders of the men, helped more sympathetically by the manufacturers, as time went on, culminated in the establishment of the second Potteries Board of Arbitration.

The arbitration of the new Board afforded a compromise between the method of branch arbitrations—as originally favoured by the first Board, formed in 1868—and general appeals, affecting all branches alike. The compromise indicated that the workmen had accepted the position that wages, as a whole, were to be influenced by general conditions of trade, but, on the other hand, it recognised each branch as a separate unit, possessing the right to make its own voice heard upon questions peculiar to itself.

By Rule 19 it was agreed that while "the general wages question, as it related to the condition of the markets," should be arbitrated upon as one case for the whole trade, when a general appeal had been made by either side, yet "each branch should have the right, at such arbitration, to make special reference to any question or subject that specially concerned its interests or modes of working." The oven-men's branch, however, enjoyed a special privilege, for the Rule which followed provided that when the Umpire had finished the hearing of a general arbitration, "he should then consider the case of the oven-men, and give to them a separate award." There was no reason why the oven-men should have been so favoured beyond every other branch, but they had all along been the strongest in Union, and the most obstinate in regard to the re-establishment of the Board, and the concession to them was much more a tribute to their might than a recognition of any right which they possessed, entitling them to this distinction. The other branches, however, gained what they desired in regard to those "technical questions" which Mr Brassey had declared to be an intrusion into a general arbitration, for Rule 21 enabled any branch to make "a separate and special appeal to the Board for change in prices, on any special ground that might seem to them to justify such a change," but such an appeal could only be made when there was no general arbitration taking place, and not more than two branches could appeal for such special arbitrations at the same time. A further advantage obtained by the workmen was that the Umpire was given power to call in an accountant to "verify any figures or statements made in evidence," providing that such verification did not expose the business of any firm.

These two Rules represented the concessions made by the employers for the constitution of a Board which should remedy defects in its predecessor. *En revanche*, however, the employers insisted upon stipulations being made in the Rules which should stereotype certain customs of the trade. For instance, the questions of "good-from-oven," and the Trade Rules — questions of bitter conflict in 1872-3—were expressly excluded from the consideration of the Board, and the second of the Trade Rules re-affirmed the sanctity of the tradition of Martinmas.

The new Board had little work to do. The workmen did not feel that the time was ripe for a general appeal on the wages question—not because of any doubt as to the favourableness of the conditions of trade so much as on account of the weakness of their Union. As a matter of fact, they had found that Boards of Arbitration meant weak Unions. There was always a nucleus of the better class of workmen who kept a Union alive, and so long as a Board of Arbitration existed, its official dealings were only with the organised workmen, who alone were members of that Board. But the decisions of the Umpire affected all alike in the sense that it set the standard by which all were governed. A manufacturer might not sub-scribe to the Rules of the Board, and might take no

part in its proceedings, but if a reduction in wages
were decreed, he would, without hesitation, adopt
that decree, which would, of course, thenceforth affect
all the men in his employ, whether they were in
Union—and, therefore, by the branches, represented
on the Board—or not. And so it had come about that
the bulk of the working potters had come to regard
it as a matter of little importance whether they were
in Union or not, as, at any rate, with a Board of
Arbitration in existence, there would always be a
little band of Unionists, who would act as their
spokesmen, and plead the cause of Union and non-
Union potters alike; and they knew very well that
the best terms possible would be obtained for them,
notwithstanding that they held aloof from any practical assistance, and were interested only in the
result. Therefore they withheld their weekly six-
penny contributions, and looked upon it as money
saved when others were fighting their battles for
them. The ranks of the various Unions had thus
become sadly thinned, and the disappointment which
followed the arbitrations of 1879 and 1880 had contributed to the result which this *laissez faire* point
of view had mainly brought about; and so, ever
since 1880, the leaders of the men had been preaching
to them the obvious doctrine that the value of an
Arbitration Board to workmen largely depended
upon the strength of the organisation of the workmen engaged in the trade with which it was
connected, and that the existence of a Board of
Arbitration in no sense superseded the necessity
of Union.

Some of the old branch Unions had fallen almost to pieces, and the leaders of the men decided that it would be a better plan to start a new and general organisation than to attempt to revive or reconstruct these branch associations. The National Order of Potters therefore came into existence. It was formally started in 1882, and was largely composed of flat-pressers, but its constitution embraced the membership of workers in every branch. The aim of its promoters, however, was to interfere as little as possible with those branches which still maintained a healthy organisation, whilst leaving it a matter of free choice to all working potters to decide whether they should join the larger and more heterogeneous organisation, or identify themselves exclusively with their branch Union, where it existed. Provision, however, was made for general and concerted actions by the Executive of the National Order and the representatives of the branch organisations. The National Order of Potters grew but slowly. A steady campaign of Unionism was carried on for several years, and continued even after the re-establishment of the Board of Arbitration.

The employers, too, had been engaged in the task of organising their ranks, and about the time of the Brassey arbitration, they formed themselves into the Staffordshire Potteries Manufacturers' Association. The North Staffordshire Chamber of Commerce was no longer a body chiefly composed of pottery manufacturers—the growing local industries of coal and

iron now had their representatives in that Chamber,
and the pottery manufacturers were impelled to form
a distinctive body of their own. Their Association
included about one-fourth of the total number of
manufacturers, but in importance and influence its
members were vastly superior to those who remained
outside it. Just as Trades Unions are composed of
the better class of workmen, so it may be truly said
that the Manufacturers' Association was composed of
those employers who most felt the responsibility of
their position, and were animated by a sincere desire,
whilst justly protecting their own interests, to recognise the rights—though perhaps often opposing the
effort to assert them—of those in their employ.   The
aim of the Association, however, provided rather for
a united opposition against those who, in Union,
were opposed to them, than for any mutual action
in regard to their own affairs.   Within the scope of
such an organisation are, of course, two main questions: The relations of its members, as a body, to
their workmen, and the relations of themselves to
each other; and those two main questions may be
subdivided, or simplified, into two other: wages and
selling prices.   The position of the Association in
regard to the question of wages was that of coherent,
united action.   Upon that point, at least, they must
be unanimous—and were.   Partly as a measure of
protection, and partly out of a jealous consideration
of each other's commercial advantage, they recognised their body as an entity complete in itself, which
must look with a "single eye" upon the wages which

it paid. Upon the other question, however, the entity became split up into isolated and independent fragments, for amongst its Rules was the following:—
"The only action that the Manufacturers' Association shall take with respect to selling prices, etc., shall be that the Secretary be *at liberty* to call meetings of manufacturers engaged in particular trades, for the purpose of considering these matters, and taking independent action with respect to them; but the action taken by such meeting shall not be considered as binding upon members of the Manufacturers' Association as such."

The manufacturers therefore were united in facing the enemy, but declined to bind themselves by any observances in their own camp. "Wages" was the bugle-call which brought them together — "selling prices" dismissed them to their tents, and in that retirement they carried on the internecine war amongst themselves which, by a strange paradox, then became a *casus belli* against the opposing side. Little wonder that the workmen spoke of the Manufacturers' Association as "a union to keep down the men, rather than to elevate the prices of the trade." The Rule we have quoted destroyed the last vestige of justification for the claim that wages should be governed by selling prices—or, rather, we should say, reduced to nought the contention that even if a direct relation could be established between the two, and the method could be made "practicable," it could be any longer urged as equitable. The manufacturers insisted that wages should decline with selling prices, and they formed themselves into an Association having for its main object united action in opposing an advance, or insisting upon a reduction, in wages; and yet in the Rules of their Association they purposely deprecated and provided against any uniform action upon the question of selling prices, by which those wages were nevertheless to be governed. If, on the other hand, they had agreed in their Association to take united action in maintaining selling prices when they could, and had so given a guarantee that when prices had declined they had declined through causes over which the united body had no control, and despite its efforts, the manufacturers could have gone to an Umpire armed with a weapon against which any protest from the workmen would have been useless. They would, in fact, have brought about an approximation to such a condition in the potting trade as made the selling prices doctrine so applicable and natural in the iron trade. The workmen had always urged that the manufacturers were setting up a standard for their wages over which they (the workmen) had no control, but if the employers had agreed to united action in selling prices, they could then have said, with unassailable right: "These are matters over which we, too, have no control—both sides alike must be governed by a force beyond themselves." There was no need why, if their attitude in regard to this question was to be of so purely a negative character, they should have referred to the subject at all in their Rules, but they were guilty of an additional *bêtise* in thus going out of their way to gratuitously support the arguments of the workmen, by announcing that so far from selling prices being a matter for their concern and control, it was a matter upon which they pledged themselves not to take any controlling action whatever.

CHAPTER XI

AFTER A CENTURY'S STORM AND STRESS

THERE was no active controversy between the two sides for several years. The Board of Arbitration was usefully employed in the settlement of minor disputes, but this work was done by the Committee of Conciliation, composed of equal numbers of both sides, to whom the cases were first submitted. The workmen had not forgotten their "pennies," but they had little confidence in being able to convince an Umpire that trade was in such a flourishing condition as to justify a verdict in their favour. As a matter of fact, trade was bad, and selling prices were still gradually declining. The employers then seem to have awakened to the view that, for their own sakes, something must be done. They, too, could not hope to convince an Umpire that a further reduction in wages must be the moral outcome of this continuous decline in prices, and they therefore saw that competition amongst themselves had reached such a point that they alone would suffer from it. So then they began to call meetings, and discuss the question; and in 1888 it seemed that abstract discussion would result in definite action. The result, however, is best told in the following extract from the report of the Association for 1889 :—

"An attempt had once more been made during the year to raise selling prices, and although this Association *is prohibited by its Rules* from taking any action with regard to selling prices beyond calling meetings of manufacturers engaged in particular trades for the purpose of considering and taking independent action, yet the members of your Committee individually rendered all assistance in their power to bring about a successful issue to so desirable an object. Numerously attended meetings were held, and at first it appeared that they would result in success, but as is unfortunately nearly always the case when important questions affecting manufacturers arise that can only be crowned with success by the several manufacturers affected thereby acting in unity, in this attempt, as in many former ones, failure was brought about to a great extent because a few manufacturers in the district did not see their way clear to act in harmony with the general body of manufacturers. Thus the time and labour bestowed by the Special Committee were thrown away; and we need not remind members of the Association that every successive failure makes it more difficult to induce manufacturers, who have the welfare of the trade at heart, to work on Committees when they so often see their time and efforts wasted."

The above extract does not clearly indicate whether there was a lack of unanimity amongst the members of the Association, or whether the hopes of the Association were frustrated by the abstention from the movement of those who remained outside the Association, but we believe we are right in attributing the failure of the effort to the apathy of those within the Association, who justified their inactivity by pointing to the Rule upon selling prices which we have quoted.

In the following year, 1890, the workmen came to offer their assistance. The manufacturers had said that they could not agree amongst themselves to increase selling prices, and the workmen now blandly inquired: "Will you agree to let us coerce you?" The representatives of the workmen met the employers, and submitted to them a proposal for joint action, the pith of which is given in the following words from the address which the workmen had prepared :—

"What you could not do, the working potters, by your help, may be able to accomplish. To you, as the only organised body of manufacturers, we must of necessity appeal in such a matter as this, and, though you do not represent all the manufacturers, you, by reason of the individual and collective importance of your firms, represent a large proportion of the productive and employing power of the district trade. What you decide to-day can become the rule of the trade to-morrow if your decision be backed up by the willing co-operation of the working potters. We are convinced we can promise this co-operation if you will agree to an equitable revision of prices on the basis we have suggested. To put it tersely: You give the workmen the advance in wages, and they will guarantee to obtain it also from those who are not in the Manufacturers' Association, and also that those who will not 'act in harmony with the general body' of manufacturers as to selling prices, shall not have working potters to employ unless they do act in harmony with the Manufacturers' Association.

"Many of those who persist in selling at the lowest prices also persist in paying lower wages than we believe is averaged at the firms of which your Association consists; and we, therefore, have a substantial reason of our own for making all to 'toe the score' of justice to the capital and labour of the trade. We, at least, owe no obligation to those who are not members of your Association as to not altering prices in the middle of the trade year, for they are not members of the Board of Arbitration, do not acknowledge its Rules, and reduce wages when they can.

"What we then request from you is that you will consent to the formation of committees to at once proceed to the revision of the wages list of each branch of operatives, with the view to incorporating the 10 per cent. advance in the prices for labour. We are convinced that the course we recommend — the honest co-operation of capital and labour in the trade — is the only course that will save the potting industry from impoverishment and commercial degradation. You know now, as the representatives of the workmen confidently predicted at the time, that the reduction of wages decreed by Lord Hatherton was an unmitigated evil to manufacturers as well as to operatives, for cheap labour has intensified competition among the makers of pottery, who are now harder pushed by a greater number of needy competitors than ever before.

"This present condition of the trade had its nearest parallel more than fifty years ago, and it was then met and conquered* by the very same action that we now recommend — namely, a combination of manufacturers and workmen to keep up wages and selling prices. If you refuse us what we ask, you force us to make an appeal to the Board at Martinmas, and even if you are able to again

---

* The attempt was only partially successful, as shown in Chapter I.

P

convince an Umpire that the time had not come for an advance, then you would only be proclaiming the weakness and poverty of the trade, and every argument you adduced against the workmen would only tell against yourselves in any effort to obtain that advance in selling prices which you desire.

"On the other hand, if we succeeded in obtaining a verdict in our favour by arbitration, it would not carry the stipulation binding upon us which we are now prepared to agree to, that we should assist you in the manner we offer in the effort to raise selling prices. In every way, therefore, it is the best for you, as it is for us, and the whole trade, that the plan we have sketched out should be adopted to ensure fair profits for employers and reasonable remuneration for labour."

It was a proposal ideal in its object, and capable of being put into practice, for there can be no doubt that, with an improved organisation, which must further have been stimulated by the condition attaching to the proposal of a 10 per cent. increase in wages, the men would soon have possessed a power which would have brought any recalcitrant manufacturer, under-selling his fellows, to his knees. The employers, however, refused the offer of co-operation—and the suggested increase in wages. Probably they refused the offer because of the condition which attached to it — possibly they felt some repugnance at the proposal of co-operating with their workmen against their own class. They gave no reason, however, but merely declined the proposal. The men were keenly disappointed, and the manufacturers appear to then have been prepared for a more peremptory request

from their men, for they passed this resolution
in September 1890—two months after the meeting
at which the proposal for co-operation had been
submitted to them : "That this meeting, having
considered the *expected demand* of the operatives
for an advance in wages, is of opinion that the
present state of trade does not warrant any such
advance being conceded, but, on the contrary, imperatively calls for a reduction." To go back a
few years, the employers appear to have viewed
the approach of successive Martinmases with much
apprehension as to the possible demands of their
men, for in 1886 they passed a resolution declaring
that "although this meeting is of opinion that
present selling prices are low enough to call for a
reduction in workmen's wages, it is unwilling to
disturb the existing relations between capital and
labour, and recommends that no alterations be
notified at Martinmas next, leaving to each
member the modification of prices in any department that may be considered necessary in order
to establish, as nearly as possible, uniformity ; but
should any representatives of the operatives give
notice for an increase in wages, in that case this
meeting recommends employers to ask for such a
reduction as the state of trade imperatively requires." It is an instance of remarkable forbearance on the part of the manufacturers to have
thus restrained themselves, and made the asking
for that which the trade "imperatively required"
conditional upon the temerity of some bold and
insistent "representatives of the workmen" dis-

turbing the serene calm of the "existing relations between capital and labour"; but the points more worthy of notice are that the employers evidently expected a demand from their workmen, and that they still looked upon a decline in selling prices —which they had bound themselves not to make any united effort to raise, and which their own competition continually depressed — as the one factor which should govern the wages of their workmen. In 1887 and 1888 they passed similar resolutions. In 1889 the same substance came out in slightly different form: "That this meeting considers that if any alteration is to be made in workmen's wages, it should be in favour of the employers, and recommends that if any intimation be given by the workmen for an increase, manufacturers should give a counter-notice of a like reduction to the workmen." The manufacturers therefore seem to have experienced, for five consecutive years prior to 1890, an annual throe of apprehension as to the intentions of their workmen, but to have refrained from "wounding" unless their workmen "struck." As we have seen, however, the workmen had been engaged in perfecting their organisation, and, besides, they had come to the conclusion that arbitration, under then existing conditions, was of little promise, but that a radical effort to change those conditions was necessary. If it succeeded, so much the better; if it failed, then they would have strengthened their position by having made the effort. They made it in the proposal to which we have referred, and, as we have seen, it failed.

To leave this retrospective digression, and to return to the position in September 1890, the manufacturers showed "an intelligent anticipation of events" in "expecting" a demand of the operatives for an advance in wages. Each branch sent in a separate appeal for an increase in wages, all demanding 10 per cent. and some branches making a further claim for improved prices on certain defined articles which, in the course of the previous ten years, had been gradually reduced. The employers immediately sent in a counter-notice for a reduction of 10 per cent. The workmen complained that the counter-claim was not seriously advanced, but had only been put forward to complicate and prejudice their own claim; but, in the light of the successive resolutions to which we have referred, it is clear that the manufacturers were only carrying out their oft-repeated threat of retaliation.

But a curious development of the situation then took place. At about the time when, according to the Rules of the Board, the notices were to be sent in—that is, six weeks before Martinmas—the quarterly meeting of the Board took place. The main business of this meeting was the re-election of the Board for the ensuing year. It is to be understood that each side elected its own representatives, and there was no suggestion in the Rules that either side should have any right of objection against the nominees of the other. The manufacturers now calmly announced that they could not proceed with the work of the Board unless the workmen withdrew one of their representatives. There were two objections which they had against him—first, that he was not an operative potter; secondly, that he had recently written a letter to a newspaper in regard to the unhealthy conditions of labour in The Potteries which reflected upon the humanity of the manufacturers. As to the second objection, there can be no doubt that the form of the paragraph was indiscreet, but there was much truth in its substance. The writer of it frankly admitted the error into which a hasty pen had rushed him, and desired to withdraw the imputation of deliberate and intentional carelessness which that paragraph had directed against the employers, but he still maintained his ground in regard to the main point: that manufacturers showed an extraordinary indifference to the fearfully unhealthy conditions—capable of easy remedy—under which their employees worked.* As to the first objection, it was too ridiculous to be argued. The man against whom they had objected had established the first Board of 1868, and but for him the Board of 1885 would never have come into existence. He had been a continuous member of both Boards, from 1868 down to 1890, and there had never been the least objection to him on the ground that he was not a working potter. Moreover, two of his colleagues were not working potters—they were the paid representatives of the men. The employers made no objection to their presence, but naïvely remarked,

---

* The subsequent revelations of the unhealthy character of the potters' calling are interesting in this connection.

"You ought to be obliged to us for not objecting to you also." But the workmen took a strong stand. The objectionable paragraph was forgotten, and the struggle became one, so far as they were concerned, to maintain their unquestionable right to nominate their own representatives, and they were all the more encouraged to fight for the principle because the employers had raised it by trying to deprive them of their ablest and most trusted leader. So matters remained at a deadlock, and the Board was suspended. The excitement in the district, however, was intense. Martinmas was drawing near, and the notices were still in force. The men were prepared to strike, but their leaders urged them to continue at work, and insist upon their right to have their case arbitrated upon. Again and again the workmen appealed to the employers for the continuance of the election of the Board. The employers replied by saying: "It is entirely your fault for not having elected a representative in the place of the one to whom we have objected," a masterly evasion of the point at issue. The workmen held meetings affirming their confidence in their leader, refusing to allow him to withdraw from the fray, and making his acceptance by the employers a *sine quà non* of the continuance of the Board. The employers said: "We will not have him for a colleague," and the workmen replied: "He is not your colleague, but ours." That was just the point. But, of course, the position of the manufacturers was wholly untenable, and if the workmen had allowed them to maintain it—and for twenty years it had never occurred to the employers to occupy it before—there would have been an end to any equality in arbitration.

Martinmas was now long passed, and December had come. The leaders of the men began to fear that their followers would get beyond control, and that the district would witness an unhappy struggle such as that which had occurred ten years ago. Then they suggested to the manufacturers that, for the time being, there should be a truce in the dispute as to the constitution of the old Board, but that a special Court of Arbitration should be re-established, to deal with the wages question, and the settlement of the other question should be postponed until the pressing matter of the wages dispute was out of the way. After some hesitation, the employers accepted the proposal, but with apparent reluctance. It was agreed that the inquiry should be conducted under the Rules of the lapsed Board—or, as it turned out, the defunct Board—but that, in addition to an Umpire, each side should appoint a representative to sit with the Umpire. By the very nature of his appointment, each representative became something of an advocate, as well as a judge. He held, in short, the position of *amicus curiæ*, and in the deliberations of the Umpire each would be presumed to see that no point favourable to the side which had elected him should be overlooked. It was further agreed that, in fixing the award, the Umpire and his two coadjutors should give no indication as to whether they were unanimous or not—at that point, the advocate was merged into the judge. The employers selected as their arbitrator a gentleman of wealth and position and an employer of labour—Mr Frank James; the workmen selected Mr James Mawdsley, the leader of one of the largest trade organisations in the country—the Lancashire Cotton Spinners. He was a man of singular ability, and, though only a Trades Union official, had just been deemed by the Chancellor of the Duchy of Lancaster worthy to exercise the functions of a magistrate. All seemed to be going favourably, when a letter came from the employers inquiring, on behalf of their arbitrator, whether the gentleman appointed by the operatives "was paid for his services as a Trades Union official?" To this certainly unnecessary question, the workmen replied in terms which intimated, politely, that the inquiry dealt with a matter which was not their business. Then the employers wrote again, saying that their arbitrator had refused to meet the arbitrator appointed by the men, as, from his position as a Trades Union official he could not be supposed to be impartial, and would force him (the arbitrator for the manufacturers) into a similar position. Instead of saying nothing of so stupid an objection, and being thankful for the opportunity of selecting another and more sensible arbitrator in his place, the employers merely said that "under those circumstances, they did not see what further could be done in the matter." But the arena of the contest had now been widened, and public opinion made itself felt. That opinion was that the masters had made themselves look rather ridiculous, and they seem to have soon adopted the same view.* They hurriedly elected another arbitrator, who made no irrelevant inquiries, but met his colleague and the Umpire, and fixed the date of the arbitration.

It took place in May 1891, and lasted three days. The case for the workmen was conducted by the leader to whom the employers had objected, and he was opposed by a barrister whom the employers had called in to look after their side of the question. The arguments and facts were the same as at previous arbitrations; there was only a difference in the figures. The workmen showed increased bulk in trade, and the employers showed declining selling prices. The workmen, however, hoped much from the new Rule, which enabled the Umpire to call in an accountant; but the manufacturers anticipated that action by calling in one themselves. He gave evidence that he had examined the books of the ten firms, and the result showed that they were not in a flourishing condition. The workmen contended that the accountant should be appointed by the Umpire; and the Umpire replied that he would

* "Mr James, of course, is entitled to his opinion, but we must frankly say that we think his scruples a little over-strained. Unfortunately the manufacturers' ready adoption of Mr James' novel contention is calculated to cast doubt, not indeed on their sincerity, but on the earnestness of their desire for an arbitral settlement of the wages dispute. In that case we are afraid the men will have no alternative but to strike; . . . but the readiness of the men to refer it to arbitration, contrary to the usages of the workpeople in so many other trades, is at least a point in their favour (on the merits of the dispute)."—*Birmingham Post*, December 30th, 1890.

adopt the manufacturers' accountant as his own. Then the workmen protested that this accountancy test was not the test which the Rule contemplated, as the manufacturers had selected their own firms— of course rightly giving no clue to their identity— and an examination of the books of any ten other firms interested in the arbitration .might disclose a totally different state of affairs. The Umpire said that he would order a further examination if he considered it necessary. Apparently, however, he did not, and no more could be said. He was clearly acting within the four corners of the Rule ; but the workmen again found that what they had regarded as giving them all they needed was faulty in practice.

The employers, at the arbitration, plainly insisted that their notices for a reduction should not be regarded as merely provoked by the notices for an advance ; and the workmen struggled hard to establish a positive case, fearing that the Arbitrators and Umpire might take a short cut to their award by setting off one claim against the other, and leaving matters as they were. The anticipation was correct. The award was given a few weeks after the termination of the arbitration. It was provokingly brief, and those responsible for it had evidently profited by the 'experience of previous arbitrations, for they accompanied their verdict with no reasons. The document merely decreed that wages should remain as they were before the arbitration.

The workmen received the award very ungraciously, and looked at it as a compromise between two claims, one of which ought never to have been made. We think, however, that the Umpire and Arbitrators were really embarrassed by the lack of any definite basis in regard to the regulation of wages by selling prices. The workmen had shown an increase in trade, and that had destroyed the claim of the employers for a reduction; the employers had shown a further decline in selling prices, and that was held to disentitle the men to an advance.* But

* One feature of this arbitration was the way in which the manufacturers tried to have the best of both worlds in reconciling their allegations of decreased selling prices in the American trade—("which is the main industry of the manufacturers composing this Board of Arbitration."—Manufacturers' advocate's speech)—with the increased value of trade shown by the Board of Trade export returns. On the one hand they said: "Selling prices have gone down to such an extent that decorated ware is now sold at former undecorated prices." The workmen replied: "That may be so, but look at the increased value in the trade done—fewer packages, but increased cash value." "Ah! that," explained the manufacturers, "is because of the higher value of the decorated ware, now sent in the place of the undecorated ware formerly sent." Thus was the circle actually squared: "Comparing the number of packages sent out in these two years you will find that though the value in 1880 was less than in 1890, the actual number of packages sent out (in 1880) was greater than the number sent out in 1890. This shows of itself that the *values of these packages have increased*, and it is wholly and solely because the values of these packages have increased that the Board of Trade returns seem to show an increasing trade. But the reason for that is that the earthenware which in 1872, 1879, and 1880 was sold undecorated cannot now be sold unless it is decorated, . . . and the very things that in 1879 and 1880 were being sold as plain white granite (undecorated) *have had to be sold for the same price*, but with decoration."—Mr Boddam's speech for the manufacturers, p. 48 of "Arbitration Report." "We cannot follow them in matters taken from their own books, for we have no means of checking them; but we can impress upon you such a fact that the trade of this district with the United States has increased 60 per cent. . . . I cannot think they have any idea you believe they are serious in this applica-

it is certain that the result satisfied neither side, because of its perfectly negative character. It was exasperating to the men that nine months of strife and effort should end in the arbitration restoring them to the position in which they were before they started. The employers, however, could look more complacently upon the drawn battle. They had had little hope of obtaining a reduction, and there had been a real fear that the men might obtain an advance. Looked at from a practical point of view, therefore, they had some cause for satisfaction at the result; but all the same their sporting instincts were outraged by what may be expressively, if not elegantly described as a " fizzle." They had been indulging in a pyrotechnic display of invective and general recrimination for nearly a year, and the climax of the entertainment, instead of being a gorgeous set-piece, was an inoffensive, unexhilarating, damp squib. There was, however, one incidental grain of comfort to the workmen in the arbitration of 1891. It rang the knell of Martinmas; for the traditions of that holy day were broken by the fact that it had been agreed that the award should be retrospective from March of 1891,

tion for a reduction; if such a contingency could be expected when the trade with America shows an increase of 60 per cent., as compared with the time when the last reduction took place, there would never be a trade that would trust in arbitration again. . . . We are not put into the position of the collier with his sliding scale, and we are not like the ironworker with his Wages Board, in the North of England. The collier in South Staffordshire can have his wages regulated according to Lord Dudley's selling prices. But we have nothing to calculate from. The employers themselves fix the basis at all times."—Reply for the Operatives, p. 69.

as so much time had been wasted in preliminaries.
Henceforth, the trade year began in the spring
month, and the working potters had the satisfaction
of knowing that in any future strife with their employers they could, if dire necessity demanded it,
" go out in the fields and eat grass," as one of their
number once lamented the unpropitious season of
Martinmas, bringing its foretaste of winter, prevented them from doing.

But nothing more was heard of the Board of
Arbitration. The leader who would have ventured
to propose to the workmen that meetings should be
called to consider the advisability of re-establishing
the Board would have been more remarkable for
his courage than his prudence. As a matter of
fact, arbitration had lived its day in The Potteries.
It had had a longer continuous trial than in any
other trade—for arbitration itself had been judged
in its own tribunals, no less than the causes which
had been fought out there in its name—and it had
been applied by the very men who had done most
in England to establish its jurisdiction; for the
names of Mundella, Rupert Kettle, Brassey, and
" Tom " Hughes had all been associated with arbitration in the potting trade. But the workmen had
in the end found it wanting. It had been effective
in one sense, certainly—that it had intervened ·in
the disputes between master and man, and its
decrees had furnished endings to the issues; but
they had only prevented war, and not left peace
behind. And so the mass of workmen, at any rate,
had come in time to think that they had put a

King Stork over their heads, and their leaders—
whose counsels had always been those of moderation, holding in check the swifter inclinations of
their followers—were forced to admit that, although
they still retained their old faith in arbitration, it
had badly requited their allegiance and championship. It had been a success at the first, from causes
which we hope this narrative has clearly indicated,
and it had been carried on in after years as a concession to the spirit of a new age. But that age
had now grown older, arbitration was no longer a
novelty, and the platitudes by which it was supported had become insipid; and besides, in the
long run, whatever doctrinaires and reformers
might say, the old Adam in man chafed at the
restraint of an artificial suppression of his natural
passions.

Such reflections, we think, express pretty nearly
what the workmen - felt after the award of 1891 ;
and out of this tangle of disappointment and disgust another strike arose. There was, of course, a
proximate cause, but it was quite out of proportion
to its effect, and at any other time would have
passed harmlessly by. The strike originated with
the oven-men's branch over some alleged grievances
at one manufactory, and the employers summarily
replied by locking their gates on all branches alike.
Then oven-men and all acted in sympathy, and said
that they would fight to the bitter death, but about
what some of them scarcely knew. As a matter of
fact, the exciting material cause was effective only
because it worked through a psychological medium.

The potters suffered from a plethora of long pent-up indignation and general unrest, and there was nothing for it but to be bled. And after that they were better again and went back to work; and the only thing to be said about the strike and lock-out of 1892 is that a careful observer, knowing the explosive elements that were in the air, might have foretold that the timid award of 1891, so far from dissipating the clouds, would prove the fatal spark, and that the compromise at which it aimed would irritate all and satisfy none.

For several years matters slumbered, and until 1895 there was no development of any interest to chronicle. There were always numerous little branch disputes occurring at individual manufactories; but as there was no longer a Board of Arbitration, with its Committee of Conciliation, to decide them, and as the workmen had no heart for strikes, these disputes were left for settlement to the diplomacy of their representatives and delegates. Here and there an informal Court of Arbitration, with some local gentleman as Arbitrator, was set up to adjudicate upon a point of comparative importance; but no incident occurred of common interest to the general body of working potters which could bring them into common action. The members of the branches still in Union went to their lodges on Saturday nights to pay their subscriptions, and aired their branch grievances, and talked of "new shapes" and "longer counts," which often meant more work for the same money, and a lessened wage total at the week end; and the officials and members shook their heads, and all agreed that things were in a bad way.

And amongst the manufacturers matters were pretty much the same. Their Association was only active when advances were talked of, and when reductions were thought possible ; but the workmen had given up thinking of Lord Hatherton's penny, and the masters were relieved from the consideration of the question of selling prices in relation to wages, in deference to the attention required by the more pressing matter of selling prices in relation to profits. But the game between them and their workmen had been played down to a stale-mate, and their Association had nothing to do.

Then the workmen began to ponder a new opening for a fresh game, and got into communication with their brethren in the United States in the hope of finding one. The employers had refused their proffered help in maintaining selling prices in the home market at a remunerative level, and when the American trade was spoken of, they found a sufficient answer in the word "tariff." But the Wilson Tariff of 1894 had considerably reduced the imports on pottery — in the case of decorated goods from 60 per cent. to 35 per cent., and on plain ware from 55 per cent. to 30 per cent. The leaders of the Staffordshire potters wrote to the working potters in the States, hinting that it might be possible for international industrial relations to be established which would work for the good of the English potter and his American cousin. The American potters took the hint, and in

Q

February 1895 the Potters' National Union of America issued an appeal "To the Working Potters of England," which they introduced by the lines of Hosea Biglow:

> "Laborin' men and laborin' women,
> Hev one glory and one shame:
> Ev'rything thet's done inhuman
> Injers all of 'em the same."

"It is a certain fact," the appeal ran, "that this applies to working potters in this country and in yours, for they have one just interest in common as workers, and also one shame if they do not protect that interest, which we now appeal to you to join us in protecting. The American potting industry (and therefore our labour as part of it) up to the passing of the Wilson Bill has been in some degree protected by the High Tariff imposed upon imported English pottery goods, but now this Wilson Bill has reduced the duty upon your goods by a 'cut-down of nearly one-half. Our feeling is that the best pro tection for labour in one country is that the workmen in both countries should receive an adequate remuneration for skilled labour, according as their employment is a tax upon the physical energies and health of the man who spends his powers to live. Is such a rate of pay given in Staffordshire, or in other parts of your country?

"You can best answer that question, but we have sufficient knowledge of the fact that a dollar's worth of pay is not given to English potters for a dollar's worth of skill and sweat. Now, with such a reduction in the United States tariff, we did anticipate that a portion of the difference would have found its way into the pockets of English working potters, by an advance upon your working prices, and that such a wages increase would have prevented the English manufacturers from reducing their selling prices in our markets to the full extent of the difference between the M'Kinley and the Wilson tariffs. But, in a mad eagerness to exploit the American crockery market before it has had time, with the general trade of this country, to recover from its depression, the English manufacturers have rushed the whole business, and all the difference that the Wilson Bill makes has been more than given away by reduced prices. So labour in England and in the United States is to be crucified between forces of selfish competition, if you and we do not join together in self-protection, which would also be the best kind of potting trade protection. We have one interest, and we appeal to you to assert your rights by obtaining such an increase in wages as will in some degree place you in the position you occupied in former years.

"Why do we make this appeal?

"Because the maintenance of under-paid labour in England is a standing menace to our being able to maintain anything like a fair rate of pay here, commensurate with our position in a free country, where skilled labour is supposed to have a chance to live in decent comfort.

"In July next (1895), the agreement between the manufacturers and operatives here in regard to the wages list terminates, and we know that an advance in your wages would materially help us to keep up our wages; but if you are content in your present position, and your bosses would rather that the money went into the Exchequer of the United States than into your pockets, then we may have to oblige them, and join in action that may mean the re-imposition of a part of the duty the Wilson Bill has remitted."

The proposal of the American potters was one

which puts the protective policy of the United
States in another aspect than that from which it
is commonly regarded in England, and illustrates
very clearly what Sir Charles Dilke has written
in "Greater Britain" upon this point. "Those,"
he says, "who speak of the selfishness of protection as a whole can never have taken the trouble
to examine the arguments by which it is supported in America and Australia. In those
countries, it is no mere national delusion; it is a
system adopted with open eyes as one conducive
to the country's welfare, in spite of objections
known to all, in spite of pocket losses that come
home to all. If it is, as we in England believe,
a folly, it is, at all events, a sublime one. . . .
Hundreds and thousands of rough men are content to live, they and their families, upon less
than they might otherwise enjoy, in order that
the condition of many of their countrymen may
continue raised above that of their fellow-toilers
in old England."

The leaders of the Staffordshire potters went
straight to the Manufacturers' Association with
the statesmanlike and broad-minded proposal of
their American brethren. "Here," they said, "is
a weapon in your hands to fight against heavy
tariffs in America if you will only give us a fair
consideration in our wages, and so cut the ground
from underneath American protection by taking
away the justification for it." This was a matter,
however, which the Manufacturers' Association
regarded as beyond its scope; and it replied that

it was unable to do anything in it, and the matter dropped there and then. Apart from the leaders of the working potters themselves, the proposal seemed to interest no one. The mass of the workmen did not understand it, and in the transactions of the Manufacturers' Association it did not get beyond the letter written by their Secretary declining to have anything to do with a proposal which did not seem to concern them.* In their restricted view they were right—it was a matter which primarily concerned their workmen. But the leaders of the workmen could not undertake the responsibility of urging them to take any action to give effect to the proposal, and the subject dropped out of mind without having roused to activity either side. Two years later, the duty on pottery imported into the States went up again to a higher level, under its protection American

* " Some months ago, at a meeting of the Manufacturers' Association, at which all the leading firms trading with the United States were represented, it was resolved unanimously that on the coming into force of the Dingley tariff [which reduced the duty on earthenware] no increase should take place in discounts allowed off the gross, as it was held that manufacturers in the United States would retaliate by withholding 12½ per cent. from their workmen's wages, which they were pledged to restore. Within two months of the passing of this resolution the discount off printed ware was increased by the leading firms from 45 per cent. to 52½ per cent., a real reduction of about 14½ per cent., and the American manufacturers, as had been predicted, withheld the 12½ per cent. from their workpeople. This suicidal reduction has, of course, resulted in nothing but loss to all concerned. . . . The ordinary observer may well ask if manufacturers in The Potteries have quite lost the use of all their senses."—Mr John Ridgway, a leading pottery manufacturer *Staffordshire Sentinel*, December 12, 1898.

production increased, and the Staffordshire pottery manufacturers then began to complain of a lessened demand for English pottery goods in the American market.

The subsequent history of the Staffordshire potter may be told in a few words.

During the last few years several organisations have come to light in The Potteries of an entirely novel character. They are connected with subsidiary branches of earthenware manufacture; the brick-making trade, the jet and Rockingham teapot trade, and a select little branch of industry called the "China furniture trade," which is concerned in the production of earthenware fittings for electrical purposes. The basis upon which they were formed may be briefly stated in this proposition: that the employers formed themselves into a Union, and the workmen did the same, and the two Unions then united. The masters covenanted to keep up selling prices, and to maintain an equal rate of wages based upon those prices, and the workmen in return agreed to allow none of their number to work for any employer in the trade who proved false to, or did not act in accordance with, the Rules governing the Masters' Alliance. These combinations have now existed for three or four years, and have apparently been successful; but they would probably have had no place in this narrative but for a circumstance which is now but a few weeks old. The general earthenware manufacturers, with whom and with whose workmen this narrative has exclusively dealt, have lately made inquiries about these organisations, and have found that capital and labour may work well together.   They have determined, within the last few days of 1898, to do their part in the establishment of a similar combination for the whole earthenware trade.   There can be no doubt that the workmen will heartily second them, and that the result will be entirely beneficent.   The employers have, in short, come to see the wisdom, because now they feel the necessity, of some such system of co-operation as that which the workmen suggested in 1890, and for which they had been prepared ever since 1836.

Is it too much to hope that in this direction lies the final solution of all the differences of capital and labour, so long as economical and political conditions preserve a distinction between the two?   It was a great thing when workmen first united to protect their class—it has not been without an effect for good when, as they have often done, they have used their strength, even at some cost to themselves, to enforce their rights. The working potters of Staffordshire moved further along the line of advance when, having taught their employers to respect the strength and principles of their Union, they established a system of arbitration under which each side met on equal terms, to conclude honourable terms of peace, when conflict separated them ; and the support which the employers gave was as honourable as the steady faith which, for many years, the workmen preserved in the elemental good of a system which had nevertheless disclosed many drawbacks and disadvantages to their cause. But there could be no more agreeable conclusion to this story of the Potters' Trade Unions than to be able to say that a still further advance had been made—an advance which would reconcile many of the antagonisms of the past, and make the possibility of their recurrence in the future very remote, for it would be based upon the broad, humane and human ground that capital and labour, invested in the same enterprise, are partners and friends, upon whom lies the common duty of promoting their common good.

EPILOGUE

AN epilogue which commences by acknowledging the falsification of the prophetic pæan which has preceded it may have its disadvantages from the point of view of dramatic unity, but it cannot be denied that it exhibits in the author the desirable qualities of candour and courage; and if Prophecy be "the most gratuitous form of human error," surely a gratuitous advertisement by the Prophet of the failure of his Prophecy should be accounted the most commendable form of human penance.

Having said so much by way of anticipatory palliation, the revelation must be made that the projected Alliance between the Staffordshire Pottery manufacturers and their workmen, which seemed so likely to be realised in 1898, was almost forgotten in 1899, and in the spring of 1900 so far had the two sides apparently drifted from any ideas of alliance, that nearly 20,000 working potters had either left their work on strike or had been locked out by their employers. Nevertheless, it may be said that the Alliance which seemed so likely in 1898 has become in 1900 well-nigh inevitable; and the very events which have apparently indicated the unlikelihood of its establishment have served to prove afresh its necessity.

249

The projected Alliance received the warmest support from many of the chief employers and the better part of the workpeople, and by its adherents on both sides it was spoken of as heralding the dawn of a new and better day for the whole trade. Many preliminary meetings were held by both masters and men, and the work of organisation proceeded vigorously. Finally, in November 1898, a combined meeting of employers and workmen was held at Hanley, which apparently set the seal to the Alliance, and pronounced it an accomplished fact. The meeting was attended by 2000 workmen and the heads or representatives of nearly seventy firms —amongst them some of the largest, oldest, and most influential in the trade.

The meeting was addressed by both employers and workmen, and the burden of the speeches made was that the old methods had failed, and others must be tried; and the gratifying spectacle was witnessed of masters and men meeting on a common platform, each recognising the rights of the other, and seeking to turn antagonism into co-operation for mutual good. The employers frankly and handsomely admitted what the workmen had always contended, and what the facts of this narrative place beyond doubt — that the process of cheapening labour, adopted as a consistent policy as a remedy for low selling prices, merely encouraged the evil, and in no sense arrested it; and a deeper meaning was discerned in the platitude that the interests of capital and labour are one.*

* Mr J. Ridgway, one of the most respected of Staffordshire pottery

The resolutions, approving of the principles of the Alliance, and pledging those present to establish it, were passed without any show of dissent, the terms of the Alliance were formally signed, and the chairman of the meeting—a gentleman of local prominence officiating in a neutral capacity—acted as witness to what was called "This solemn compact."

It needs words of more than conventional meaning to adequately express the regret which must be felt by all those who have a genuine concern in industrial questions, that a movement of such a nature, and having such a force behind it, should have become abortive, if only for a time. But it had reached its point of highest promise, and steadily declined. Though supported by some of the largest and most influential firms, who had almost perfected their organisation, and acted together as the Earthenware Manufacturers' Alliance, it was bitterly opposed by firms of equal rank, who clung to the Manufacturers' Association ; and though it commended itself entirely to the Union workmen, 4000 of whom commenced paying their subscriptions to the Earthenware Operative Alliance, it could

manufacturers, said at this meeting : "He was one of the Committee which gave the advance in (working) prices in 1872—the only advance to pottery workmen which, in his recollection, had ever taken place. Since then they had been on a downward grade. Workmen's prices had been reduced, selling prices had been reduced far more. He was not there to accuse anybody, or to confess anything except one thing— that he, in common, he believed, with every manufacturer on that platform, had come to the conclusion, grounded on evidence before them for the last twenty-six years, that reduction in wages was *not* the cure for low selling prices."—*Staffordshire Daily Sentinel*, November 27, 1898.

not leaven the lump of apathy amongst the non-Union portion of the workmen.

In February 1899 it was still regarded as a progressive movement, and in May the Committee of the Earthenware Manufacturers' Alliance subscribed to a statement, addressed to the Home Secretary on the question of lead poisoning, as a body separate from the Manufacturers' Association.

But all the vitality of the movement had gone, workmen's subscriptions had ceased, and the printed notices remaining on the walls of the various manufactories of which the employers and employed had accepted the Alliance, became only another object-lesson of the disunion and supineness of those engaged in the potting industry.

Meanwhile, the prices of materials were steadily rising. Coal especially, — thanks mainly to the united action of colliery owners and miners,—had risen so much in price as to appreciably affect the cost of production. Thereupon, under the stress of this necessity, the pottery manufacturers decided that there was nothing. for it but to raise the prices of their ware, and accordingly it was done. It was a very simple business matter, and there was no suggestion of an appeal to the generous instincts of the colliery owners and workers in favour of the distressful industry—the market price of coal had gone up, and the market price of pots must follow.

And so the working potters, seeing how readily earthenware selling prices responded to the claims of coal, determined to test the sensibility of those prices to the claims of their labour. In February and March 1900, the Union workmen gave notices for a 10 per cent. advance in wages. The reply was that it was impossible to give the advance—it was an unreasonable thing to ask for it seeing that the price of coal was what it was. But the working potters had determined that the selling price of their labour must also advance—coal or no coal —and if coal must be the arbiter of their fate they could cite the claims of their kitchen fires against those of the manufacturers' ovens.

At most of the manufactories non-Union men, unaffected by the notice for an advance, were also employed, but there was a sufficient number of Unionists employed at all manufactories to stop the work entirely. The employers, therefore, gave a counter-notice terminating all contracts, and Union and non-Union workpeople then became united in the struggle.

As soon as the gates were closed people began to ask when the negotiations would begin. There was no longer a Board of Arbitration ; and no machinery existed by which the two sides could be automatic-ally brought together. The procedure on each side followed the usual course of meetings, resolutions, and letters. The manufacturers had passed a resolution three days before the general lock-out, which stated that "having considered the suggestion made by one branch for a 5 per cent. advance on July 1st, with a promise of a further 5 per cent. advance on the 25th day of March 1901," they regretted they could not "see any reason for altering the decision already arrived at — namely, that the present time is inopportune for any advance either to the before-mentioned or any branches, and that the suggestion cannot therefore be entertained, but the manufacturers will be quite willing to consider an advance on 25th March 1901, providing the state of trade will admit of it, and to meet the operatives to discuss the question in ample time before the close of the trade year."

The *Daily Sentinel*, a local paper of great influence, which took very broad views of the dispute and ably expressed them, pertinently asked, "Why should not the Manufacturers' Association meet the operatives now instead of a year hence?" and pointed out that if the manufacturers had a good reply to the workmen's request they would both strengthen their own position, and enable the operatives to at least feel the compliment had been paid them of having their intelligence appealed to, if that reply was given and explained frankly and personally in a Conference.

The manufacturers, probably feeling that something should be done to show their position in the matter, issued a notice saying that if the workmen would return to work on the old terms their cases should be individually considered. As for a Conference, what was there to confer about when they had already said that any question of an advance "could not be entertained"?

The notice of the employers was simply a naïve invitation to the workpeople to abandon their position, on the promise of a benevolent considera-

tion of a request that had been described as
beyond further consideration; or, to put it in a
locution, "If you will give up the fight we will
allow you to surrender." But the workmen were
not in the mood for surrender before the struggle
had well begun, and nothing came of the notice.

There was, however, one gratifying feature in
the strike—the total absence of bitterness on either
side. It was, in fact, an affair of honour, conducted
with the most perfect regard for punctilio—nothing
was said of capitalistic rapacity, and nothing was
heard of Trades-Union tyranny. But, equally,
nothing was being done to bring the dispute to
an end, or to get at the heart of the matter; and
whilst factories were closed, and the streets were
full of out-of-works, the dispute was degenerating
into a pretty little exercise in the art of polite
letter-writing. There was then an intervention of
vigorous and exhilarating common-sense. The two
sides were drifting still further apart when several
spectators of the quarrel—notably the Duchess of
Sutherland and the Rev. W. S. Knowles, Rector of
Hanley—interposed with the humble suggestion that
all this fiddling was out of place in a matter of such
gravity; and that the dispute could never be settled
by the "aloofness" of the disputants. They appealed
to the employers to depart from their attitude of
letting matters take their course rather than con-
descend to explanations, and pressed them to meet
the men in Conference.

It required just such a timely intervention from
some one dispassionately looking at the struggle

from outside to change the course of events. Thereafter, the two sides met, and talked things over, and the position was at once clarified. One Conference led to another, counter-proposals were made, and ultimately the manufacturers offered an advance of 5 per cent., to commence in October 1900. The representatives of the men received it favourably, and promised to lay it before their constituents, and the Conference broke up with mutual compliments upon each other's behaviour, "though," it was pleasant to read, "masters and men smoked and chatted for some time afterwards."

The chairman of the Manufacturers' Association said that the masters, in making their offer, had gone beyond what they should have done in justice to themselves, "but they were very anxious to relieve themselves of the responsibility of continuing the struggle." In this admirable spirit the men accepted the offer, which was commended to them by their old adviser, Mr William Owen; a mass meeting of potters was held to ratify the action of their delegates, and when the gates were re-opened on the 29th of May the general feeling was that the rupture had ended in a *rapprochement.**

In 1879 Lord Hatherton had decreed a reduction of 8⅓ per cent. Twenty years afterwards the potters had won back 5 per cent. of their lost wages. Moreover, they had, for the first time within the memory of a working generation, seen a strike end in their favour.

* Messrs Fielding & Co. entertained their workpeople to a day's outing in the country in celebration of the termination of the strike and lock-out.

"The men," it was written, "have won their case. They have achieved a solid and memorable victory."

It is impossible to doubt that the effect of the strike will make for good. The workmen are content to accept the advance conceded as a temporary satisfaction, but there is no question that now they have been able to make a breach in the traditional attitude of their employers, they will follow up their success at the earliest moment. The employers, on the other hand, will be compelled to raise selling prices to meet the advance in wages in October, and their anxiety will be to maintain and increase them — for they, too, have a long way to travel before they reach satisfaction. It will indeed be strange if they do not seize the opportunity of turning the growing organisation of their workmen into one of co-operation rather than of antagonism: and, in any case, the bulk of the manufacturers, like their predecessors of 1836, would welcome a strong and aggressive Union which would compel them to do that which, left to themselves, the past clearly shows they can or will not do, rather than see the trade drift aimlessly on as it has done for the last quarter of a century.

The course of events, therefore, leaves combination on one side only, or on each side, or a combination of both sides together practically an irresistible policy. The masters have always been united on one point—the necessity of keeping wages low—and now the utter fallacy of this as a policy of self-interest has come home to them. The men have always been dis-united, and the folly of dis-

R

union has only been thrown into sharper relief by a success at last obtained by united action. The masters, again, have always been dis-united on the question of selling prices, and now each individual master wishes that pressure in some form or other might be put upon his fellow-manufacturers to force them to observe rules of restraint as to selling prices by which he, for one, would be gladly bound. The question therefore remains what form this pressure should take, and it has become clear that to be most effective the pressure should come from circumstances to some extent beyond their corporate control, but within their acquiescence and support. In other words, the pendulum is swinging back again to the projected Alliance of 1898—to the workmen's proposals of 1890—to the far-sighted scheme of the manufacturers' forgotten predecessors of 1836. An industrial policy advocated by employers so long ago as 1836, revived by employers sixty years afterwards, when the whole history of the trade during the interval is seen to have proved its soundness, and opposed in 1900 by other employers who hold it to be of a revolutionary and ultra-Socialistic character, forms in itself an interesting study. It is therefore worth while to make some examination of the policy, and of the objections made against it, rather with the view of clearing the air of negatives than of attempting a final and positive judgment on its theoretical perfection.

The objections made in 1898 to the suggested Alliance were mainly divided into two classes—its immorality as a commercial creed (in which was included its economic fallacy), and its impracticability as a working scheme. There was a still further objection, but one which was too flimsy to sustain any argument either for or against. It was that the scheme was the suggestion of an outsider, Mr E. J. Smith of Birmingham, who was interested in the manufacture of bedsteads, and therefore knew nothing of the manufacture of pottery. This objection is answered by the circumstances that the working potters in 1890 proposed a scheme identical with that of Mr Smith; and that in those branches of the potting trade in which his scheme had been adopted — and particularly in the Rockingham teapot trade — the manufacturers admitted that until Mr Smith's advent into their midst they had only the haziest notion of what certain articles sold by them cost to produce, and in many cases were selling their teapots at prices which only just fell short of giving them away.* Moreover, it was an objection which stopped at the threshold of the scheme, and did not even look inside it.†

The first class of serious objectors relied mainly on the use of the term "un-English." It is an

---

* "It was clear, however, that the smaller sizes (of teapots) were being sold without any profit whatever, and the result of this negotiation has been that . . . these sizes were advanced, and have maintained the advance. Were the same investigation to be made into some of the staple lines in earthenware and china there can be no doubt that a similar result would follow."—North Staffordshire Correspondent of the *Pottery Gazette*, December 1899.

† Mr Smith explains his scheme in "The New Trades Combination Movement." Rivingtons, 1899.

epithet only to be sparingly employed, for all things English are not good, nor are they either always good or bad; and, moreover, it begs the question, and until we know what is English and what is not, the epithet itself is of little assistance. But it is a term which has often served the turn of the most arrogant type of conservatism, and in that sense was doubtless used by the pottery manufacturers who opposed the scheme. Trades Unions, compulsory education, the early Factory Acts, and free schools have all been assailed by the same term, and all have survived and have passed into acceptance by the body politic.

It is, at any rate, obvious that the same arguments which support and justify, on the grounds of morality and expediency, a combination of working-men engaged in the same trade, and a combination of employers in the same trade, must support a further combination of working-men and employers. The last is, indeed, only the inevitable and logical outcome of the former two states. Combinations of employers have hitherto had to deal with forces on each side of them. On the one hand, they kept an eye on the wages they paid to their workmen, and took care they did not pay more than they could help; and on the other, they took united action to see that they got paid for their goods as much as their customers could give them.

The pottery manufacturers have been so busily engaged in attacking and resisting attack on the one side that they have allowed the enemy on their other flank to have pretty much his own way, and he has been helped in his depredations by the manufacturers themselves, who have thus been playing at the game of robbing Peter to pay Paul. This has proved to be a very unprofitable game, and the manufacturers now see that it is time to give as much attention to what is coming into one pocket as to what is going out from the other. They have come to realise that the cleavage of interests lies between the trade as a whole, and the middleman and customer beyond him,* rather than between the two forces in the trade itself. Is it an un-English thing to acknowledge the failure of a policy that has failure written across it with unmistakable clearness, and to adopt some other policy which promises to make for commercial soundness?

But where the un-English character of the policy is supposed to lurk is in the method of "coercion" by which it is supposed to be maintained.† Under the constitution of the Alliance, no manufacturer

---

* "For a quarter of a century selling prices in the potting trade have gone consistently down. No doubt production has been cheapened, machinery has enabled a greater output to be made, materials have generally become cheaper, labour has been abundant, many things have combined to lessen the cost of pots; but, under the stress of competition, for every penny saved in production, three half-pence has been given away to the voracious customer, who is still asking for more."—*Pottery Gazette* (trade organ), June 1899.

† "One word as to the charge of coercion brought against the Alliance. What the scheme proposes to do is to stop the reckless manufacturer, not necessarily the weakest, as you assume, from damaging his fellow-manufacturers by selling below a legitimate price, allowing a reasonable margin of profit, and a reasonable wage to his men."—Mr Cecil Wedgwood, of the firm of Josiah Wedgwood & Sons, December 8, 1898.

who did not subscribe to its rules would have workmen who were members of the operative section of the Alliance to work for him. "It is not honest or English to say that if a manufacturer does not join this combination his workmen shall be withdrawn,", says one objector — the president of 'the North Staffordshire Chamber of Commerce. Leaving out the debatable question of national characteristic, wherein does the dishonesty lie? If a manufacturer persuades himself that his interest lies outside an employers' Alliance, and can persuade his workpeople that their interests lie outside their Union, no one shall say him nay, and non-Union employers and non-Union workmen may forgather in harmony, rejoicing in the unity of their disunion. Such employers and workmen may indeed formally unite in an association for the maintenance of free capital and free labour, and exercise in turn the "coercion" of a policy of proscription against the unclean thing, and they shall be unmolested; and if their Union, rooted in dis-union, stood, they would have given an interesting Gilbertian touch to the treatment of industrial problems. It has been no rare thing to see in the advertisements of certain of the daily papers the warning—or should one say "coercive" — note: "No Union men need apply." If a body of employers adopts a contrary motto in its relation to the labour it employs, it is at least exercising an equal right, leaving out of consideration any question of the comparative honesty or enlightenment of the two methods.

The strange thing is that these objectors to the

honesty and English character of the proposed
Alliance all admitted that something must be done
to raise and maintain selling prices, but none had
a better plan to suggest than that the manufacturers
in the trade should come to some agreement in the
matter, "and honourably abide by it." This is a
proposal which has not even the merit of novelty,
and has the demerit of having been tried for twenty
years and having failed most completely. But, on
the ethical part of the question, it is difficult to see
the difference in principle between an organisation
of employers — whether called the Manufacturers'
Association or by any other name — pledged to a
certain course of action, and providing for a monetary
penalty in the case of breaches of the rules, and an
organisation of employers and workmen bound together for precisely the same object, though enforcing
a penalty which cannot be expressed in monetary
terms. In each case the association is entirely voluntary, and the principle the same ; but in the case
of the Manufacturers' Association the result of the
successive efforts to maintain selling prices has been
that those who have honourably adhered to the
agreement have practically been labouring under
the disadvantage of a self - denying ordinance by
which the less scrupulous members have profited,
until it became too obvious, and the movement fell
to pieces, to be afterwards renewed and to pass
through the same stages to the same end.* But

* "The Manufacturers' Association held its annual meeting recently
and issued a report thereof to the Press, from which it appears that
this body opposes the scheme. . . . It may in fairness be asked,
What has the Manufacturers' Association done for the trade? It has

all this talk of coercion, honesty, and un-English attributes becomes the merest nonsense when one reflects that the effort of seventy manufacturers to form themselves into an Alliance with their workmen was not so much the outcome of any sudden benevolence towards their employés as the deliberate expression of their revolt against the backsliding and treachery of their own class, and the realisation that their traditional enemies might, after all, prove to be their friends.

As to the objections to the scheme on economic grounds, these mainly consisted of a tiresome reiteration of the relentlessness of the law of " supply and demand "—a phrase which has probably done more harm, as apparently summarising and stereotyping a system of philosophy, than any other phrase consisting of as few and as simple words, readily to be remembered and repeated by the multitude. One would have to delve deeper than a phrase in order to get at the economic bottom of the matter, but those who used the phrase forgot, or ignored, the fact that this law, like most others, has been baffled or breached by human ingenuity; and that the equation between supply and demand is mainly adjusted by competition. In other words, the inexorability of the law may be considerably modified by a modification of the circumstances

been in existence many years, and has several times arranged for an increase in prices, which has never been maintained. The only point upon which action has been possible has been in resisting any advance in wages, and if an Association has no better results to show than this, it should not stand in the way of other attempts to organise the trade."
—North Staffordshire Correspondent of the *Pottery Gazette*, Dec. 1898.

upon which it is based, and a combination of individuals may accomplish what a number of individuals acting independently would not do. If this combination of individuals (dealing with an article which is not of elemental utility, and the production of which is not a monopoly) attempted to force up its price beyond what was fair and reasonable, which under these circumstances practically becomes that which the customer is prepared to pay, then indeed they would invoke the operation of the law of supply and demand, just as much as the individual who attempted to defy the same force.

But the objectors on this ground failed to see that the individual is not necessarily the final unit, but that a collection of individuals may also be the unit, and that by the very fact of their combination they have, to that extent, made a breach in the law of supply and demand in its relation to values. To apply the point in less technical language, it is ridiculous to suppose that the final and "natural" price of a dinner service is precisely and inevitably that which the keenest and most reckless competition amongst individuals may fix, and that by no possibility would that dinner service be purchased if offered by a combination of individuals who, taking into consideration the cost of its production and the reasonable profit which they required, offered it at a price which secured a recognition of those essentials.

The Alliance was even spoken of as a "conspiracy to defraud the public," and it was gravely questioned whether it would not be indictable on that ground. As to the public, it is big enough to take care of itself, and it would effectually check any conspiracy to force upon it a dinner service it did not want at a price it was not prepared to pay by leaving the dinner service in the shop. The argument that a combination of employers and workmen for the purpose of regulating selling prices and wages must tend to put an "artificial value" on the article produced must also claim that Trade Unions put an artificial value on labour, and that a combination of manufacturers acting alone must also tend to put an artificial value on the goods they offer for sale; and if, after defining what is an artificial and what a natural value (a definition which might summarily close the controversy), that argument is maintained, it must involve, in order to be effective, the demonstration of the economic fallacy of all combination movements. Moreover, the price of an article may be equally an artificial one when below a "natural" standard as when above it.

The question of foreign competition was also raised, but it is particularly foreign to the question at issue. The programme of the projected Alliance involved no such claims of English exclusiveness and superiority as to commit the Staffordshire pottery manufacturers to take no notice of the competition of their foreign rivals where it made itself felt, but to persist in offering to the Africander or the New Zealander — or even to the Englishman—an article marked two shillings which the gleeful German could offer and sell for one. The sole ground for any effort to raise and regulate selling prices in the Staffordshire pottery trade

—whether by one form of combination or another —is that there is a field and margin on the hither side of foreign competition which might be profitably cultivated were it not for the competition of Staffordshire manufacturers in adjoining towns, or in the same town, or probably in the same street.*

From the workman's point of view, he can have nothing to lose by an alliance with the manufacturer on the lines suggested. His Union would be buttressed by the compact (and the whole history of the potters' Unions has shown their lamentable weakness), just as he would help to uphold the combination of his employer. Formerly he was told that his wages were dependent on

---

* " Our potting industries have suffered nothing from foreign competition in comparison with what they have suffered from the foolish competition amongst our own manufacturers. No manufacturers in the world can touch us in the manufacture of earthenware, and yet our manufacturers have permitted dealers and exporters to cut down the prices on goods that they could not get elsewhere."— Editorial in the *Pottery Gazette*, the manufacturers' trade organ, October 1898.

Mr F. Winkle, one of the largest manufacturers in The Potteries, is quoted as "recognising that the competition which has brought the trade to its present state is not due to German and French competition, but to unbridled competition amongst English potters themselves."—*Pottery Gazette*, December 1898.

Whilst these sheets were passing through the press, the English China Manufacturers' Association held their annual dinner on January 16, 1901. They are a body distinct from the earthenware manufacturers with whose trade this book deals, but they, also, are learning the same lesson. " One of the speakers remarked that the unfair competition of one manufacturer with another was really worse than foreign competition, and a broad hint was given to the operatives that a strong workpeople's organisation that would prevent manufacturers from under-selling one another would be of benefit to all concerned." —*Staffordshire Sentinel*, Editorial, January 17, 1901.

selling prices; and when he asked upon what selling prices depended, he was handed a tabloid of compressed truth called "the law of supply and demand," and told that he would find it easy to swallow, and that it would give him instant relief from perplexity. For a time it worked all right, but the effect soon wore off, and he came to see that selling prices, if ultimately governed by a stern law, were, before that point was reached, the sport of the reckless competition in which one manufacturer indulged, and to which another succumbed.* If the workman can be assured by an arrangement which has for the security of its observance the interest of the employers themselves, and the force which he can exercise, that selling prices shall be maintained by united action up to the point when they must give way to

* The working potter, however, should remember that he has had some share in this result. At the arbitration, before Mr Brassey, in 1880, Mr John Ridgway, one of the most reputable of the manufacturing body, said: "Workmen charge us with under-selling. Their action forces that — by the different rates at which they work at different manufactories" (p. 39). Cause and consequence are here interwoven, but the workmen must take some share of the blame. *Per contra*, however, the workmen offered to take in hand the under-selling and under-paying manufacturer in 1890, but the Manufacturers' Association did not give him the encouragement he asked for—an advance in wages on the part of the members of that Association, to justify action against those who under-sold and under-paid. The largest and best employers have never seen an enemy in their workmen's Unions, and have had cause to regret their weakness. But it is precisely this weakness of the best of each side that has made an alliance between them so necessary. If either manufacturers or workmen as a body had been loyal to their own class, they would have compelled union on the other side. But dis-union on one side has engendered dis-union on the other.

outside forces beyond their control, then he is at
least as sure of getting his "natural" share of the
value he helps to create as if he, through his Union,
acting as an antagonistic body to his employer,
and therefore inviting resistance, demanded a price
which could not be given—or accepted a rate below
that which the conditions of trade would afford.
He becomes, in fact if not in name, a partner of
his employer, and if he sacrifices his "independence"
as an aggressive Trades Unionist it is only because
he has secured a recognition of that interdepend-
ence of capital and labour which has been the
laudable theme of every industrial reformer.

And, as for employers and workmen together,
there is the consoling fact that the whole law and
government by which the social machine is governed
and ordered is based upon the principle that in
order to preserve the individual it is necessary to
assert the power of the community.

But all these cobwebs of abstract speculation
may be brushed away by the broom of common-
sense. For the Staffordshire potter, master and
man, the question is a very simple one—How can
a fair profit and a fair wage be assured? Combination has never passed on either side beyond
a half-hearted stage; strikes 'have failed, arbitration
has left things in the air, and wages and profits
have chased each other in an eager descent. Any
plan that can arrest this descent, and bring about
an upward tendency, is to be welcomed with open
arms; and if to do so is to embrace an economic
heresy, so much the worse for economic theories

that cannot square with the imperative law of self-preservation.

Political philosophers evolve theories of political and social perfection, and Utopias are founded. here and there in distant Western states, which flourish for the day of enthusiasm, and on the morrow of disillusionment provide a sale of effects which offers a desirable opportunity for the invest- ment of the unregenerate and outside speculator. Economists propound theories of what should or must be, and the middleman reaps where free labour, working for starvation wage, and free capital, growing lean on unrestricted competition, have sown. It should be no reproach to either the intelligence or the morality of labour and capital in the potting trade if they adopt measures which, even if empirical, point to a better goal than that to which they have been led by following the old and well-worn road of individualistic caprice.

If theories of industrial economy raise them- selves as ghosts in the path, may they not rise superior to superstitious fear, and walk through the shadow to the substance beyond? And if it is said that posterity will put its finger on the fallacy, and show them where they were wrong, may they not, thinking of their *present* need, reply that they are the heirs of a policy which has left them only an encumbered estate for a legacy;—or, in lighter vein, ask, What has posterity done for them? and add, That sufficient for the evil of the day is the cure thereof.

BURSLEM, *May* 1900.

ON THE DANGEROUS PROCESSES IN
THE POTTING INDUSTRY

IT is, of course, useless to deny that a large proportion of the trades in this country are detrimental to the health of those who work at them. Some are so directly, some indirectly, but rare are the cases when it can be said that health in the simple material sense of the word is improved by a man's manual toil in a centre of manufacture. This being the case, it is hardly to be wondered at that custom in this matter has bred indifference. A man must work if a man would eat, and the surroundings in which he works seem usually of minor importance to those who benefit by his labour. The ranks of humanity who work to exist are serried. The falling out of one means replacement by another, and the trade itself need not suffer. And to no one indeed can blame be completely assigned. Altruism and Commercialism are not twin brothers. The man who employs labour to live, and the man who labours to exist are both a necessity, the natural outcome of social conditions; and so long as there are no startling disclosures in mortality

271

statistics, so long as the man who works receives a fair wage, according to existing standards of wage, and the man who pays it does so with the occasional panacea of a soup ticket and a flannel shirt, there appears to be no ground for interference. The reformer may groan and rebel at heart, but if, under such conditions, he agitates loudly, his agitation is tossed back to him by the sneers of a self-absorbed public, like a spent bullet.

These assertions, be it said, are made in relation to the normal condition of affairs existing in our manufacturing towns, but here and there the abnormal obtrudes itself and compels attention. Trades may be usually unhealthy—on occasions they are dangerous to life; not thus actually implying death, but, by causing cessation of activity in brain and limb, bringing about the horror of death in life. In the category to which such threatening trades belong, the potting industry may not be omitted. Granted that a large number of those employed in the manufacture of china and earthenware suffer comparatively little, granted that the manufacturers themselves who employ labour are hampered by peculiar difficulties in the carrying out of improvements in their trade, a very fair number of men and women, a number that may be counted in hundreds, are still liable through their occupation on the pot-banks to death, or to acute suffering. It will require all the supervision which may be exercised by the State, one of whose chief functions now is to shield the worker from preventable evils in his employment, all the improvements which mechanical skill may effect, all the enthusiasm of the employers and the good sense of the employed, to minimise the evil, and, possibly, to abolish it.

Here I strike a note of hope. The revelations of past years have been startling enough to rouse at last public opinion from apathy, and to excite public interest in the individuals whose suffering is the outcome of poisoning by raw lead. Through observation even the most sceptical have been convinced that the suffering is preventable.

Those who are stricken by this ill, are not "carried in cart loads from our streets," as a master potter lately, with lack of taste, has gibingly told us is the common belief in the country—it is here and there, and among the weakest that the poison creeps ; but protection is due to the individual child of the State as well as to the crowd, and such protection shall be secured when occasion, as it is now doing, cries for it.

The author, in the earlier chapters of this book, has placed clearly before his readers the position of The Potteries, and the conditions of trade there.

S

It therefore merely remains for me to offer some explanation of the insanitary conditions of potting, and to explain a little more clearly why certain processes are dangerous, apart from a mere disregard of the necessity for a certain cubic air-space per individual in many factories, and of ventilation remediable by architectural or mechanical means, which means have been largely adopted during the last few years.

The potter suffers a special injury from the nature of the material with which he works. These injurious materials consist (1) of clay and flint, which give off a siliceous and very finely divided dust, with which the air was often thickly impregnated; and (2) carbonate or oxide of lead, forming part of the glazing mixture with which some portion of the workers come into manual contact, or which they breathe as part of the dust-laden air where they work. The inhalation of the siliceous dust is the cause of an insidious pulmonary malady amongst the workers which has had for generations a name special to it in the locality,—that of "potters' rot"; the absorption of lead into the system, though capricious in its effects on various individuals, produces that lead poisoning to which I have alluded, and of which so much lately has been heard in Parliament, and read in the Press.

There is something peculiarly pitiable about this asthma of the potter and "potters' rot," in the worker's patient acceptance of it as incidental to his employment, and his bravery in following his daily work until driven to bed, and possibly to his coffin, at an age far before the ordinary period of man's decease, to be mentioned in the mortality returns merely as a victim to bronchitis, phthisis, or general debility.

Dr Arlidge, in his standard work on "Diseases of Occupations," touches to some extent on this point, when, speaking of the generally baneful character of all dust, as such, apart from any special noxious properties it may possess, he says: "In one sense, indeed, it is unfortunate that it does not for the most part awaken attention by any immediate tangible consequences. Its disabling action is very slow, but it is ever progressive, and until it has already worked its baneful results upon the smaller bronchial tubes and air-cells . . . it is let pass as a matter of indifference—an inconvenience of the trade."

It is in this light that it has been regarded by the operative potter for generations—even for centuries. As it was with his father before him, so with him—there seemed nothing more to be said. It was not that the evil was not recognised—in the earliest days of his industrial struggles the unhealthiness of his trade always figured in his appeals to his employers as a circumstance that was entitled to consideration in dealing with the matter of wages—but just as an axiom is stated without exciting controversy, so the statement of a fact which in 1820 had been accepted as such for over a hundred years, passed without further comment.

Probably the earliest public reference to this aspect of the potters' trade is to be found in the preamble to the Letters Patent granted by George the First on the 5th of November 1713, to Thomas Benson of Newcastle-under-Lyme, for his invention of the method of grinding flint stones by water. This is interesting enough to reproduce in full:

"Whereas, our trusty and well-beloved Thomas Benson, of Newcastle-under-Lyme in our County of Stafford, engineer, hath by his petition humbly represented to us that in Staffordshire there is a manufacture carried on of making White Pots, the chief ingredient of which is Flint Stone, and the method hitherto used in preparing whereof has been pounding or breaking it dry, and afterwards sifting it through fine launs, which has proved very destructive to mankind, insomuch that any person, ever so healthful or strong, working in that business cannot possibly survive over two years occasioned by the dust sucked into his body by the air he breathes, which, being of a ponderous nature, fixes there so closely that nothing can remove it, insomuch that it is now very difficult to find persons who will engage in the business to the great detriment and obstruction of the said trade, which would otherwise by reason of the usefulness thereof be of great benefit and advantage to our Kingdom. That the petitioner has with great pains and expence invented and brought to perfection an Engine or new method for the more expeditious working the said Flint Stone whereby all the said hazard and inconveniences attending the same will effectually be prevented; that he has, at his own charge, made several experiments of his said invention whereby he fully knows the same will answer the ends above purposed in every particular, to the manifest improvement and advantage of the said manufacture, and preserving the lives of many of our subjects employed therein, and proposes to perform the same in the manner hereinafter described—viz.: The Flint Stones are first sprinkled with water, insomuch that no dust can rise to the hurt or damage of the workmen; then crushed as small as sand by two large wheels of the bigness and shape of millstones, made of iron, to turn round upon the edges by the power of a water-wheel, and afterwards conveyed into large pans made of iron, for that purpose circular, in which there are large iron balls which, by the power of the water-wheel above named, are driven round by such a swiftness of motion that in a little time the flint stones so broken are' made as fine as oil itself without the use of launs, and when so done, by turning of a cock, empties itself into casks provided for that purpose and so kept therein for the uses above-mentioned; and having humbly prayed us to grant him our Royal Letters Patent for the invention, according to the Statute in such case made and provided; We being willing to give encouragement to all arts and inventions which may be of public use and benefit, are graciously pleased to gratify him in his request."

It is a far cry from the days of the husband of the luckless Sophia Dorothea to the Factory Act Department of the Home Office of 1900, but during all the intervening years the working potter has suffered from the same evil dust "sucked into his body by the air he breathes."

Those most liable to disease by dust are those whose work is concerned with the actual shaping of the ware, and amongst these the flat-presser—the maker of plates—has the greatest liability. It may be necessary to explain to the uninitiated that it is only after the flint stones have been ground and have passed with other ingredients into a plastic state (afterwards to become dry, and be given off into the air in the form of dust), that the clay comes into the hands of the potter, to be worked by him into the shapes required.

In an obituary notice of a flat-presser who was an official of his Trades Union, *The Potter* of August 18th, 1860, says: "For a flat-presser he has exceeded the average age, the years of his life numbering fifty." This is in accord with the statement made by Dr Arlidge, from his experience as physician of the large North Staffordshire Infirmary, that the "mean age at death of male potters aged

20 and upwards was 46½ years, whilst that of non-potters stood at 54."

The many years' study given by the late Dr Arlidge to the Diseases of Potters—which, doubtless, led him to enlarge his field of inquiry into other occupations, and to produce the work by which he will be remembered—practically furnished all the statistical information which was available on the effects of the dusty processes of the trade. In his book, "The Diseases of Occupations," he prefaces his chapter on "The Manufacture of China and Earthenware" by the statement that "this manufacture stands foremost among those wherein the employment is distinctly chargeable with the production of disease." Further, he says, "The vital statistics of the pottery business . . . tell a sad tale of disease and early death," and he cites Dr Ogle as showing that the mortality rates give a comparative figure "only exceeded in the table by the figures for costermongers" (a class in which is included many of irregular employment, some leading an almost vagrant life, and all leading lives of exposure to the weather for many hours a day), "Cornish miners, and inn and hotel servants. This excessive mortality is in greatest part due to the phthisis and diseases of the respiratory organs, the deaths from these two causes being represented by 1118, while the number for all males is only 402;

so that the mortality under these two headings is almost three times as great in this industry as among average males." Dr Arlidge then gives statistics furnished by "the very extensive out-patient practice" of the North Staffordshire Infirmary, showing that of 800 patients treated, all of whom were engaged in some process of pottery manufacture, 36·57 per cent. of the male potters suffered from bronchitis as against 18 per cent. amongst non-potters. "Whence arises the astonishing high ratio of bronchitis among male non-potters is demonstrated by the following table of registered illness of pressers—a class of workmen exposed more than any other to dust inhalation:—

MALES.—Pressers, 263.

Bronchitis was present in . . 55·5 per cent.
Phthisis   „   „   „   . . 17·8   „
Stomach Disorders were present in . 10·6   „
Cardiac lesions   „   „   „ . 2·28   „
Epilepsy was present in .   .   .   1·52   „   "

Even more striking is this paragraph from the Report presented to the Home Secretary by the Potteries Committee of Inquiry which sat in 1893: "Analysis of the mortality returns for males above 14, for the year 1890, of the parish of Stoke-on-Trent, including the county borough of Hanley, the boroughs of Longton and Stoke, and the large town of Fenton, shows that of the total mortality from all causes among potters, bronchitis accounted for 42 per cent., pneumonia and pleurisy 8 per cent., pulmonary consumption 21 per cent. Grouping bronchitis with lung inflammation, the result thus stands: That, in the case of the potters, 50 per cent. died from chest diseases, as distinguished from pulmonary consumption, which on its part carried off 21 per cent." No wonder that the Report proceeded to state: "The inference is consequently unavoidable that potters suffer an excessive mortality in following their occupation, and that the mineral dust they inhale is largely accountable for it."

At this stage it may be interesting to specify the particular branches in the many divisions of the potting industry which must be tabulated as dangerous processes through the use of lead :—

Dippers and Dippers' Assistants.—When the ware has been printed and the oily matter burnt out, or when, as in the case of some ware, without being printed at all, it is taken into the dipping-house, the dipper coats it with a layer of glaze by plunging it into a bath containing the glazing material very finely ground held in suspension in water.

Ware-Cleaners after Dippers. — When the ware has been dipped it is the duty of the ware-cleaner to examine all the pieces to see if they are properly dipped and to remove all superfluous glaze by scraping with a knife or otherwise.   When the ware is cleaned dry, this creates dust, which, of course, contains lead.

Glost Placers.—After it has been glazed and cleaned the ware is placed in another set of "saggers" for firing.   This is done by "glost placers," who also very often clean ware, thereby becoming liable to dust.   Much of the mortality amongst glost placers is due, however, to disease of the circulatory system consequent upon disorganisation of the rhythmic action of the heart caused by the sudden transitions from extreme cold to extreme heat and *vice versâ* in placing the saggers in bungs in the glost oven, and by the sudden muscular strain in lifting and carrying the saggers, which is very great.

Majolica Paintresses and Glaze Blowers.—In some branches of the general earthenware trade, glaze is applied by painting or blowing.   The percentage of lead contained in majolica is as much as 40 to 65 per cent.

Ground-Layers and Colour-Dusters.—When the ware has been fired after glazing, much of it is decorated by applying enamel colours to the surface of the fired glaze. The colours or metals used for this purpose are mineral pigments fluxed with a large proportion of lead compounds, so that when exposed to a moderate heat the melting of the fluxes will fuse the colour into the surface of the glaze.   They contain on an average 58 per cent. of lead.

Litho-Transfer Dusters.—They dust the colour, in the form of a powder (containing a lead-flux) upon prepared sized sheets, which then become decorative transfers. Owing to the extreme fineness of the dust, this is one of the most dangerous processes.

A few words of technical explanation may here be necessary to show in what manner, and why, lead is used in pottery manufacture. The ware, having been shaped, undergoes a first firing—called the biscuit fire—which transforms it from soft clay to a hard, baked body, and it is then in what is called the biscuit state. It is porous, and this involves the process of glazing to fit it for domestic use. It is therefore dipped in a glaze consisting mainly of silica, alumina, alkalis, and lead. The silica and alumina are essential components of a durable glaze, and, roughly speaking, the more of them that can be crowded in an earthenware glaze the more stable the glaze. But of themselves they do not possess the requisite glazing property of softness and fusibility, under the conditions in which they are used ; nor, it is contended, does the amount of alkaline matter admissible in a reliable glaze sufficiently soften the hardness of the silica and alumina to convert the mixture into a satisfactory glazing material. It is therefore necessary to import into this mineral mixture the metallic substance of lead, which, being easily fusible, fluxes the other materials, and enables the glaze to do its appointed work. It is used in glazes in varying proportions, according to the class of ware made. Roughly speaking, the higher the class of ware, the lower the quantity of lead used. Translucent china glazes contain about 17 per cent., opaque earthenware glazes about 22 per cent., majolica (known to the public as "art" pottery) 40 or 50 per cent., jet and Rockingham ware (common black and brown teapots) 60 per cent. and even more.

Liability to lead poisoning resolves itself mainly into a question of the amount of dust to which the worker is exposed, the danger varying accordingly. In the operations of ware-cleaning, ground-laying, colour-dusting and litho-transfer dusting, dust is necessarily produced. This lies on the face, hair and clothing, clogs the pores of the skin, and (greatest evil of all) inhaled through mouth and nose passes through the lungs into the blood.

One must acknowledge frankly that the dangers of the trade are capricious in their attacks, that while one constitution is quickly a prey to great suffering, another may work in like circumstances with complete immunity from anything worse than "malaise" or somewhat lowered vitality. But to the susceptible constitution, be it of man or woman, the blood, instead of being the source of renewal and fertilisation to the working tissues, becomes a poisoned stream which carries the poison in its course and deposits it here and there in the tissues. When the blood is thus vitiated all the organs of the body soon become impaired.

"To account for such divergences," says Dr

Arlidge, "it is common to appeal to constitutional peculiarity, or what is called idiosyncrasy; and there is no denying the operation of this cause; nevertheless, in the majority of cases, the difference is to be explained on more obvious grounds, existing in carelessness at work, indifference to cleanliness of the person and clothing, in reckless eating and drinking in the place of work, and in wearing the clothing begrimed with glaze, whereby the poison· is carried to the homes. Lastly, ill-constructed, dirty, confined shops and want of free ventilation contribute an important factor."

In ground-laying, colour-dusting, etc., the worker is constantly inhaling the fumes of lead from the colour over which she is bending, and her mouth gets so full of the sweet taste of the lead that she speedily loses her appetite and seems to live, as it were, on lead. Workers frequently say they are unable to eat, but that the lead "seems to feed them up." Dirty or careless workers sometimes actually put the colour into their mouths.

Majolica paintresses and dippers get, in the case of the former the fingers, and in the case of the latter the whole hand and forearm, covered with glaze. This dries quickly, and unless care is taken to remove it frequently a thin coating of dry glaze gathers on the fingers and arm, whence it is con-tinually conveyed to the lips, nostrils and face, whenever the fingers are put to mouth, nose, or eyes. Then, again, a dipper is usually all over splashes and daubs of glaze; his hands, arms, clothes, hair and beard are covered with pulverised glaze; dust is produced and taken in by the respiratory organs and enters the system with the inevitable results.

There is no doubt that the dipper also absorbs a certain amount of lead through the skin. It penetrates into the glands and is there acted upon by the carbonic acid, water and oleaginous materials contained by the sweat. The question as to whether this is sufficient to account for the dropped wrist is a debatable one—though expert opinion is inclined to the negative.

Ware-cleaning is usually carried on in the dipping-house in close proximity to the tub, and the dipper is therefore exposed almost as much as the ware-cleaners to the dust which arises.

Cleaning ware over a trough of water does not always, in the opinion of many operatives, do away with the dust, as much of it still falls about and upon the clothes of the workers. This leaves a general surrounding of dust which must blow about from time to time, and the dipper has therefore to contend with the evils of another branch of the trade as well as his own.

Glost placers, except when they are ware-cleaners

also, ought not, strictly speaking, to incur much risk. They do, however, get a good deal of lead on their hands, which of course renders them liable to plumbism.

Ware-cleaners and glost placers inhale the dust in the form of the silicate and carbonate: ground-layers, majolica paintresses and litho-transfer printers inhale the dust formed by the colour compounds. Any operative in a lead process who fails in the slightest detail to carry out the rules with regard to food, takes the lead direct into the stomach with whatever food he or she is foolish enough to consume under such conditions. In "placing" ware it is the dry glaze which the glost placer gets on his fingers. The ware is allowed to dry after dipping, and when the placer grasps it to place it in the sagger the glaze dust adheres to his fingers: it is probable also that a good deal must fall from the pieces of ware on to his clothing. When a glost placer also cleans his own ware he does not use a knife, as the women ware-cleaners do, but rubs the edges of two pieces of ware against each other; he then dusts these off on his clothes or apron, thereby actually covering himself over with dust, which, of course, gets shaken about with his every movement.

It is a peculiar thing, too, that women ware-cleaners clean the ware *towards* instead of *from* them, which must increase their liability to inhale dust. For this there does not appear to be any reason except habit.

Having stated the case at its worst, it is good to turn to the best, and to give full measure of praise to those efforts, however imperfect some may think them, which have been made since 1891 to deal with an evil such as I have described.

From the first establishment of the potting industry in Staffordshire down to the year 1891, no attempt whatever had been made to alter the conditions which produced these lamentable results in the trade. The potters themselves only vaguely realised the state of affairs when the publication of statistics showed them the extent of the evil with which they had grown so familiar.

The various Factory Acts had only affected the pottery industry to the same degree as they had affected other industries, and practically concerned themselves only with the hours of labour of women and young children, and the whitewashing of the workshops, laying no sacrilegious hands on the conditions of adult labour.

But in 1891 the Factory and Workshop Bill was introduced into the House of Commons, and this measure, when amended, contained provisions empowering the Secretary of State to make Special Rules at his discretion for trades declared by him to be dangerous to health. The whole virtue of the

Bill, however, lay in the manner in which it was amended. Originally designed as applicable mainly to the textile trades, and not of very great moment even for that restricted purpose, it became a measure of prime importance, carrying the principle of Governmental supervision of trades to a point of very wide application. The working potters of Staffordshire were largely responsible for this.

The sanitary aspect of the potter's trade had just come into something like organised local prominence, and was being talked of—not so much as a fact, as an evil. The potters saw in the Bill introduced by the Home Secretary an opportunity to secure some protection against the conditions of their trade, and their leaders proceeded to London to indulge in the pastime known as "lobbying." They gained the ear of several prominent members of the House — and particularly of the late Mr A. J. Mundella and Sir Henry, now Lord, James —and gave these members a liberal education in the darker side of the potter's trade. They collected statistics, and drew up a statement which they sent broadcast among the members of the House of Commons, and so prepared the ground. The result was that an amendment was moved extending the provisions of the Bill to the manufacture of china and earthenware as well as to wool and cotton, giving protection to workers in "dusty processes."

T

From this amendment, amendments grew. It began to be asked whether the china and earthenware trade alone involved "dusty processes," and next whether danger to health in employment arose only through dust. The Bill was sent to the Standing Committee, and emerged very different to the original idea of its promoter, for it left the beaten track of general factory supervision, and gave the Home Secretary the right to investigate the conditions of labour in special industries, to declare them dangerous where the conditions warranted the declaration, and to make special rules applicable to them. Thus white-lead processes, lucifer-match making, paint and colour making, and the industry of enamelling iron plates were brought, with the manufacture of pottery, under the object-glass of the Factory Act Department, and the measure marked a new era in factory inspection. By the potters it was spoken of as their "charter of health," and this was no hyperbolical phrase, for from the Act of 1891 sprang all the remedial efforts which followed.

The Home Office almost immediately declared the potting industry to involve processes "dangerous to health," and a set of Special Rules was framed by the Factory Act Department for the consideration of the Home Secretary, and this step was followed by the appointment of the Committee to which reference has been made. It consisted of local medical men (the late Dr J. F. Arlidge and Mr W. D. Spanton), Professor Laurie, and superintendent and local Inspectors of Factories. They were instructed by the Home Secretary to "make inquiry into the conditions under which the manufacture of pottery is carried on, with the object of diminishing any proved ill-effects in the health of the workpeople engaged therein."

The Committee sat for eight days, taking evidence from masters and men, and visiting many manufactories in the district. They recommended the adoption, with trifling amendments, of the Special Rules which had been provisionally issued as being likely to diminish the effects of the dust; but in regard to lead-poisoning their investigations into the use of glazes free from lead, or into the treatment of lead by fusion—"fritting" lead—so as to render it comparatively harmless, as had been suggested for a remedy, and in some cases had been adopted—did not go very far. The Special Rules made it incumbent upon manufacturers to provide suitable over-alls and head coverings for those workpeople employed in processes in which lead was used, to sweep and keep clean the workshops, to provide washing appliances, to forbid the taking' of meals in the workshops in which lead was used, and—most important of all—to provide efficient means for the removal of all avoidable dust in all dusty processes. And upon the workpeople were imposed correlative obligations — that they should wear the over-alls provided, wash their hands before leaving the works, not take their meals in the forbidden parts, and the like.

The Committee concluded its report by saying: "The results of our inquiry appear to us, sir, to justify your action in having declared processes in the manufacture of pottery to be dangerous and injurious to health. If it should be decided to adopt and enforce the Special Rules we have recommended, we hope that manufacturers and workpeople will accept them and cheerfully obey them, with a view of taking away from one of the most beautiful, interesting, and useful of our manufactures the reproach of being also one of the most unhealthy."

Some of the Special Rules were opposed by the manufacturers; and with the view of obviating cumbrous arbitration proceedings, as provided by the Act, Mr G. W. E. Russell, Under-Secretary of State for the Home Department, presided, in April 1894, over a Conference of employers and workmen with the object of endeavouring to arrive at a mutually satisfactory code of rules. The Conference was a good example of the advantage of the conciliation method over that of arbitration.

Mr Russell plunged into the mass of bewildering technicalities and contradictions, to which he had come as a stranger, as though they were his daily element; and the perusal of his report cannot fail to be of the greatest interest. His skill and imperturbable good temper evidently extracted the maximum amount of concession from each side.

But the employers struggled somewhat against many of the Rules, debated at great length at one stage of the proceedings as to what was "avoidable" and "unavoidable" dust, particularly concentrating their opposition on the point of the erection of fans in some of the old and dilapidated manufactories, declaring this would be "impracticable" and "impossible," and would involve the closing of many. Mr Russell's ironic remark, "I must honestly confess that it seems to me, so far as I am competent to judge, that this objection of impracticability is only a more solemn way of saying it is expensive, and that everything is impracticable which is expensive," was accepted by the manufacturers in all seriousness. "Yes, a thing to be practicable must come within a man's means," said one of the chief employers.

This little scene of eight years ago rings a strangely familiar note at the present time.

The Rules agreed to at this Conference were accepted by some 470 manufacturers, but about

100 carried the matter to arbitration. These were mainly Longton china manufacturers, and though they succeeded in obtaining slight verbal advantages over the Rules accepted by the 470 manufacturers who had been represented at the Conference, the result of the working of this second set of Rules is that not a single factory in Longton is now without fans worked by mechanical power for the removal of dust, although it was in the hope that "other means" would be held to be "efficient" that they went to arbitration.

I believe that in spite of "mechanical means" having been duly insisted upon by the Factory Inspectors of that time, not a single manufactory stopped work for a day on account of the revolution.

These Special Rules, however, although promising to be highly effective in dealing with the evils of dust, practically left untouched the evils of lead-poisoning, and in May 1898 the Home Office took steps to discover how far lead-poisoning was a necessary incident of the manufacture of pottery. The Home Secretary instructed Professor T. E. Thorpe, the eminent Director of the Government Laboratory, and Dr Oliver, an expert on lead-poisoning, to make a detailed investigation into all the circumstances attending the use of lead compounds in the manufacture of pottery ; but primarily to investigate " How far the danger may be diminished or removed by substituting for the carbonate of lead ordinarily used either (*a*) one or other less soluble compound of lead — *e.g.* a silicate (of lead); (*b*) leadless glaze."

It must be said that the justification for the use of lead, from a practical point of view, is that it is very effective and reliable in its work, and that no substitute, used *directly* under the same conditions, has been found to do its work as well. But that is not to say that a glaze, without lead, may not be so combined as to do its work and still fulfil all practical essentials.

The form of lead used is either carbonate or oxide, and it is used in the raw state. In this state it is readily soluble in the digestive juices of the body — hence lead-poisoning. Its pathological effect is thus described by Dr Arlidge in his brochure, "The Pottery Manufacture in its Sanitary Aspects":

"The other dust noted — viz. that of lead—exhibits injurious results exceeding those of all other kinds of dust in severity, by reason of its highly poisonous properties. The group of maladies provoked by it go by the useful general name of Plumbism; a condition represented by colic, paralysis, severe brain phenomena, and general deterioration of the blood and nutrition of the body. The poison finds its way gradually into the whole mass of the circulating blood, and exerts its effects mainly on the nervous system, paralysing nerve force, and with it muscular power. Its victims become of a sallow, waxy hue; the functions of the stomach and bowels are deranged, appetite fails, and painful colic supervenes. The loss of power is generally shown first in the fingers, hands and wrists, and the condition known as 'wrist-drop' soon follows, rendering the victim useless for the work. The palsy will extend to the shoulders, and after no long time to the legs also. Other organs frequently involved are the kidneys, the tissue of which becomes permanently damaged, whilst the sight is weakened or even lost."

The recital of statistics and the narration of peculiarly horrible individual cases would serve no useful purpose. The general truth of the evil of lead-poisoning in the pottery trade has in times past been challenged by some manufacturers, and deplored by most, but now is admitted by all; and admitted, moreover, as justifying entirely the action of the Home Office in seeking for a remedy.

The investigation made by Professor Thorpe and Dr Oliver was very exhaustive. They visited many manufactories in The Potteries, and witnessed all the processes in which lead is used, and extended their investigations to the pottery manufactories on the Continent. Their report in 1899 stated that "beyond what might have been effected by the Special Rules issued by the Home Office in 1894, there had been little or no improvement during this period of five years."

The returns of Mr J. H. Walmsley, H.M. Inspector for the District, showed that the number of persons "working in the lead" in The Potteries was 4703. The number of cases certified as suffering from lead-poisoning in the three years, 1896-7-8, was 1085, of whom 607 were females, and 478 males. There was therefore ample justification for their inquiry, which was pursued in two directions. Fritted lead had been introduced in the trade before 1894, but was only in very restricted use. Glazes without lead had been made and offered to the trade for even a longer period, but were not in regular use in a single instance, and were declared by the manufacturers to be wholly impracticable. The same objection was made to a less degree in regard to fritted lead, but upon this point the objection was not so positive and absolute as in the case of leadless glazes. Still, it was said that if fritted lead were compulsory, factories would have to be closed, a prediction which had been made in regard to most efforts at similar reforms. But the practical evidence on the point of the perfect adaptability of fritted lead was too strong for the contention of impracticability to have any weight with the Home Office experts in 1898, and upon this point they limited their inquiries to the question of the comparative solubility and safety, as revealed by chemical treatment, of various forms of fritted lead, showing conclusively that the lead could be so fritted as to be rendered practically harmless. On the question of leadless glazes, however, they were very positive as to their possibility, though they were not able to point to the same body of actual evidence of use as in the case of fritted lead. Still, they committed themselves to the deliberate and italicised statement in their report to the Home Secretary: "We have no doubt whatever that leadless glazes of sufficient brilliancy, covering power and durability, and adapted to all kinds of table, domestic, and sanitary ware are now within the reach of the manufacturers," and the conclusions at which they arrived "from their inquiries at home and abroad, and from the observations and experiments they had made," extending over nine months, were: (1) "That by far the greater amount of earthenware of the class already specified" (forming seven-tenths of the whole produced) "could be glazed without lead in any form. It has been demonstrated without the slightest doubt that the ware so made is in no respect inferior to that coated with lead glaze. There seemed no reason, therefore, why the operatives should still continue to be exposed to the evils which the use of lead glazes entailed." (2) "That there were certain branches

of the industry in which it would be more difficult
to dispense with lead, but that there was no reason
why the lead used in these cases should not be
fritted so as to be rendered comparatively harmless,
and so greatly diminish the evil of lead-poisoning
in those branches"; (3) "That the use of raw lead
should be absolutely prohibited"; and (4) "That
young persons and women should not only be
medically examined every month, but be prohibited
from working in lead, and male workers should be
subject to systematic medical inspection.

This report certainly raised a great outcry
amongst the manufacturers. The prevailing tone
was one of remonstrance against being taught their
business by outsiders, and the optimistic statements
of the experts in regard to the practical stage which
leadless glazes had reached were vehemently assailed
by spokesmen on the part of the manufacturers.
The fear was felt that the Home Office might
precipitately adopt the views of the experts in
regard to leadless glazes, and decree their compulsory use, but even those whose faith in leadless
glazes was strongest would ·have shrunk from this
as an immediate measure.

The Manufacturers' Association memorialised the
Home Secretary, declaring their willingness to adopt
fritted lead, but praying for a reasonable time to
effect the change, and protesting against the idea

of there being any possibility of the abolition of
lead. Gradually the panic subsided. It was seen
that the Home Office did not contemplate taking
any rash step, and as a matter of fact nothing was
done until December 1899, when a notification was
issued from Whitehall to the effect that within six
months of that date manufacturers would be expected to have discontinued the use of raw lead
entirely. It was also proposed that those who used
leadless glazes should be freed from the operation
of certain special rules ; and an indication was given
that within another two years the Government
might require that the lead should be so fritted as
to produce in the dipping-tub an amount of soluble
lead not exceeding 2 per cent. of the total mixture.
No restriction was placed, as had been feared, on
the amount of lead to be used, but a manufacturer
would be free to use as much lead as he liked
provided that it was fritted, and ultimately it was
hoped to so frit it as to decrease its solubility to
the degree named. The Government has thus done
nothing "to drive the trade out of the country."
Manufacturers have within the last twelve months
been gradually and patiently adopting fritted lead,
and though it may be necessary to extend the
time beyond the limit foreshadowed in December
1899,—postponed afterwards for another six months,
until January 1901,—there is no doubt that a period

will be reached when raw lead will have entirely disappeared from pottery glazes.

The Manufacturers' Association has practically accepted the new Home Office Rule, issued in the summer of 1900, with the exception of a few unimportant and apparently reasonable recommendations made by them in regard to certain minor operations in which a very limited use of raw lead may be found still necessary.

The prejudice against universally adopting leadless glaze has certainly some *raison d'être*. Manufacturers are naturally reluctant to take any precipitate step in changing their method of glazing, inasmuch as the glazing of the ware is the last process to which it is ordinarily subjected, and the risk of disaster therefore becomes a serious one. Some enlightened manufacturers have already adopted leadless glaze partially, and have recognised the possibility that, after all, the resources of civilisation may not fall exhausted and powerless before one particular substance among the countless products of nature, but that a respectful treatment of leadless glazes will receive by renewed experiment practical justification. It is a pity that so many others prefer an attitude of downright denunciation, rather than one of knowledge, open-mindedness and inquiry.

Undoubtedly the various precautions due to outside pressure and command during the last year or two have sensibly diminished the number in the returns of those suffering from lead-poisoning; the periodical medical examinations of females, involving the rejection of those physically unfit for further employment, being perhaps from one point of view the most effectual of all innovations. The opposition of the manufacturers to outside pressure as it affected their position—while encouraging all restrictions on their workpeople—has been salutary in precisely the same sense and in the same measure as the distrust of conservatism is useful in checking any hastiness in political or social reform, and, by making the reform difficult, causing its desirability to be demonstrated. One hesitates to believe in the words of a contemporary journal that there may be yet "a high mountain of mediocre ability, routine methods, and self-satisfied complacency to be overcome." Rather with another writer one acknowledges that "Economic and industrial problems are now so complicated, and the interests involved are so many, that organic changes become continually more difficult to imagine and to accomplish." But there can be no two opinions that the point has been reached when the right road stretches most surely before those who care for the welfare of the workers of The Potteries. Some, on the one hand, who care not at all, may hold aloof; some there are, on the other hand, who, disappointed in the attainment of greater things, can find no content in the lesser, expecting too quickly the fulfilment of their hopes. These forget that "time is not measured by the years we live," and that of all the processes of evolution through which this strange hoary world of ours has passed, and is passing, no process moves more slowly than that of the moral and intellectual enlightenment of the ignorant and the indifferent.

Let, however, the *via media* be taken unquestioningly by the master and the workman of good intention ; let them in mutual trust and confidence, even if stronger trade combinations are a necessity of the position, accept the inevitable and mould the inevitable to mutual profit and advancement. The Government has done much, the manufacturers may do more—not only in the letter of reform, but in the spirit thereof—by passing from the pettiness of recrimination and continual antagonism to reform, to a higher altitude where every advantage may be taken of scientific discovery and enlightened education, and where, infused with a new energy and enthusiasm, they may make their trade not only one of the most beautiful, but in organisation one of the most perfect in the world.

MILLICENT SUTHERLAND.

APPENDICES

U

I.—WAGES AND HIRINGS IN OLDEN TIMES

Mr Llewellyn Jewitt, in "The Wedgwoods" (1865), quotes some interesting entries from the original accounts kept by Thomas Whielden, the second partner of Wedgwood, from 1747 to 1754, showing the "rate of wages paid to potters when Josiah Wedgwood first began business," and giving some curious instances of the hiring from Martinmas to Martinmas.

1747.

			£	s	d
Jany.	27.	Hired Jno. Austin for placeing white, etc., pr. week	£0	5	6
		Pd. his whole earnest	0	3	0
Feb.	14.	Then hired Thos. Dutton	0	6	6
		Pd. one pr. Stockin	0	3	6
		Earnest for vineing [veining] ware	0	15	0
		1 pr. Stockin	0	2	6
		Pd. in part	0	1	0
		Pd. do. in 7 yds. cloth	0	8	9
	16.	Hired Wm. Keeling for handleing	0	6	0
		Pd. his whole earnest	0	1	0
	20.	Hired Wm. Cope for handleing and vineing cast ware, for [per week]	0	7	0
		Pd. his whole earnest	0	10	6
	28.	Then hired Robt. Gardner per week	0	6	6
		Earnest	0	10	6
		Pd. him toward it	0	1	0
		I am to make his earnest abt. 5s. more in something.			
March	8.	Then hired Jno. Barker fr. ye huvels @	0	5	6
		Pd. earnest in part	0	1	0
		Pd. it to pay more	0	1	0

1747.
March 26. Then hire George Bagnall for fireing
     for this year for .   .   . £0 5 3
   Full earnest, 5s.
   Pd. in part 0 2 6
   Hired for 1750   .   .   . 0 5 6
April 9. Hired Siah Spode * to give him from
     this time to Martelmas next,
     2s. 3d. or 2s. 6d. if he Deserves it.
   2nd year 0 2 9
   3rd year 0 3 3
   Pd. full earnest   .   .   . 0 1 0

1749.
June 2. Hired a boy of Ann Blowers for
     treading ye lathe, pr. week   . 0 2 0
   Pd. earnest 0 0 6
   Then hired Elijah Simpson for turn-
     ing, he is to have pr. week   . 0 8 0
   Whole earnest   .   .   . 2 2 0
   Pd. in part 1 2 0

1751.
Jan. 11. Then hired Saml. Jackson for Throw-
     ing sagers and fireing, pr. week . 0 8 0
   Whole earnest   .   .   . 2 2 0
   Pd. in part 1 2 0
   Pd. more 1 1 0
Feb. 9. Hired Jn. Edge for pr. week   . 0 6 0
   He is to have earnest   .   . 0 5 0
   And a new pr. stockins   .   . 0 2 0
   Pd. in part 0 1 0
   Hired his sn. Saml. for   .   . 0 1 3
April 6. Hired Wm. Kent per week .   . 0 7 6
   To give for earnest .   .   . 0 12 0
   Pd. in part 0 1 6
   To give a new shirt at 16d. per yd.

* This refers to the apprenticeship of Josiah Spode, the founder of the celebrated family of potters of that name. In the same journal, under the year 1752, "Josiah Spoad" is hired "for next Martelmas— pr. week, 7s."; and in 1754, "Hired Siah Spode, per week, 7s. 6d."

1751.

April 6. Hired Ann Blowrs Girl & Boy—

Girl	.	.	.	£0 0 9
Boy, Joseph	.	.	0 2 0

To give earnest, Testament.

Dec. 26. Then hired Cupit pr. week . . . 0 2 3

Pd. earnest 0 0 6

I am to give him a old pr. stockins, or somthing.

1752.

July 22. Hired George Bayley for 2 years—

1st year .	.	.	.	0 3 6
2d year .	.	.	.	0 4 0

To give him a pr. shoes each year.

1753.

June 21. Hired Wm. Marsh for 3 years. He is to have 10s. 6d. earnest each year, and 7s. per week. I am to give him a old coat or somthing abt. 5s. value.

Aug. 29. Hired Westabys three children, per

week 0 4 0

Pd. earnest 0 0 6

Hired John Everall per week . 0 4 6

Pd. earnest 2 pr. stockin . . 0 4 0

1 shillin in Cash . . . 0 1 0

To have a handkershef.

1760.

Dec. 3. Hired Joseph ——'s son to look after my flint mill. He is to have 6s. pr. ton for grinding & to find his own candle's. To pay £3 a year for the Mill House.

Pd. earnest 0 0 6

Nothing further—unless I chuse to give him a old coat—he is to work for me at any time when I want. His father is to assist him in anything he can do about the mill.

"Ann Blowrs Girl" had evidently given satisfaction to her employer, and had been set to paint sprigs and flowers upon the ware, securing a consequent rise in wages, for under the year of 1752 there comes the following entry:—

Aug. 24. Hired little Bet Blowr to learn to
flower £0 1 0
1st year per week . . 0 1 0
2d year ,, . . 0 1 3
3d year ,, . . 0 1 6

II.—THE USE OF MACHINERY AND ITS EFFECT ON WAGES

"ONE of the most bold attempts to cheapen the process of potting manufacture was made some two years ago, and is even now in course of perfecting, by Mr George Wall of Manchester. A machine for the manufacture of flat-ware has been invented, and nearly brought to perfection by that gentleman. Charles James Mason, Esq. of Fenton, was the first to introduce it to the Staffordshire Potteries, but the spirited opposition of the operatives, together with some defects in the machine itself, caused Mr Mason to abandon it after a few weeks trial. The machine is so constructed as to be made to work either by steam or hand power. In its first and most rude form it was capable of producing by the power of one man and a boy as much ware as is now produced by six adult operatives. But there was one great defect in nearly all the ware thus manufactured. Independent of the want of polishing, hair-cracks almost invariably made their appearance in the backs of the ware after firing. This defect has not, as yet, been overcome; and it is a question of much doubt whether it ever will be overcome. Some of the most practical men of the trade believe that no mechanical appliance can ever remedy the evil alluded to. The ductility of clay requires something more than a fixed immovable tool to fashion the ware. Human touch and skill are required to avoid the suppression or compression of air which doubtless produces the hair-cracks in Wall's machine-made ware, a defect which nothing but volition and skilled manipulation can remedy. . . . Mechanical appliances may increase perhaps to an enormous extent the *production* of potting goods, but they would not increase the *consumption*; the result of which would be increased competition among the employers, to the injury of all, and a sorrowful depression in the social and domestic condition of the employed. Let it be hoped that such a calamity will never be sought by potting manufacturers, on the one hand ; and, at the same time, never tolerated by the operatives on the other."—"The Art and History of the Potting Business," a booklet published by the Potters' Printing Society, Hanley, 1846, and written by William Evans, the Trades-Union leader of that day.

"Mr Ackrill then proceeded to read the masters' statements. . . . It was also argued that the American operatives did not resist the application of machinery, as did the English workmen. Hence articles must be produced at a moderate cost in order to sell largely" (p. 4). "Mr Shaw, manufacturer, said in times past the workpeople threw great difficulties in the way of the adoption of machinery, and asked the witness [a manufacturer] if in America he found the workmen threw any difficulties in the way of the employers' use of machinery?—Witness: Quite the contrary. Mr Shaw: Have you met with any opposition to the use of machinery on the part of the workpeople in this neighbourhood?—Witness: Yes, I have in some cases, where they threw every obstacle they could in the way. Mr Eardley [a workman]: Was it not because you have introduced women to do the men's work?—Witness: No, it is not so. Mr Eardley: Have you not done so?—Witness: Yes, we have had to do so, being compelled thereto. Mr Shaw remarked that it was employing women to do what they could do. The Umpire: Then the operatives object to the women, and not so much to the machinery. Mr Eardley: Do the women get sufficient wages to support a man and his family?—Witness: Certainly not, because they do not work as a man would do" (p. 5). "Mr Shaw:

Notwithstanding the outlay on the machinery, you still lose by its introduction?—Witness [a manufacturer]: It is no advantage. Umpire: It seems curious that the tables are turning in a few minutes, for only a few minutes ago you said it was an advantage to have machinery, and now you say it is not.—Witness: It is an advantage so far as the comfort of the workpeople, but not the masters. Mr Shaw: So far as I am concerned, the introduction of machinery is a direct profit to the workmen, and a decided loss to the masters" (p. 10).—Report of Arbitration, on an appeal of employers for a reduction in wages, before The Potteries' Stipendiary Magistrate, Mr J. E. Davies, January 1877.

"He then referred to the benefits conferred on the workmen by the introduction of improved machinery, including the jolly, all of which involved a large expense, and for the repair and maintenance of which, the deductions ($7\frac{1}{2}$ per cent.) made from workmen *barely paid the outlay.*" —Evidence of Mr Pinder, manufacturer, before Lord Hatherton Arbitration, 1879.

"The mechanical appliances that I have referred to are of a simple and inexpensive character. First, there is what is called a 'jolly' or 'monkey.' Instead of the platemaker holding the tool in his hands, the profile, or tool, is fixed upon the lever, and the man, by pulling a handle, brings the tool upon the bat of clay out of which he has to make the plate. The other contrivance which has contributed to the undoing of the flat-presser as a wage-earner is called the steam-spreader, or batter-out. This makes the bats of clay out of which the workman makes his plates, instead of his having to beat them out himself. The man has, however, in most cases, to pay for attendance upon this mechanical batter-out, and so it is not a complete saving of all cost in the preparation of his bats. The general charge for the use of this contrivance has taken the shape of 3s. in the £ off the workman's gross earnings, which often means

4s. 6d. in the £ off his own wages. This heavy charge is made, although the putting down of a steam-batter only costs the manufacturer a few pounds, and the total cost of it is in several months repaid to him by the charge upon the earnings of the hapless flat-presser."—Mr Wm. Owen's opening speech for the Operatives, Report of General Arbitration of 1891 (p. 12).

"Before I leave the flat-pressing branch altogether, let me say that cheapened production in this department is not limited to the decreased prices [consequent upon the use of machinery] that I have quoted. Through the introduction of this awfully mis-named apparatus called the 'jolly,' women now make, at some manufactories, the smaller-sized plates. I could, but will not, dwell upon the unwomanly character of this work—it is neither good for the living female nor the future offspring—but will merely point out that the cost of producing plates is on the average still further reduced through the cheap labour of the women. All this women-labour in this department has been introduced since 1872" (*Ibid.* p. 13).

"Of course, these labour-saving appliances act in this way; they do at a cheaper rate that which was previously paid for as manual labour at a higher rate, and if they had not done so they would not have been introduced at all. Therefore, it is by reason of these things, which are merely mechanical, that the men complain so bitterly that they have lost the plums—that is to say, the easy and light work by which they made their wages with less trouble, because of the labour-saving machines leaving them the more delicate work that could not be done by the machines, and which has still to be done by manual labour. . . . I regret to say that the introduction of labour-saving appliances has come too late to allow the manufacturers to share the profit with the men."—Speech by Mr H. T. Boddam, barrister-at-law, in opening the case for the Manufacturers, Arbitration of May 1891 (p. 50).

"The manufacturers also introduced labour-saving appliances, and, as a last resort they appealed to the men to help them to keep their trade by asking such of them who could afford, by a little more careful application and perhaps a little harder work, to assist them by some slight reduction in wages, and it was in consequence of that that notices were issued . . . to those persons who, they submit, are in a position, by a little more industry and care, to get the same wages as they have got before, even though prices are reduced by the labour-saving appliances which were introduced with this idea. What I mean is this—(we said): 'When the labour-saving appliances are introduced, if we alter your prices we shall not really lower your wages if you work right up to the collar'" (*Ibid.* p. 51).

"With regard to cup-makers and saucer-makers, they are gradually being driven out of the market by women labour, and if they don't care to take our terms we can supply their places with women and apprentices. We do not wish to do so. We think, if the workman will put himself to the collar, he can make so much with the assistance of the labour-saving appliances, with a 10 per cent. reduction, that he will be able to continue to earn an average wage. We believe if they choose to work a little harder they can make wages almost exactly the same as they obtain to-day. If, however, they prefer the luxury of ease to added industry, well, of course, we say they must take the consequences, because we are not in a position to give them any luxurious prices at the present time" (*Ibid.* p. 51).

"They are working up to the collar pretty well now. . . . There is a great deal of misapprehension as to what working potters can do. There is one thing they can do—they can put on a spurt occasionally, but if you will take into account all the conditions of the lives of the potters, you will readily see that they cannot be on the spurt always. How is it possible for the flat-presser, who has to make 45 per cent. more plates, to stand over his machine and work at full strain until he becomes part of the machine itself? Is he going to get further into the collar?"—Reply for the Operatives (*Ibid.* p. 70)

III.—THE WAGES OF POTTERS

"When we are told that trade is bad in The Potteries, we are aware that the master potter is not the only one who suffers from that condition. . . . When there is a fall in selling prices, the manufacturer has no alternative but to curtail his working expenses in one way or another. The easiest way of doing this is by reducing the amount of the weekly wages bill. For upwards of a quarter of a century, prices paid to the workers in the pottery trade have steadily declined. The loss to the workers has been a double one—the reduction in the rate of wages has been accompanied by such changes in the character of the articles made as have militated against the wage-earning power of the operators. Some manufacturers who, by virtue of their name, have been able to maintain the prices of their goods, have not allowed their workpeople to suffer from the indirect reductions [of alterations in shapes and sizes] we have just instanced. But many others, who have been willing to deal liberally with their employés, have yet been compelled to keep down their wages to the lowest possible amount. This has not been from inclination, but sheer necessity, and the result has been an undercurrent of dissatisfaction on the part of the employés that, coming to the surface at intervals, has produced no little friction between them and their employers. We think we are right in saying that every section of the potting trade admits that this is a true statement of the condition of affairs."—*Pottery Gazette* (manfacturers' trade organ), January 1899.

It is a matter of singular difficulty to arrive at any definite knowledge of the average earnings of the Staffordshire potter. Almost every reference to his wages deals with the rate at which he is paid for various articles, and any comparisons instituted are those between the price paid for such an article at one period, and the price paid at another. The question is further complicated by a reference to sizes, and again to shapes. It is obvious that it would convey no information to quote any figure showing that, for example, at a certain period "Hand-basins, size 6, Shape Regina," were made at so much each, or per score; unless one also knew how many such articles a workman could produce in a week when exclusively employed in making that article. But the work of each operative, within the limits of his branch, is of a somewhat varied character—a hollow-ware presser, for instance, may make half-a-dozen different articles, each article varying in shape, size, and price; and the weekly wage-earning capacity of any operative in any branch varies according to many circumstances, but mainly depends upon his branch, his individual skill, the quality of the work entrusted to him, and the rates and custom prevailing at the manufactory at which he is employed. It is, therefore, extremely difficult to give a summary average of a potter's earnings, but a few instances, given as representative cases, may be first cited.

In 1836 the Chamber of Commerce issued a return of wages paid at the principal manufactories, which showed that in 1833-4 an average workman earned between 17s. and 21s. a week, a woman about 6s. to 11s., a child of fourteen from 3s. to 3s. 6d. In 1836-7, according to the same authority, the average earnings of a man had risen from 21s. to 28s., of a woman from 10s. to 15s., and of a child from 3s. 6d. to 4s. 6d. per week. Probably the figures given were correct, though the source is partial, and inasmuch as the purpose of the figures was to show the improvement that had taken place in wages at the time of the strike of 1836, it is possible that either the rate of wages in the first period was unduly depressed, or in the later period slightly exaggerated. But the same objection applies to all the figures given, at any period, and by either

side—they are all vitiated by being the statements of
interested parties, using those figures for their own purposes; and never in the course of the history of the potting
trade has any attempt been made to arrive at a correct
estimate of wages for the sake of the information in itself—
the figures given upon that matter have always been employed as arguments, and neither side has ever completely
accepted the figures of the other.

In 1843, an oven-man asserted that his wages for a
week's constant work amounted to 17s. only, but there
is nothing to suggest that his case was representative of
the whole of his branch, the average earnings of the
members of which appears to have been, at about that
time, 24s. for adults. At the arbitrations before Mr Davies
(in 1877) and Lord Hatherton (in 1879), the evidence of
the workmen went to show that the rate of wages prevailing
in all the branches, so far as an average could be taken,
did not amount to 30s. a week; but, on the other hand,
the manufacturers quoted instances in which the wages
were considerably higher. At the Brassey arbitration, it
was officially stated, on behalf of the hollow-ware pressers,
that at few firms was the average in that branch as high as
30s., and that if all the hollow-ware pressers in a whole
town—journeymen, and not apprentices—were taken, the
average would not come out higher than 25s. a week. The
flat-pressers spoke particularly of the effect of machinery
upon their wages, and the following may be given as an
example: — A flat-presser, working by hand, produced
twelve score of ware, which, after paying his attendant
labour and various deductions, earned for him £1, 13s. 6d.
as the result of a week's work; after the introduction of
machinery, he was able to make eighteen score a week, but,
owing to a consequent reduction in the price, was only
able to earn £1, 4s. 7½d. Another said that by the same
process his wages had been reduced to £1, 2s. from

£1, 8s., others admitted that they could earn £1, 10s., whilst some declared their earnings to be as low as 20s. a week. At the same arbitration, the turners (one of the higher branches) declared that they could not, upon an average, command 30s. a week, the printers spoke of 25s. to 30s., and the oven-men said that 4s. to 4s. 7d. per day was the average rate of payment at the various manufactories, and that 27s. 6d. was the highest wages earned by an ordinary journeyman oven-man, working from sixty to seventy hours per week.

In 1891, a flat-presser, a good and steady workman, receiving the best kind of work, and employed at a good manufactory, said he could earn £1, 11s. to £1, 12s. a week, but others spoke of £1, 5s, £1, 2s. 6d., and £1, 1s. as representing their average earnings. The employers, however, gave £1, 9s. 5d. as the average earnings, for twelve weeks, of a flat-presser. The hollow-ware pressers declared that the best work yielded only £1, 8s. to £1, 10s., and the employers gave an average of a certain hollow-ware presser, for twelve weeks, as £1, 17s. 10d., of a printer £1, 9s., and of an oven-man £1, 8s. 9d. The last two figures do not show a very great discrepancy from those of the workmen; but it is practically impossible to arrive, by any process of arithmetic, at anything more than an approximate estimate of a potter's average earning, and, taking the statements of both masters and men, it appears as though the average wages, in 1 ter periods, fluctuated on either side of 30s. a week, but that many more potters were earning wages less than that sum than above it.

In the absence of any absolutely reliable and impartial return of the wages paid, it is necessary to take the figures given in the course of the various arbitrations that have been held, and the following are the results of the collation of these particulars, tabulated according to the various branches:—

FLAT-PRESSERS.—A branch engaged in making flat-ware — plates and dishes, as distinguished from hollow-ware — formerly made by hand, but now by machine, and also including saucer-makers and cup-makers, articles also made by the "jigger." The flat-pressers are the worst paid of any branch, and particularly the maker of plates. They pay the wages of their attendants out of their gross earnings.

PLATE-MAKER.—"I shall call one witness who will prove by his wage bills that whereas he could earn £2, 2s. 6d., he is now earning about £1, 5s. per week, and for that sum, which is left to him after paying his attendants, he has to make, considering his losses in the oven and in the clay state, 440 dozens of plates per week. . . . Averaging all sizes of plates together, every dozen costs about 1d. for the making. Now, a dinner-set of 121 pieces, for twelve persons, includes 7 dozen plates, which would mean, so far as the flat-pressers are concerned, at 20 per cent advance (asked for), less than 2d. per dinner-set. Will the manufacturers contend that it would be impossible for such an advance in selling prices to be obtained as would give this advance in wages? . . . Now, the Umpires must yield to the common-sense of my statement, after the figures I have given as to the prosperous state of this trade, that manufacturers could, so far as the flat-presser is concerned, afford to add 2d. to the 539 pence that is put down as the selling price of the common dinner-set, and I may add that the price of the richest dinner-set that is produced in earthenware need not be increased to any greater extent by this addition to the flat-presser's wages."—Opening statement for workmen, Arbitration of 1891.

"There is no desire to reduce the wages of plate-makers, because their wages at the present time, according to our view, are as low as we could reasonably ask them to be, and, therefore, they are excepted from the reduction asked for."—Manufacturers' case, Arbitration of 1891.

This branch obtained an advance in 1871-2, equal to about 7 per cent.; reduced by Lord Hatherton's arbitration, 1879, by 8¼ per cent.; appealed for restitution of Lord Hatherton's "penny" before Mr Brassey, in 1880, unsuccessfully; appealed in 1891 for an advance of 20

X

per cent. (other branches asking for 10 per cent.) unsuccessfully; strike in 1900 resulted in 5 per cent. increase; general feeling among the employers at the time favourable to this advance. Have suffered loss through machinery, and increased sizes of articles made at same price as smaller ones formerly.

" He had worked full time for the last 13 weeks, and his average earnings for himself and attendants were, £2, 17s. 6d. He paid his attendants £1, 5s. 9d., leaving him £1, 11s. 7d. The proposed reduction of 10 per cent. would reduce his wages by 5s. 9d. on the gross, as he could not think of reducing his attendants who were by no means over-paid. Then he had to buy his own sponges, at a cost of 8d. to 1s. per week."—W. Gibson, flat-presser, Hatherton Arbitration, 1879.

" His average earnings for self and attendants were £1, 8s. to £1, 12s. He had two attendants at 13s. a week, leaving his nett earnings, 19s." (Probably a poor workman.)—Flat-presser's evidence, *ibid*.

" I earn 30s. a week. I pay 5s. rent, firing, 2s., school-wage, 2s., and rates, 1s. That leaves me £1 to clothe and feed 9 of us. That is below poorhouse fare, which is, I think, 2s. and something per head."—Weaver, flat-presser, Brassey Arbitration, 1880.

Average of plate-makers' earnings, given by manufacturers, at Arbitration of 1891, £1, 9s. 5d. per week. Workmen contended that this was 10 per cent. above the average.

CUP- AND SAUCER-MAKER.—"How little it would be upon a tea-set to give an advance (10 per cent.) of wages to the saucer-maker may be readily computed by the Umpires, when I tell them that for 4s. or 4s. 6d. 720 saucers are made. The additional expense upon a tea-set would be even less than the flat-presser's 2d. upon a dinner-set."—Operatives' case, Arbitration of 1891.

" With regard to cup-makers and saucer-makers, they are being gradually driven out of the market by women labour, and if they don't choose to take our terms we can supply their places with women and apprentices."—Advocate for manufacturers, on cross-appeal for 10 per cent. reduction, Arbitration of 1891.

Advanced in 1872; reduced by Lord Hatherton, 1879, 8⅓ per cent., or 1d. in the shilling; unsuccessful in arbitration (with every other branch) in appeal for advance, 1891; advanced by strike, 1900, 5 per cent.

"The man is a good average workman, and can work both by hand and jolly. When working by hand he could make twelve score dozen per week. There are 36 cups counted to the dozen, and 720 to the score. He was paid by hand 6s. 6d. per score, so that the twelve score would amount to £3, 18s. He employed three attendants, to whom he paid 24s.; and a woman sponger, to whom he paid 1s. per score, so that would be 12s.; he paid his employer 2½ per cent. to mill the clay, which would be 2s.; and the reduction (of Lord Hatherton) had to come off the gross amount of £3, 18s., so that would be 6s. 6d. more, which left him £1, 13s. 6d. But by the employer investing £2 in a jolly, the man's price was reduced from 6s. 6d. per score to 4s. 3d.—a reduction of 2s. 3d. between hand-made and jollied. I am not going to say that he is not able to make so much work by the jolly as by hand, for I find he makes eighteen score dozen by the jolly at 4s. 3d. per score. This amounts to £3, 16s. 6d. He is obliged to employ four attendants, to whom he pays £1, 12s. There is also the sponger, to whom goes 18s.; the use of pug-mill, 1s. 10½d. This leaves the man £1, 4s. 7½d. for eighteen score cups."—Evidence of George Bloor, Brassey Arbitration, 1880.

Arbitration of 1891:—Workmen's evidence—£1, 5s. for cup-maker, and £1, 5s. 8d. for saucer-maker. Employers' evidence—Cup-makers (women), £1, 7s. 6½d., saucer-maker (man), £1, 7s. 1d.

DISH- AND BASIN-MAKER—"What would the 10 per cent.

advance upon these low prices mean on a toilet-set? It would mean less than a penny on every twelve hand-basins, or the twelfth part of a penny per toilet-set. Would there be even one face less washed in a Staffordshire-made toilet-set because of this enormous advance to the basin-maker? . . . Now, there are twelve dishes included in a dinner-set that I have taken as an illustration; and 10 per cent. on the dish-maker's prices would only mean increasing the cost of the dinner-set by about three halfpence."—Workmen's case, Arbitration of 1891.

"There are the dish-makers and the hand-basin-makers. They can already earn wages which I venture to submit will bear some slight reduction."—Employers' cross appeal, Arbitration of 1891.

Fluctuation of wages as in other departments of flat-presser branch; the same decrease in earning-power through increase of sizes and introduction of more difficult shapes.

"Gross earnings, £4, 5s.; reduced by Lord Hatherton's award (1d. in the shilling) on the gross amount (7s. 1d.) to £3, 17s. 11d.; attendants' wages, £2, 12s. 0d.; leaving nett wages, £1, 5s. 11d., out of which he has to pay for pugging of clay, gas, and sponges."—Evidence of basin-maker, Brassey Arbitration, 1880.

"Previous to Lord Hatherton's reduction, could earn from £1, 17s. to £2. At present prices I could not earn more than 25s. if I did my best."—Evidence of basin-maker, Arbitration of 1891. Wages of basin-maker given by employers, 1891, £1, 17s. 10d.; dish-maker, £1, 13s. 8d.

HOLLOW-WARE PRESSERS. — In 1891, workmen's census showed 1873 journeymen, and 993 apprentices. Have suffered through increase in sizes, and easy work being taken from them to the "jigger," leaving difficult work to be made by hand, reducing earning capacity. Gradual informal reductions in working prices; formal advances and reductions same as in other branches, but advance in 1872 only partial.

"Bread and butter plates, that were made by the hollow-ware presser at 1s. 2d. per dozen, are now made by the flat-presser (on the "jigger") at 5s. per score dozen—a reduction of 300 per cent. Sponge-bowls have been taken to the jigger, and cost 50 per cent. less to make; soapboxes for which the hollow-ware presser received 1s. 10d., are now made on the jigger at from 9d. to 1s. per dozen," etc.—Operatives' case, Arbitration of 1891.

"We say that the hollow-ware presser can earn, at the (proposed) reduced 10 per cent., if he chooses to work with a little added industry for six days, even more than he makes at the present time."—Employers' advocate, Arbitration of 1891.

"Since 1872, my average wages have not been more than 30s."—Workmen's evidence, 1877 Arbitration.

"Average wages, £1, 10s.; rent, 4s.; rates, 8d.; coal, 1s. 6d.; school pence, 10d.; books and newspapers, 6d.; sick and benefit clubs, 2s. 6d.; leaving £1 for food and clothing."—Workmen's evidence, Arbitration of 1879.

"An average of 24s. to 26s. full time." "An average of £1, 8s. 1d. working four days a week. In cross-examination, an average of £2, 2s. 9d. for certain weeks, but working full time. Had the best work; at his place 3 men averaged £2 per week, but 38 men averaged 10s. a week less, some £1 less. Average for whole manufactory, about 26s."—Workmen's evidence, 1891 Arbitration. Evidence of employers: average of £1, 15s. 8½d. for general hollow-ware; £1, 11s. 10½d. for ewer-makers.

MOULD-MAKERS.—Makers of the mould in which the ware is made, "requiring much skill and the application very often of original contrivance." The use of machinery has made their work more exacting in finish. Altogether a highly skilful branch for an operative.

"Ours being the stage or portion in the process of manufacture next following the modeller or designer, it requires a considerable amount of training and skill."—Workmen's case, Arbitration of 1891.

"The mould-makers have received notice of a reduction equal to 15 per cent. These mould-makers, I will show conclusively, make almost fabulous wages. They come and go generally at times which suit themselves, and are a superior class in every way; and in the circumstances can afford, if anybody can, to have a percentage taken off."—Employers' advocate, Arbitration of 1891.

Received no advance in 1871-2, as did other branches, but were included in Lord Hatherton's reduction in 1879. Have received no advance since.

Workmen's evidence of average wage: £1, 10s. to £2, 5s.—Brassey Arbitration of 1880.

Workmen's evidence in 1891 Arbitration: £1, 16s. to £2, 2s. "We (Doulton's) employ three mould-makers, and their average earnings for the first 13 weeks of 1891 were £3, 2s. 11½d., £2, 11s., and £2, 3s. 1d."—Employers' case, 1891. Manufacturers' statement of average earnings of mould-makers, at twelve places, £2, 3s. 4d. per week.—Arbitration of 1891.

THROWERS.—"The throwers' case is an interesting one, and illustrates the great changes that have taken place in potting during the period covered by the great arbitrations in this trade. The thrower's wheel—the first machine, perhaps, in any industry—no longer occupies the prominent producing position it once did, for most of the articles that were made by the thrower are now taken away from the wheel, and are either pressed or made on the jigger. Seventy-five per cent. of these articles have been taken away from him, and the articles left to him have been increased in size."—Workmen's case, Arbitration of 1891.

"Taking the thrower as an example, that which was formerly entirely done by the men is now done on the machine by women and boys equally well for the purposes of the manufacturer, and the result is that machinery drives out these men from positions which they previously held alone. If there were any added wage given to the thrower at the present time the result would be his extinction the more rapidly."—Manufacturers' case, Arbitration of 1891.

The thrower is probably the most complete example of manipulative skill in any industry. It is his work, giving shape to shapeless clay by the movement of the fingers, which best illustrates the saying of "clay in the hands of the potter."

"A thrower who worked a week would get £2, 10s. to £2, 15s. in 1875 to 1879" (reduced by Lord Hatherton in 1879), "but it is a fair average man who gets £2 now."—Workmen's case, 1891. Average of thrower's earning stated by manufacturers, 1891, to be £2, 10s. 3½d.

TURNERS.—They finish on the lathe the work of the thrower, and sometimes the rougher work of the jiggerer. Like the thrower, they have suffered by much of their work being taken to and completed by the jigger, and by increase of sizes. The introduction of the steam lathe has reduced prices. They pay their attendants.

"Head-turner, £2, 2s., average of others, £1, 6s., ordinary turners, £1, 13s. Average at different firms: £1, 8s., £1, 4s. 9d., £1, 5s., and £1, 7s. 6d."—Workmen's case, 1891. Manufacturers' average of turners' earnings, £1, 14s. 2½d.

Were only partially advanced in 1872, but reduced same as other branches in 1879 by Lord Hatherton.

HANDLERS.—No material increase in 1872; reduced by Lord Hatherton in 1879; further reduced 1885; sizes larger, prices rather less than formerly. They pay their attendants.

"It is impossible for a handler to get more than 5s. per day, and, after paying attendants and other deductions, his day's wages are brought down to 4s. 2d."—Workmen's case, 1891. Employers' statement of average earnings, 1891, £1, 17s.

PRINTERS.—The printer prints upon tissue paper from the copper-plate, which he passes under his press, the design which is to be imprinted on the ware; this is then transferred to the ware by the transferrer (a woman), and the paper is washed off, leaving the print behind, by a girl attendant. In 1872 there were in The Potteries district 705 printers (journeymen and apprentices), with 1500 women transferrers and girl assistants; in 1879, 807 printers, with 1620 women and girls; in 1891, 1223 printers (journeymen 822, and apprentices 401), with 2500 women and girls. The wages are paid on the basis of the "count"—*i.e.* 5½d. is paid for each dozen of ware printed; but the "count" decides how many pieces shall go to the dozen. In recent years the count has been lengthened —new patterns have largely been taken as long counts, and short counts have become long counts. The shorter the count the fewer pieces to be printed to the dozen. Advanced in 1872, reduced in 1879, prices unaltered, but counts gradually lengthening ever since.

"Our wages are insufficient to meet our rents, rates, firing, insurance for sickness and death, religious and social charities (!), clothing for ourselves and families, and twenty-one meals per week for parents and children; and a printer cannot work ten hours a day at a press and over a hot stove on red herrings and broth. If an English operative cannot obtain substantial food, he loses his native stamina, and will sink to the inertness of a Continental operative. Living in towns, we cannot go out full-rigged in a smock-frock, hob-nailed boots, and for our head-gear a fourpenny tommy-cap."—Evidence of John Goodwin, printer, Brassey Arbitration, 1880.

"The printer's position is a dignified one. His occupation is not a laborious one. There are certain drawbacks—the mixing of paint [colour], and having to allow a reduction for soap are objectionable, no doubt—but to stand and turn a handle and pass a thing backwards and forwards is not a very laborious occupation. For some years past, for my own amusement and information, I have visited various potteries in the district, and I have always admired the dignified ease of the printer's position. We say that the printer can afford to allow us ¼d. a dozen."—Employers' advocate, Arbitration of 1891.

"I say a good printer can earn £1, 13s. 9d., paying 1s. 4½d. out of that (1s. for oil, 3d. for soap, and 1½d. for tar), if he comes at breakfast-time on Monday and works the usual hours until 2 o'clock on Saturday."—

Mr Ridgway's evidence (manufacturer), Arbitration of 1877. "We admit that printers can earn that amount, but we affirm that whilst at Mr Ridgway's place the deduction would be only 1s. 4½d., in general it is 5s. for mixing colour, size, cutting, tools, and so on."—Workmen's case, Arbitration of 1877.

"Printer, £1, 13s. 9d., gross; 5s. deductions, leaving £1, 8s. 9d. nett, working full time and producing 120 dozens; journeywoman transferrer, 15s. gross, deductions, 2s. 8d., nett, 12s. 4d.; apprentice, 10s. gross, deductions, 2s. 8d., nett, 7s. 4d. Average for journeymen generally, £1, 5s. 9d."—Summary given in 1879, by workmen.

"So far back as 1836, nearly half-a-century ago, we, as printers and transferrers, were paid more than we received previous to the reduction of last year (1879). There has been a gradual reduction, whenever a manufacturer had an opportunity of making it."—Statement of George Ingleby, printers' representative, Brassey Arbitration, 1880.

Evidence being given on the part of the workmen that the printers averaged £1, 5s. 8d., Mr Powell, leading for the manufacturers, said : "We say the average is £1, 7s. 1d." —Brassey Arbitration, 1880. "A journeywoman transferrer earns 12s. 10d.; deductions, 2s. 6d., nett, 10s. 4d. Journeywomen transferrers, as a rule, are married, and pay 3s. or 4s. for nursing."—Workmen's evidence, 1880.

"Here is an article we counted as 24's—it is now counted 36's. That is 50 per cent. added on that article. There are places where tea-pots counted as 12's previous to 1884, are now counted as 15's. There are articles that have been doubled from 6's to 12's, as in vases, comports, and all that sort."—"120 dozens of ware is considered an average week's work. It is £1, 11s. 3d. for 120 dozen. A man has to pay 3s. for mixing colour, and 3d. for soap, as well as 6d. to the girl who cuts papers—the cutter we call her. That reduces his wages to £1, 7s. for the full week. Holiday times and other things will reduce the full time by half-a-day a week, and in that case his nett wages are £1, 4s. 6d. A woman transferrer earns 13s. 9d., less 2s. 4d. for the cutter, and 1d. for soap."—Workmen's case, 1891 Arbitration. Average earnings of journeymen printers as stated by manufacturers, 1891—£1, 9s. 2d.

OVEN-MEN.—"No labour upon a manufactory is so heavy, and they must be men of strong constitution, or they are soon out of the ranks. Their work includes the carrying of the ware and the sagger to the bench, the placing of the ware in the sagger, the carrying of the full sagger to the oven and the lifting and placing of it in the oven. Then, after firing, the oven has to be drawn; the saggers to be carried out, to be emptied, and the ware carried into the warehouse, and this makes up the tale of the oven-man's work. . . . During the last winter the clay they have used for 'wads' has been frozen on the bench outside; and after that they have had to go to work in the oven in heat which has singed the flannels with which their hands and heads have been swathed. When the oven-men receive the advance they are asking for, it will not amount, for the journeymen, to 5d. per hour."—Opening statement for workmen, Arbitration of 1891.

"A question has been much pressed by the workmen as to whether the manufacturers thought 5s. was too much to find the comforts which every man needed. He said 5s. was not too much, but unfortunately political economy and England could not afford to pay it, and if he were asked whether, compared with skilled labour, 5s. was too much for an oven-man, he held that it was above the market price. . . . Lord Hatherton : A good hedger and ditcher is a very valuable man.—Mr Jones : So is a good placer a very valuable man, but that is no reason why we should pay 5s., when in the country (for farm labourers) they pay 3s. or 3s. 6d., including everything."—"Mr Pinder (manufacturer) : Before the pug-mill was introduced, women were selected, many of whom were physically strong, for the wedging of the clay, a toil that was perhaps the most laborious on the manufactory. In that respect it could only be matched with oven-work."—" Mr Clement Wedgwood: Two or three years ago witness's brother had gone round on a (Continental) tour of inspection, and from the notes he gathered that the wages of oven-men—who his Lordship had heard were well worth 5s. a day—were there only 2s. 6d. and 2s. 9d. per day. This was, he thought, a proof of the co-operation of men and masters abroad."—Extracts from employers' evidence, Hatherton Arbitration, 1879.

"Witness: He had worked in France. It was a fact that there were two Frenchmen to carry a sagger up in the oven, but an Englishman put it on his back and did it himself, besides placing 20 more saggers in a day. He does three times as much work as a Frenchman. He could not stay in France, as he feared for his life, having introduced so much more work for them to do. Lord Hatherton: All this is very interesting, no doubt, but I fail to see how it bears on the point before us.—Mr Oakes: Yes, the employers say foreign competition interferes with them, as French manufacturers get their work done cheaper than in England."—Extract from workmen's case, Hatherton Arbitration, 1879.

"The amount of work that an English navvy will get through in comparison with an Italian is almost incredible."—Mr Brassey, Arbitration of 1880.

"The oven-men have received a notice to the effect that the reduction in their branch would be equivalent to 3d. a day. It is true these men have to work hard, but in these days to pay more than 4s. 6d. or 4s. 3d. for such work is not the rule."—Employers' advocate, Arbitration of 1891.

"I take my average at 5½ days a week (though that is not always the case) at 5s. a day, which brings me in 27s. 6d. a week, which, with my, children's 3s. per week, makes me 30s. 6d. Out of that I pay 3s. a week for rent, 3s. for coal and light, which, with my 1s. 6d. for my clubs, makes 7s. 2d. Then I have to pay 1s. for school wage for my children, which makes me 8s. 2d. I take out of 21s. 10d., 2s. a week for my clothing for myself and family, and that won't cover it, which leaves me 2d. short of a pound to support my family. There are eight of us in the family, and I think that under the present circumstances, the oven-men should not be reduced."—Evidence of Mr Thomas Edwards, oven-man, Davies Arbitration, 1877. (No reduction was awarded.)

"At different manufactories different rates were paid for oven-men. At one firm the average was 4s. 2d. per day; at another 3s. 9¾d. (names given)."—Lord Hatherton: "I think we have got enough to show that the oven-men do not all get 5s. a day."—"Other evidence having been given, Lord Hatherton said again enough had been quoted to show that oven-men did not get 5s. a day as a whole."—"Mr Spooner gave evidence showing that of 10 firms, with 68 ovens, employing 155 men, the average wages of oven-men were 4s. 6d. per day."—Evidence of workmen, Hatherton Arbitration, 1879, p. 20. (In 1872 advances were made to oven-men, making their day wage 5s. Lord Hatherton decreed a reduction of a penny in the shilling in 1879.)

"Mr Edwards was entering upon the question of the price of provisions, when the Umpire said this was not an element of which he could take cognizance.—Mr Edwards said inasmuch as the employers sought to show what a large percentage of their money went in materials—coal and borax, etc.—he wished to show in what food 50 per cent. of his earnings went. He had to cut up twenty-eight loaves a week, and the price of flour had risen."— Workmen's case, Hatherton Arbitration, 1879.

"You will see that our work has been increased" (by new methods of placing the ware in the saggers, by which more ware was consequently placed in the oven), "and our wages reduced from an average of 4s. 7d. per day."— Workmen's case, Brassey Arbitration, 1880.

In 1891 wages had not materially changed, but the oven-men complained of the increase of the apprentices in each "set" throwing more work on the journeymen, who were responsible for the whole job. Manufacturers gave evidence of the average wages of oven-men being £1, 8s. 9d. Reduction of wages asked for by the employers (3d. per day) and advance of 10 per cent. asked for by oven-men were both refused at Arbitration of 1891.

Maximum earnings of the "clay-branches" when working full time:

Class.	Gross Earnings.	Deductions.	Nett Wages.
Dish-maker . .	£2 12 0	Mould-runner, 7s. Sponger, 10s.	£1 15 0
Plate-maker . .	2 10 0	Mould-runner, 8s. Tower, 12s.	1 10 0
Jiggerer of chambers, pails, etc. . .	3 10 0	Mould-runner, 9s. Fettling, etc., £1.	2 1 0
Cup-maker (woman) .	2 0 0	Mould-runner, 8s. Sponger, 12s.	1 0 0
Saucer-maker . .	2 0 0	Batting, 8s. Mould-runner, 8s. Sponger, 10s.	0 14 0
Saucer-maker (man) .	2 15 0	Batting - out and Mould-runner, 16s. Sponger, 10s.	1 9 0
Basin-maker . .	2 12 0	Mould-runner, 9s. Sponger, 11s.	1 12 0

Comparative wages of workmen in hollow-ware branch :

A man making soup-tureens at 7s. per dozen can earn .	£2 5 0
The same man making jugs at 9d. ,, ,, .	1 0 0
,, ,, cover-dishes at 3s. ,, .	1 16 0
,, ,, ewers at 2s. 6d. ,, .	1 10 0
,, ,, tea-pots at 2s. 6d. ,, .	1 10 0
,, ,, gravy-boats at 1s. 2d. ,, .	1 5 0

The above figures are supplied by a manufacturer in 1900, and represent the possible earnings of workmen when working full time, and when "not waiting for clay or steam."

Calculated on basis of 5 per cent. advance obtained in 1900.

IV.—THE WEAKNESS OF THE POTTERS' UNIONS

THERE are in the North Staffordshire Potteries district about 400 earthenware manufactories, including "china" works, a term used locally, in contradistinction to the trade acceptance of the term "earthenware," which forms the staple branch of the industry. These factories employ 50,000 operatives, of whom about 27,000 are males, and 23,000 females; and of these about 21,000 males, and 16,000 females are above eighteen years of age, and may be considered available for trades unions. But there are only 5000 enrolled members of the various branch unions, and these consist almost entirely of male operatives.

The Women's Trade Union League endeavoured to form a separate trades union for some of the women-workers in 1893, but the class to which the League chiefly appealed—the transferrers—was, when in union at all, affiliated to the journeymen printers' society, and little headway was made in the propaganda. This proportion of 10 per cent. of the total operative class, in union, appears to have been in later years the high-water mark of pottery trades-unionism. The Union of 1843, with all the incentive of early successes, the enthusiasm of the emigration movement, and the panic caused by the introduction of machinery, "never exceeded in numbers 2000 members," according to the statement of the leader of that day, Mr William Evans, in his pamphlet of 1846; and this number bore about the same relation to the total roll of operatives of that day.

Excluding female workers and males under eighteen years, as being unavailable for trades union membership, it would appear that only about one in four of the "effective" male

334

operatives have been members of their unions, even in the palmiest days of unionism during the last half-century. Indeed, the potters have never had, since the Union of 1836, an organisation of such strength and completeness as those which satisfy the spirit of unionism in most other trades to-day. Several special circumstances may be given to account for this. In the first place, the very advantage of their concentration and insularity, as a body, produced, contradictorily enough, a carelessness which would not have been found had they been more scattered, and so felt a greater need of union; secondly, the custom of an annual settlement of prices has always h d the effect of relaxing the union spirit during the greater part of the year, and stimulating it only when Martinmas came round, then to let it slumber again until the time came for prices again to be fixed for another annual term; and, thirdly, the consistently moderate policy of their leaders, particularly in their commendable desire to make arbitration paramount, has, during later years, caused the men to rely more upon the conciliatory machinery which they had set up than upon their own strength. The latter circumstance conveys a useful warning to other trades which may adopt, or have adopted, arbitration.

Still, after making all allowances for those special conditions, there has always remained a large margin of non-unionism only to be accounted for by apathy on the part of a large section of the working potters. They have, on the whole, been as well and wisely led as any body of working-men in the kingdom, but they have never supplied their leaders with adequate materials for the effective championship of their cause; and this weakness on their part has necessitated, in turn, the moderate policy of their leaders. "Organise," and "Arbitrate" have proved two conflicting cries, although identical in purpose. It is an interesting commentary on the aims and effects of trades unionism

that this enforced conciliatory attitude of the leaders of the
potters, which should have commended itself to the employers, and which (if there is any meaning in the platitudes
of the capitalistic class upon the extravagant demands of
labour, and the possibility of mutual goodwill between
employers and employed when "agitators" are out of the
way,) should have produced harmony between master and
man, has proved ineffective in establishing good relations
between the two sides. The leaders of the men have
always said, "Arbitrate if you can, but unite first and in any
case." The body of workmen have remained deaf to the
call for nine months out of every year, and then have expected their leaders to undertake the responsibility of strikes
on the strength of nothing but unusual fervour as Martinmas
and a crisis approached, and a few weeks' increased subscriptions to the Union funds.

It is not too much to say that if the working potters had
been led by "agitators" of true agitating proclivities—for
some emphasis is necessary when that name is indis-
criminately applied to all who take the side of labour—
and had given them power to make "agitation," even of a
ruthless and unreasoning type, effective, they and their
employers would have gained more than by the essentially
wise and honourable policy which their apathy has forced
their leaders to adopt, even as a matter of caution as well
as of conviction. The workmen would have then been
able to insist upon their claims, to their own advantage, and
would have forced their employers to adapt themselves to
circumstances by checking their own competition amongst
themselves, and so giving to the trade a stability which
would have been to their profit also. But all this could
have been done quite as well—if not better—if the working
potters had solidly supported the leaders they have had, and
so had combined the advantages of numerical strength and
good direction.

V.—WHERE AND HOW THE WORKERS LIVE

No manufacturing district can escape the defects of its quality, but "The Potteries," from several special causes, is unutterably unlovely. The traveller passing from one end to the other would see no interval between the six towns of which it is composed, and Tunstall ends, as Longton began, the pilgrimage, in a view of the walls of manufactories lining the main streets and the side streets—the conical tops of smoking ovens peeping over and behind them—with frequent interludes of two-storeyed shops and rows of cottage houses. The tale is continued even to Golden-hill, beyond Tunstall, and, if you are again deluded by a name, to Silver-dale, which lies outside the strictly Potteries area, forges and collieries only take the place of potters' ovens and mill chimneys. And as for the classic suburbs of "Florence" and "Etruria"—vassals to Longton and Hanley—or even the more modern, if equally modest, claim of "Dresden," they are merely sly and deliberate examples of the irony of nomenclature.*

Starting from Longton, which rejoices in a Town Council, you run into the arms of Fenton Local

---

* "It would be irony to speak of the magnificence of the Pottery towns—he referred to the warm hearts of the people who lived in that district."—The Earl of Stamford, at Hanley, November 8, 1900.

Board, pass thence through the domain of the Corporation of Stoke - upon - Trent, are handed on to the County Borough of Hanley, and having thus reached the zenith of municipal glory, pass with a gentle descent through the incorporate town of Burslem, to end the journey within the realm of the Tunstall Local Board.

This seven-mile main road—which has two intervals, each of half-a-mile's length, of villa houses —cuts through the centre of the towns and townships in which the pottery workers work and live. The footpaths are fairly well paved, the roads are possibly all that the principles of Macadam and the ministrations of a steam-roller can make them ; but the clayey subsoil keeps the rain-water on the surface, and the mud of the roads is blackened blacker by the droppings from the jolting coalcarts which pass along the thoroughfares to the manufactories. These coal-carts are followed by poor and ragged little boys and girls, sent out by their mothers—and often accompanied by them— to pick up in baskets, buckets, or folded dress-fronts, the small coal which falls from the carts. Occasionally, a tolerably large lump is furtively loosened, and when the next jolt in its charity sets it free, there is a scramble for the prize.

The Potteries is in its interests and definite characteristics just as much one town as Manchester, Liverpool, or Birmingham. Its powers and action, however, are split up between six separate governing bodies, and the opportunity of natural amalgamation which was offered by the formation of County

Councils' under the Local Government Act of 1888 was allowed to pass. Hanley did, indeed, take unto itself the dignity of a County Borough, by virtue of its superior population, but for any good that this act did to the rest of The Potteries, Hanley might just as well have set up to be a Republican State. But Hanley is in every respect, save population, acreage, and rateable value, precisely like Burslem, as Tunstall is like Longton, and as all are like each other.

The effect of thus having an industry (whose products are undoubtedly beautiful, but the production of which involves conditions that are undoubtedly not) straggling through the whole length of the district, is that the whole partakes of the character of its worst part, and there are no oases of a purely residential character. Birmingham has its Edgbaston, but The Potteries is all Soho. The residential quarters lie outside it—Wolstanton and Newcastle barely escape The Potteries (and all its "works") by the providence of nature in setting them on a hill—and the favoured spots for those who are not compelled to live where they work lie farther out, to Trentham, Stone, and Sandon to the south, and northwards even unto Alsager and Congleton in Cheshire. Possibly the greatest advantage incidental to living in The Potteries is the hope of being able to make enough money to live out of it.

The topography of The Potteries is very varied. You may pass down a street to find that its exit is barred by a mound of ashes, higher than the houses, gathered from furnace fires long since extinct, or of shale, raised from a coal-pit. The coal-pit is probably disused, and a dome of bricks covers the shaft on a neighbouring mound. You may pass up a road, and discover through an interval in the rows of houses that the playground of the children at the "backs" verges on a yawning marl-hole, deeper many times than the houses. These pimples of pit-mounds and these pock-marks of marl-holes scar the features—otherwise none too fair—of The Potteries. Man's faith cannot move pit-mounds, so houses are built on the lower slopes, and the monarch of the range stands an eternal sentinel at the back doors. But the deep places of the earth may be made level, and the marl-hole which yields no more marl is filled up, in the course of time, by cart-loads of broken pots and shards, with an occasional variation of cinders, from the manufactories. Dirty women and dirty little children may be seen sifting the contents of these carts before the dust of their falling has cleared away. They wait there all day for the carts, but what they hope to find is a mystery, as manufacturers sometimes pay for the privilege of thus getting rid of the rubbish of their works, and at any rate give it away. What they have taken from the earth they thus give back to it. When a marl-hole is nearly filled up, it swims within the ken of the speculative builder, and a row of cottage houses soon rests upon its foundation of fifty yards of broken pottery. One wonders whether Macaulay's New Zealander will stay long on the ruins of London Bridge, to the neglect of the archæological research which excavations in The Potteries might satisfy.

Each town has thus its ups and downs of building levels. The exigency of the presence of a pit-mound or of a "shord-ruck" in the centre of a plot of ground may demand that the space left unoccupied shall be filled up with more broken pots, until that particular piece of ground has reached an independent and exclusive level of its own, without reference to its neighbour. Its neighbour may be a plot of virgin ground, hitherto undefiled, yet on a much lower level. Or, to vary the metaphor with the matter, a few cottages may rest on mother earth, yet no longer enjoy nature's equality, for around and above them stretch acres of broken shards, whose advancing tide must one day engulf them, so that a street may pass over their chimney-tops.

The Potteries is thus, and inevitably, mainly a place of muddy, squalid streets, insignificant public buildings, smoky atmosphere, pot - works, and higgledy - piggledy rows of small houses. Nine-tenths of its population are of the working - class, and its well-to-do live mostly in their little colonies outside. The character of a neighbourhood must inevitably have some effect on the dwellers within it, but, apart from a certain habit of thought which may be styled "independence" — the result of the self-contained character of the district and its trade —the inhabitants of The Potteries bear up well against the aesthetic disadvantages of their surroundings. Each town has its free library; schools of art flourish amongst them, and remind one of the innately beautiful side of the trade in which they are engaged; musical societies, which have successfully competed with some of the best choral combinations in the country, have many adherents and supporters; and Hanley holds one of the best of the provincial musical festivals.

Like most Midland centres, it is devoted to "sport," but unfortunately takes it in a form which yields little. The attentions of the bookmaker are by no means scorned, with the inevitable moral effect; but probably an even equal amount of harm, physical if not moral, is done by the religious worship which is paid at the shrine of the successful "forward," "half-back,"—or "goal-keeper," for choice. It will probably be regarded as unenlightened heresy to say so, but one certainly fails to see, in the absence of conviction from the enthusiasts, what "sport" can possibly lurk in the occupation of several thousands of men standing in a sodden field in the football and rainy season to watch twenty-two men enjoying an exhilarating game in which only twenty-two men can take part. One cannot look too austerely upon the few available amusements of the working-class, but it is unquestionable that many a flat-presser, working all week in a hot and dusty shop, has accelerated his death by watching the performances, on a Saturday or Monday afternoon, of the heroes of his local football team. It is, moreover, their exploits that furnish his main theme of conversation during the working week, and it is a sad reflection that the only retribution that overtakes the two groups of eleven men each, who are the cause of all this absorption of doubtful advantage, is that their portraits are published as special supplements to "football editions." This excessive passion for watching other people enjoy themselves (a sadly perverted form of "hero-worship") when contrasted with the intellectual and industrial aspirations of their fathers, who sought education all the more earnestly because of the difficulties in the way of acquiring it, and were all the more zealous trades unionists because the Law looked on trades unionism out of the corner of its eye, probably accounts in no small measure for the apathy towards trades union-ism among the younger generation of the pottery workers of to-day. It also suggests the aphorism that possibly everything is worth struggling for, but nothing is worth the struggle. For the rest, a small section satisfies its sporting instincts by pigeon - flying; and there are again a few others who, "struggling towards the light," find their aesthetic desires solaced by brass band "contests" —a term appropriately applied to these vigorous exhibitions.

Coming now to the homes of the workers, generalisation is no longer possible. Nothing in modern social advancement is more remarkable than the way the "working-class" has developed within itself, and established different grades. The aristocracy is divided into the "smart set," and the intellectual or simple aristocrat; the middle class varies more in its manners than its money: but there is a much greater range from the lowest to the highest among the millions of workers whose earnings average from 10s. to 50s. per week than amongst those whose incomes vary from £1000 to £10,000 per year. The masses, in fact, have classes of their own, and it is precisely because of the narrow margin which is allowed for gradation that the differences in their ranks are so well marked.

Amongst the working potters, the higher branches —throwers, turners, and firemen—earning £2, 10s., and in some cases considerably more per week, keep up a home which time and opportunity may allow to pass, without much noticeable change, into that of the manager, or even the small manufacturer. The hollow - ware presser, engaged on "good work," and earning £2 per week, can keep up a very decent average artisan's home; the oven-man at thirty shillings a week, the printer at twenty - seven, and the flat-presser at eighteen to twenty - five, have perforce to be content with what they can get and their money will buy. But individual habits and family conditions finally settle the rank to which the worker belongs. A sober and thrifty flat-presser, with the aid of the earnings of his children able to work, keeps open a small and moderately comfortable home. If, on the other hand, he has a large family of young children, is of careless and improvident habits, and has a wife who works as transferrer, or in the warehouse, at 15s. to 18s. a week, the home becomes neglected, and the whole family may sink to the lowest level of its class. Probably this

matter of the wife working because none of the
children are yet old enough to work, in order to increase the family earnings, just when her attentions
are most urgently required at home, accounts a
good deal for the fact that many families, in which
the parents are in regular work, though not in
receipt of high wages, live in houses whose condition, externally and internally, suggest that they
are occupied by those in the most casual and pre-
carious employment. The mere fact of a wife
working at all is an incentive to domestic disorder
and squalor. She lives an independent life, forms
a circle of acquaintances of her own, and when
work is done is much more inclined for the continuation of her independence elsewhere than at
home. The husband comes to regard her as a
pillar of the household of equal importance to
himself, on the same grounds—if he is out of
work, she will help to keep it going—and so he
concedes to her as her right the same indulgences
and enjoyment as he takes himself. She goes her
way "after hours," and he goes his, and it is no
unusual thing for wife and husband, each with
their following, to meet in the same public-house
and treat each other. The result of all this to
the home is easily imagined. So potent a factor
in the production of domestic disorder is this
question of the working wife and mother, that it
is not too much to say that, given a husband
earning low wages in one of the badly - paid
branches of the trade, and a wife going out to
work, with a small family at home—nothing but

the most exemplary virtues on the part of husband
and wife can keep a decent home decently together. The conditions are such, however, as to
make the commonest virtues difficult, and so the
cause reacts on the consequence.

In a series of articles of remarkable interest dealing
with the housing of the poorer working-class in The
Potteries, published in the *Staffordshire Sentinel*
during October 1900, Father O'Rourke, of Hanley,
is quoted as saying:

"'I have seen among my own people, the Irish, six
sleeping in one bed—three at the foot and three at the
head.' And while on the question of dirty homes, Father
O'Rourke expressed himself very clearly on the subject
of female labour in the factories. 'I don't see how it
is possible,' he said, 'for a woman to properly attend to
her household duties and to go out to work all day. I
know cases where more is lost by want of attention in
the home than is actually earned by the woman herself
on the pot-bank—that is, more is lost in cash, apart from
any consideration of comfort which the hand of a woman
can impart to all domestic arrangements.'"

There are probably a thousand houses in The
Potteries in which disorder and dirt are the direct
outcome and result of the wife and mother working
all day, and bestowing half-an-hour's care on the
house whilst "tidying herself up" for the recreation
of the evening.

The bulk of the working population, however, lives
fully up to the average of their class with their
earnings. There are scores of rows of houses, built

within the last ten or twenty years (but often, unfortunately, "jerry" built), with two living-rooms
and a kitchen-scullery downstairs, and two or three
bedrooms, whose occupants are respectable and
cleanly, whose earnings range from 25s. to 35s. per
week, and whose rents vary from 4s. to 5s. 6d. If
there is a son or daughter of working age, earning
6s. to 10s. a week, and the wife is a domestic woman,
the household goes on fairly easy with the combined
earnings—though the working daughter is careful
to assert her right to the satisfaction of an excusable
vanity by hypothecating enough for her Sunday
finery—often tawdry and flimsy enough, but, even
so, showing pathetically the desire, and the limitations for its satisfaction, of a relief from the drab
of the working week. But there is no margin for
holidays, illness, accidentals, or spells of out-of-work
—it is a constant struggle to keep the home together
in ordinary comfort, and any slight variation in either
earnings or spendings will disturb the balance.
These conditions, with slight variations, according
to family conditions, prevail in the case of about
half the working population; about one-eighth
belongs to a higher class, where the heads of the
family work in the better paid branches; and the
remaining three-eighths overlap into a class which
lives in dirty, overcrowded houses, is dependent on
the pawn-shops at frequent crises, is in regular
but ill-paid work, or only fitfully employed, and
embraces the merely unfortunate, and the idle and
dissolute, all undergoing pretty much the same
vicissitudes with varying degrees of merit. How

they are housed will be seen by quotation from recent investigations.

A few days before Lord Rosebery, when addressing a meeting of the Christian Social Union, in the Holborn Town Hall, upon the impending elections in November 1900, for the new municipalities of London, advised that two questions should be put to intending councillors—(1) "Are you a builder, and, if so, what have you built?" and (2) "Are you a property-owner, and, if so, what sort of property do you own?"—the *Staffordshire Sentinel* commenced a series of articles dealing with the housing of the people in The Potteries, and advised that this inquiry, even more concise and direct than those suggested by Lord Rosebery, should be addressed to candidates for municipal honours in the County Borough of Hanley: "Are you the owner of any slums?" The articles, which clearly showed that The Potteries abounded in the malodorous attributes of a great city, considerably astonished and shocked The Potteries people, whose one fault is probably that of being too self-satisfied to indulge in introspection. The Special Commissioner commenced his articles by saying:

"Much is said of London, its wickedness, its immorality, its over-crowded homes, its dens of vice. On a smaller scale, The Potteries possesses all these; yet there are not wanting people who would shut their eyes to the truth, and go merrily on until the sore shall have so spread that nothing shall be able to stay its wide-reaching and evil effects."

The process by which houses become dilapidated,

and tenants become resigned to the dilapidations, thus saving the compunctions of the slum landlord, could not be better described than in the following passage :—

"In many cases, time was when these quarters were inhabited by a respectable working-class population, by women and men who took a pride in their homes and in their children too. But the time came, when, owing to the greed of a landlord, or the unscrupulousness of an agent, or from some other cause, one house, or perhaps a row of houses, was allowed to get out of repair. The tenant asked for improvements, but nothing was done. Then, when the artisan could patch up no longer, he left, and the next state of that dwelling was worse than the first. The new-comer was one who cared nothing for the pride of home. To live, to live anyhow, was the only consideration. . . . The same thing happened, perhaps, two doors away, and respectable people living between felt that they were sinking with the neighbourhood. They must either move, or find the level of their neighbours. So they moved, and others, very different, filled their places, and thus the quarter degenerated, and the class of inhabitants sank lower and lower, until no self-respecting person could dwell in the vicinity. As time went on, more people drifted that way. There were rooms, or part of rooms, to be had cheaply here. With the majority there was no care for decency, and insanitary lodgings did not frighten them. They 'dossed' here at night; during the day no one could find them. Meanwhile the landlord went on receiving the rent, which he had increased, as he, or his agent, understood that lodgers were taken in. He was not worried to put the place in repair by the tenant now. If they did not like it they could 'clear out'; there were plenty of the same class waiting to come in."

A snapshot of the interior of these habitations is here developed:

"A room 11 feet square. In it there are two bedsteads, standing close together. A mattress rests on both. There is a little boy in the room, and, when questioned, he tells you that his father and mother and himself and seven brothers and sisters—ten in all—pass the night in the room. Ask him how so many manage to sleep in so small a space, and he explains that they lie lengthwise and crosswise, adding, while a tear slowly finds its way down his blackened face, 'I don't sleep much, but I 'ave to stop quiet.' The only covering by night is the clothes these poor wretches wear by day. The stench is horrible; the mattresses are sodden. There is no means of ventilation except through the broken pane of glass in the window, boasting at night the cover of a paper bag. The windows do not open; they have not opened for years. If you attempted to move them, they would fall out into the roadway. What a sight for the doubting Thomas [a Town Councillor] breathing sweet air outside!"

The moral of Lord Rosebery's warning that no Londoner should vote for those who had any interests of their own to serve could not be better enforced than by the following passage:—

"It is a hard job to fight overcrowding in The Potteries, I am told. There are so many vested interests that you can hardly advance an inch without treading on somebody's toes. 'Vote for workmen's dwellings to be erected! No member of the Council will vote for the erection of new property in Hanley if it is ever likely to come into competition with their own.' Thus said a well-known member of our civic body."

Then follow detailed descriptions of the interiors

of these dwellings — details of thirteen persons, amongst them adults of both sexes, sleeping in two rooms no larger than cupboards; of families already overcrowded in two rooms taking in another family to lodge. In rickety tenements, with the walls covered by filth, and an absence of sanitary arrangements as completely primeval as could be wished, the Commissioner "asked for the name of the landlord, but failed to get it. The rents, I was told, were collected by an agent, and that agent was Mr ——, one of the best-known men in the Borough."

In some of these hovels, lodgers are admitted on payment of 4d. per night. The accommodation offered by the "bedrooms" having, after all, a final limit, "beds are made up" downstairs on the floor—a euphemism which merely means that the space is let. It is true that the *clientèle* is mainly of the loafing class;

"But there is also another class, and a pretty numerous class, too, who do not hesitate to patronise 'cottage lodging-houses.' Their work is carrying and drawing ware. For a day's work they receive 2s. 9d.; but it is casual labour. When they have been paid at night they have no further claim upon the manufacturer. To-morrow may bring nothing to their coffers, nor the next day; so they 'doss' for 4d. per night on floor, bench, or table."

The sanitary inspectors have all their work cut out, for

"Longton has always some outbreak of infectious disease which must be attended to, and throws a large amount of extra work upon the department. · But even in the brief space that is left for house-to-house inspection, they must take care how they tread, for the slums of Longton are the choice investments of many of its most prominent citizens."

Who owns these things, and takes money for them? The newspaper says again: "As to the landlords, it is painful to have it pointed out that so much of the worst property in our towns is owned by leading townspeople, some of them bearing a name for philanthropy and religion." The cynic would have expected it. Some of the worst property in Hanley, where the tenants were ruefully contemplating the necessity of "flitting" because the building was unsafe, where "the rain comes in, and there is not a whole pane of glass in the window" of the bedroom, was the property of—The Hanley County Borough. This body had "adopted" the vital clauses of the Housing of the Working Classes Act of 1890.

Such are the revelations made by the courageous conduct of a newspaper, fulfilling its highest function, though fluttering complacent local dove-cotes. It tells, of course, the worst side of the tale, but black shades off into grey, and only higher up does white prevail. The Potteries is not singular in being a provincial district possessing slums, nor are all its landlords of the type of Mr Bernard Shaw's Sartorius; nor are the poorer tenants of the poorer houses all dirty and vicious, and addicted to the habit of breaking the window-panes in the early and more frivolous stages of Saturday night dissensions, and of taking down the back-doors and uprooting the

staircases in an emergency for fuel. But it is precisely because of these negations, and differences,
and qualifications, twisting themselves through the
general mass of facts, that the complications of the
social problem are to be seen ; and the problem is
not to be solved by the cheery boast of a Pottery
Mayor, speaking of the newspaper revelations upon
an occasion when most mundane affairs take on a
couleur de rose, that " He did not know of any
slums in The Potteries, and if there were any he
did not want to know where they were. There
were houses in Florence fit for a prince to live in "—
for a prince of " Florence," probably, though hardly
of Firenze. In proportion as the civic conscience
thus sleeps soundly after dinner, the voice of the
reformer must speak above conversational pitch.

The whole social problem is honeycombed with
contradictions and difficulties, and the mention of
one complication in the social life of The Potteries
microcosm—that of female labour, to the neglect
of the home, leading to the contemplation of a
question which summons up a hundred other questions that are root-fibres in the general social growth
—only shows with what difficulties the path of the
reformer is beset.

The politician has had his day with representative
government, religious liberty, freedom of the Press,
and the removal of general and obvious political disadvantages ; and his work, though not completed, now
merges into that of the social reformer. The very
recrudescence of " Imperialism," rightly understood
and properly directed, involves a recognition of the

z

brotherhood of Englishmen as a stage in the far-off millennium of the brotherhood of man; and is the expression of the feeling that if England is to stand well either with or against the world, she must develop and increase the well-being of those who live within her borders, who are and who make England. And in this sense the action of the Legislature, whether in spreading education, cleansing slums, or in protecting industrial workers, is as truly Imperialistic as any Royal declaration read from the steps of the Exchange. Otherwise, Imperialism merely means the growth of a prize-apple with a rotten core. But to lament, as a recent writer has done,* that an advanced political party with an historic name should put its hand to other work with so much of its old work done, is to lament that the crop should be gathered after the seed has been sown. That a great

* Mr James Annand, in a series of articles commencing in the *Daily News* of January 10, 1899, and since republished. The *f* expound very clearly the political creed of the Liberal from the point of view of the individualist: "All restrictions upon human freedom, from the true Liberal standpoint, are in the first instance evils, and are only to be tolerated because, unhappily, they are occasionally needful." "The Factory Acts apply to women and children. It is a distinct and different thing to apply the principle of the Factory Acts to grown men." "Liberalism declares that Parliament best serves the purposes of its being, best serves the interests of all its citizens and the ends of good government, by *confining itself to the great things of the commonwealth*." "If, however, the temptation comes to them in the specious guise of proposed legislation for the preservation of health and life in, say, 'dangerous trades,' . . . or in the proposal to fix a working day of eight hours for adult men" . . . "the true line of Liberal advance lies not among these questions, but away from these questions. They are the bye-paths, and not the main avenues—the minor incidents, not the main scheme."

work has had to be done in clearing the barnacles from the hull of the ship of the Commonwealth is not to say that alterations are not required above the water-line. And because political disabilities, appealing to the liberal-logical mind—going half-way down to first principles—as crying for removal, have been largely removed, we cannot shut out the claims of a more subtle perception, in which expediency and a wider sense of human responsibility are blended. To give all men an equal chance in life so far as rests with the political rules of the game is not to say that in life's handicap some of the shorter - winded shall not be given a better sporting chance. Life is too greatly tangled for the ancient associations of a name — Liberal or Conservative — to fetter the action of those who come into the world seeing much work done, but much yet to do. If, for instance, we are frightened by the cry of the sacredness of the individualism of the adult, and are reminded that our effete grandmotherly care should be limited to the young and the feminine, we may for the moment forget "political principles" in the recollection that over the adult was thrown the protecting mantle of the State in the reign of a petulantly parental monarch who courted a revolution rather than court the will of his people; and if William the Fourth signed an Act of Parliament which decreed that his meanest subject should not be paid his wages in pig's liver—however much he might appreciate that delicacy—but in the coin of his realm, we may take comfort in the fact that the "independence" of the individualistic adult was settled so long ago.

Whether the thread is gradually disentangled by a public will acting through a Government as its instrument, or by capricious philanthropic effort, is immaterial. What is material is that, if need be, a Government should serve the purposes of man, and not man serve the purposes of a Government fancifully limited to certain functions because the outlook of a political party, narrowed to its age, did not contemplate a more distant horizon; for the aims and limits of a Government made by man are as artificial as the Government itself, and a Government to answer man's needs should be as expansive as man's conception of his own needs or of his duties to others.

It must be inevitable, in any state of society, and under any form of government, that when the highways of obvious political principle have been traversed, the mazes of social life and its disorder shall be explored; and in England at least one may hope that the national spirit of compromise, —which is progressing to a Social Democracy whilst its Monarchy takes deeper root*—will round off the corners of logical difficulty when they obtrude too sharply; for the social problem no more than the human character can be mapped.

---

* *Note.*—Thanks to the splendid wisdom and example of Queen Victoria, who, as those words pass into type, ends her glorious and beneficent reign, bequeathing to her successor the loyalty of an Empire, and a Throne which, having become the pride and deliberate symbol of a self-governing people, rests upon surer foundations than any claims to Divine Right.

out with the rectangular regularity of a chess-board.

Not the least of the tasks before the social reformer is that of the decent and cleanly housing, even of the unclean poor—

> "When the poor are hovell'd and hustled together, each sex, like swine."

The work can only be finally accomplished by the permeation of education through the general mass, but its greatest immediate hope lies in the fact that it has come to be a part of the creed of the pessimist, and is no less a refuge for his higher instincts than it is the duty of the professed Christian.

THE END

THE RIVERSIDE PRESS LIMITED,
ST BERNARD'S ROW, EDINBURGH

CPSIA information can be obtained
at www.ICGtesting.com
Printed in the USA
LVHW081624020919
629646LV00008B/286/P